THE ART OF THE NOVEL

The Art of the Novel

CRITICAL PREFACES

By

Henry James

WITH AN INTRODUCTION

By

Richard P. Blackmur

CHARLES SCRIBNER'S SONS, NEW YORK
CHARLES SCRIBNER'S SONS, Ltd., LONDON

INTRODUCTION

BY

RICHARD P. BLACKMUR

INTRODUCTION

I

THE Prefaces of Henry James were composed at the height of his age as a kind of epitaph or series of inscriptions for the major monument of his life, the sumptuous, plum-coloured, expensive New York Edition of his works. The labour was a torment, a care, and a delight, as his letters and the Prefaces themselves amply show. The thinking and the writing were hard and full and critical to the point of exasperation; the purpose was high, the reference wide, and the terms of discourse had to be conceived and defined as successive need for them arose. He had to elucidate and to appropriate for the critical intellect the substance and principle of his career as an artist, and he had to do this—such was the idiosyncrasy of his mind—specifically, example following lucid example, and with a consistency of part with part that amounted almost to the consistency of a mathematical equation, so that, as in the *Poetics,* if his premises were accepted his conclusions must be taken as inevitable.

Criticism has never been more ambitious, nor more useful. There has never been a body of work so eminently suited to criticism as the fiction of Henry James, and there has certainly never been an author who saw the need and had the ability to criticise specifically and at length his own work. He was avid of his opportunity and both proud and modest as to what he did with it. "These notes," he wrote in the Preface to *Roderick Hudson,* "represent, over a considerable course, the continuity of an artist's endeavour, the growth of his whole operative consciousness and, best of all, perhaps, their own tendency to multiply, with the implication, thereby, of a memory much enriched." Thus his strict modesty; he wrote to Grace Norton (5 March 1907) in a higher tone. "The prefaces, as I say, are difficult to do—but I have found them of a jolly interest; and though I am not going to let you read one of the fictions themselves over I shall expect you to read all the said Introductions." To W. D. Howells he wrote (17 August 1908) with very near his full pride. "They are, in general, a sort of plea for Criticism, for Discrimination, for Appreciation on other than infantile lines—as against the so almost universal Anglo-Saxon absence of these things; which tends so, in our general trade, it seems to me, to break the heart. . . . They ought, collected together, none the less, to form a sort of comprehensive manual or *vademecum* for aspirants in our arduous profession. Still, it will be long before I shall want to collect them together for that purpose and furnish *them* with a final Preface."

In short, James felt that his Prefaces represented or demonstrated an artist's consciousness and the character of his work in some detail, made an essay in general criticism which had an interest and a being aside from any connection with his own work, and that finally, they added up to a fairly exhaustive reference book on the technical aspects of the art of fiction. His judgment was correct and all a commentator can do is to indicate by example and a little analysis, by a kind of provisional reasoned index, how the contents of his essay may be made more available. We have, that is, to perform an act of criticism in the sense that James himself understood it. "To criticise," he wrote in the Preface to *What Maisie Knew*, "is to appreciate, to appropriate, to take intellectual possession, to establish in fine a relation with the criticised thing and make it one's own."

What we have here to appropriate is the most sustained and I think the most eloquent and original piece of literary criticism in existence. (The only comparable pieces, not in merit

INTRODUCTION

of course but in kind, are by the same author, "The Art of Fiction," written as a young man and printed in *Partial Portraits,* and "The Novel in 'The Ring and the Book,'" written in 1912 and published in *Notes on Novelists;* the first of which the reader should consult as an example of general criticism with a prevailing ironic tone, and the second as an example of what the same critical attitude as that responsible for the Prefaces could do on work not James' own.) Naturally, then, our own act of appropriation will have its difficulties, and we shall probably find as James found again and again, that the things most difficult to master will be the best. At the least we shall require the maximum of strained attention, and the faculty of retaining detail will be pushed to its limit. And these conditions will not apply from the difficulty of what James has to say—which is indeed lucid—but because of the convoluted compression of his style and because of the positive unfamiliarity of his terms as he uses them. No one else has written specifically on his subject.

Before proceeding to exhibition and analysis, however, it may be useful to point out what kind of thing, as a type by itself, a James Preface is, and what kind of exercise the reader may expect a sample to go through. The key-fact is simple. A Preface is the story of a story, or in those volumes which collect a group of shorter tales the story of a group of stories cognate in theme or treatment. The Prefaces collocate, juxtapose, and separate the different kinds of stories. They also, by cross-reference and development from one Preface to another, inform the whole series with a unity of being. By "the story of a story" James meant a narrative of the accessory facts and considerations which went with its writing; the how, the why, the what, when, and where which brought it to birth and which are not evident in the story itself, but which have a fascination and a meaning in themselves to enhance the reader's knowledge. "The private history of any sincere work," he felt, "looms large with its own completeness."

INTRODUCTION

But the "story of a story" is not simple in the telling; it has many aspects that must be examined in turn, many developments that must be pursued, before its centre in life is revealed as captured. "The art of representation bristles with questions the very terms of which are difficult to apply and appreciate." Only the main features can be named simply. There is the feature of autobiography, as a rule held to a minimum: an account of the Paris hotel, the Venetian palace, the English cottage, in which the tale in question was written. Aside from that, there is often a statement of the anecdote and the circumstances in which it was told, from which James drew the germ of his story. There is the feature of the germ in incubation, and the story of how it took root and grew, invariably developing into something quite different from its immediate promise. Then there is an account—frequently the most interesting feature—of how the author built up his theme as a consistent piece of dramatisation. Usually there are two aspects to this feature, differently discussed in different Prefaces—the aspect of the theme in relation to itself as a balanced and consistent whole, the flesh upon the articulated plot; and the aspect of the theme in relation to society, which is the moral and evaluating aspect. Varying from Preface to Preface as the need commands, there is the further feature of technical exposition, in terms of which everything else is for the moment subsumed. That is, the things which a literary artist does in order to make of his material an organic whole—the devices he consciously uses to achieve a rounded form—are rendered available for discussion, and for understanding, by definition and exemplification.

These are the principal separate features which compose the face of a Preface. There are also certain emphases brought to bear throughout the Prefaces, which give them above all the savour of definite character. Again and again, for example, a novel or story will raise the problem of securing a compositional centre, a presiding intelligence, or of applying the method of indirect approach. Again and again James emphasises the necessity of being amusing, dramatic, interesting. And besides these, almost any notation, technical, thematic, or moral, brings James eloquently back to the expressive relation between art and life, raises him to an intense personal plea for the difficulty and delight of maintaining that relation, or wrings from him a declaration of the supreme labour of intelligence that art lays upon the artist. For James it is the pride of achievement, for the reader who absorbs that pride it is the enthusiasm of understanding and the proud possibility of emulation.

None of this, not the furthest eloquence nor the most detached precept, but flows from the specific observation and the particular example. When he speaks of abjuring the "platitude of statement," he is not making a phrase but summarising, for the particular occasion, the argument which runs throughout the Prefaces, that in art what is merely stated is not presented, what is not presented is not vivid, what is not vivid is not represented, and what is not represented is not art. Or when, referring to the method by which a subject most completely expresses itself, he writes the following sentence, James is not indulging in self-flattery. "The careful ascertainment of how it shall do so, and the art of guiding it with consequent authority—since this sense of 'authority' is for the master-builder the treasure of treasures, or at least the joy of joys—renews in the modern alchemist something like the old dream of the secret of life." It is not indulgence of any description; it is the recognition in moral language of the artist's privileged experience in the use of his tools—in this instance his use of them in solving the technical problems of *The Spoils of Poynton.* James unfailingly, unflaggingly reveals for his most general precept its specific living source. He knew that only by constantly retaining the specific in the field of discussion could he ever establish or maintain the principles by which he wrote. That is his unique virtue as a critic, that the specific object is always in hand; as it was analogously his genius as a novelist that what he wrote about was always present in somebody's specific knowledge of it. In neither capacity did he ever succumb to the "platitude of statement."

It is this factor of material felt and rendered specifically that differentiates James from such writers as Joyce and Proust. All three have exerted great technical influence on succeeding writers, as masters ought. The difference is that writers who follow Joyce or Proust tend to absorb their subjects, their social attitudes, and their personal styles and accomplish competent derivative work in so doing, while the followers of James absorb something of a technical mastery good for any subject, any attitude, any style. It is the difference between absorbing the object of a sensibility and acquiring something comparable to the sensibility itself. The point may perhaps be enforced paradoxically: the mere imitators of the subject-matter of Proust are readable as documents, but the mere imitators of James are not readable at all. It is not that James is more or less great than his compeers—the question is not before us—but that he consciously and articulately exhibited a greater technical mastery of the tools of his trade. It is a matter of sacrifice. Proust made no sacrifice but wrote always as loosely as possible and triumphed in spite of himself. Joyce made only such sacrifices as suited his private need—as readers of these Prefaces will amply observe—and triumphed by a series of extraordinary *tours de force*. James made consistently every sacrifice for intelligibility and form; and, when the fashions of interest have made their full period, it will be seen I think that his triumph is none the less for that.

There remains—once more before proceeding with the actual content of the Prefaces—a single observation that must be made, and it flows from the remarks above about the character of James' influence. James had in his style and perhaps in the life which it reflected an idiosyncrasy so powerful, so overweening, that to many it seemed a stultifying vice, or at least an inexcusable heresy. He is difficult to read in his later works—among which the Prefaces are included—and his subjects, or rather the way in which he develops them, are occasionally difficult to coördinate with the reader's own experience. He enjoyed an excess of intelligence and he suffered, both in life and art, from an excessive effort to communicate it, to represent it in all its fullness. His style grew elaborate in the degree that he rendered shades and refinements of meaning and feeling not usually rendered at all. Likewise the characters which he created to dramatise his feelings have sometimes a quality of intelligence which enables them to experience matters which are unknown and seem almost perverse to the average reader. James recognised his difficulty, at least as to his characters. He defended his "super-subtle fry" in one way or another a dozen times, on the ground that if they did not exist they ought to, because they represented, if only by an imaginative irony, what life was capable of at its finest. His intention and all his labour was to represent dramatically intelligence at its most difficult, its most lucid, its most beautiful point. This is the sum of his idiosyncrasy; and the reader had better make sure he knows what it is before he rejects it. The act of rejection will deprive him of all knowledge of it. And this precept applies even more firmly to the criticisms he made of his work—to the effort he made to reappropriate it intellectually—than to the direct apprehension of the work itself.

II

Now to resume the theme of this essay, to "remount," as James says of himself many times, "the stream of composition." What is that but to make an *ex post facto* dissection, not that we may embalm the itemised mortal remains, but that we may intellectually understand the movement of parts and the relation between them in the living body we appreciate.

Such dissection is imaginative, an act of the eye and mind alone, and but articulates our knowledge without once scratching the flesh of its object. Only if the life itself was a mockery, a masquerade of pasted surfaces, will we come away with our knowledge dying; if the life was honest and our attention great enough, even if we do not find the heart itself at least we shall be deeply exhilarated, having heard its slightly irregular beat.

Let us first exhibit the principal objects which an imaginative examination is able to separate, attaching to each a summary of context and definition. Thus we shall have equipped ourselves with a kind of eclectic index or provisional glossary, and so be better able to find our way about, and be better prepared to seize for closer examination a selection of those parts of some single Preface which reveal themselves as deeply animating. And none of this effort will have any object except to make the substance of all eighteen Prefaces more easily available.

There is a natural division between major subjects which are discussed at length either in individual essays or from volume to volume, and minor notes which sometimes appear once and are done, and are sometimes recurrent, turning up again and again in slightly different form as the specific matter in hand requires. But it is not always easy to see under which heading an entry belongs. In the following scheme the disposition is approximate and occasionally dual, and in any case an immediate subject of the reader's revision.

To begin with, let us list those major themes which have no definite locus but inhabit all the Prefaces more or less without favour. This is the shortest and for the most part the most general of the divisions, and therefore the least easily susceptible of definition in summary form.

The Relation of Art and the Artist. The Relation of Art and Life. Art, Life, and the Ideal. Art and Morals. Art as Salvation for its Characters. These five connected subjects,

one or more of them, are constantly arrived at, either paren-
thetically or as the definite terminus of the most diverse discussions. The sequence in which I have put them ought to
indicate something of the attitude James brings to bear on
them. Art was serious, he believed, and required of the artist
every ounce of his care. The subject of art was life, or more
particularly someone's apprehension of the experience of it,
and in striving truly to represent it art removed the waste and
muddlement and bewilderment in which it is lived and gave
it a lucid, intelligible form. By insisting on intelligence and
lucidity something like an ideal vision was secured; not an
ideal in the air but an ideal in the informed imagination, an
ideal, in fact, actually of life, limited only by the depth of the
artist's sensibility of it. Thus art was the viable representation
of moral value; in the degree that the report was intelligent
and intense the morals were sound. This attitude naturally
led him on either of two courses in his choice of central characters. He chose either someone with a spark of intelligence
in him to make him worth saving from the damnation and
waste of a disorderly life, or he chose to tell the story of some
specially eminent person in whom the saving grace of full intelligence is assumed and exhibited. It is with the misfortunes
and triumphs of such persons, in terms of the different kinds
of experience of which he was master, that James' fiction almost exclusively deals.

It is this fact of an anterior interest that largely determines
what he has to say about *The Finding of Subjects* and *The
Growth of Subjects*. Subjects never came ready-made or complete, but always from hints, notes, the merest suggestion.
Often a single fact reported at the dinner-table was enough
for James to seize on and plant in the warm bed of his imagination. If his interlocutor, knowing him to be a novelist, insisted on continuing, James closed his ears. He never wanted
all the facts, which might stupefy him, but only enough to
go on with, hardly enough to seem a fact at all. If out of

politeness he had to listen, he paid no recording attention; what he then heard was only "clumsy Life at her stupid work" of waste and muddlement. Taking his single precious germ he meditated upon it, let it develop, scrutinised and encouraged, compressed and pared the developments until he had found the method by which he could dramatise it, give it a central intelligence whose fortune would be his theme, and shape it in a novel or a story as a consistent and self-sufficient organism. James either gives or regrets that he cannot give both the original *donnée* and an account of how it grew to be a dramatic subject for almost every item in the New York Edition.

Art and Difficulty. Of a course, a man with such a view of his art and choosing so great a personal responsibility for his theme would push his rendering to the most difficult terms possible. So alone would he be able to represent the maximum value of his theme. Being a craftsman and delighting in his craft, he knew also both the sheer moral delight of solving a technical difficulty or securing a complicated effect, and the simple, amply attested fact that the difficulties of submitting one's material to a rigidly conceived form were often the only method of representing the material in the strength of its own light. The experience of these difficulties being constantly present to James as he went about his work, he constantly points specific instances for the readers of his Prefaces.

Looseness. Looseness of any description, whether of conception or of execution, he hated contemptuously. In both respects he found English fiction "a paradise of loose ends," but more especially in the respect of execution. His own themes, being complex in reference and development, could only reach the lucidity of the apprehensible, the intelligibility of the represented state, if they were closed in a tight form. Any looseness or laziness would defeat his purpose and let half his intention escape. A selection of the kinds of looseness against which he complains will be given among the minor notes.

INTRODUCTION

The Plea for Attention and Appreciation. The one faculty James felt that the artist may require of his audience is that of close attention or deliberate appreciation; for it is by this faculty alone that the audience participates in the work of art. As he missed the signs of it so he bewailed the loss; upon its continuous exertion depended the very existence of what he wrote. One burden of the Prefaces was to prove how much the reader would see if only he paid attention and how much he missed by following the usual stupid routine of skipping and halting and letting slide. Without attention, without intense appreciation an art of the intelligent life was impossible and without intelligence, for James, art was nothing.

The Necessity for Amusement. James was willing to do his part to arouse attention, and he laboured a good deal to find out exactly what that part was. One aspect of it was to be as amusing as possible, and this he insisted on at every opportunity. To be amusing, to be interesting; without that nothing of his subject could possibly transpire in the reader's mind. In some of his books half the use of certain characters was to amuse the reader. Henrietta Stackpole, for example, in *The Portrait of a Lady,* serves mainly to capture the reader's attention by amusing him as a "character." Thus what might otherwise have been an example of wasteful overtreatment actually serves the prime purpose of carrying the reader along, distracting and freshening him from time to time.

The Indirect Approach and *The Dramatic Scene.* These devices James used throughout his work as those most calculated to command, direct, and limit or frame the reader's attention; and they are employed in various combinations or admixtures the nature of which almost every Preface comments on. These devices are not, as their names might suggest, opposed; nor could their use in equal parts cancel each other. They are, in the novel, two ends of one stick, and no one can say where either end begins. The characterising aspect of the Indirect Approach is this: the existence of a definite created sensibility interposed between the reader and the felt experience which is the subject of the fiction. James never put his reader in direct contact with his subjects; he believed it was impossible to do so, because his subject really was not what happened but what someone felt about what happened, and this could be directly known only through an intermediate intelligence. The Dramatic Scene was the principal device James used to objectify the Indirect Approach and give it self-limiting form. Depending on the degree of limitation necessary to make the material objective and visible all round, his use of the Scene resembled that in the stage-play. The complexities of possible choice are endless and some of them are handled below.

The Plea for a Fine Central Intelligence. But the novel was not a play however dramatic it might be, and among the distinctions between the two forms was the possibility, which belonged to the novel alone, of setting up a fine central intelligence in terms of which everything in it might be unified and upon which everything might be made to depend. No other art could do this; no other art could dramatise the individual at his finest; and James worked this possibility for all it was worth. It was the very substance upon which the directed attention, the cultivated appreciation, might be concentrated. And this central intelligence served a dual purpose, with many modifications and exchanges among its branches. It made a compositional centre for art such as life never saw. If it could be created at all, then it presided over everything else, and would compel the story to be nothing but the story of what that intelligence felt about what happened. This compositional strength, in its turn, only increased the value and meaning of the intelligence *as* intelligence, and *vice versa*. The plea for the use of such an intelligence both as an end and a means is constant throughout the Prefaces—as the proudest end and as the most difficult means. Some of the specific problems which its use poses are discussed in the Prefaces to the novels where they apply. Here it is enough to repeat once more—and not for the last time—that the fine intelligence, either as agent or as the object of action or as both is at the heart of James' work.

So much for the major themes which pervade and condition and unite the whole context of the Prefaces. It is the intention of this essay now to list some of the more important subjects discussed in their own right, indicating where they may be found and briefly what turn the discussions take. The Roman numerals immediately following the headings refer to the volume numbers in the New York Edition.[1] The occasional small Arabic numerals refer to material within the various prefaces according to their pagination here.

The International Theme (XII, XIV, XVIII). The discussion of the International Theme in these three volumes has its greatest value in strict reference to James' own work; it was one of the three themes peculiarly his. It deals, however, with such specific questions as the opposition of manners as a motive in drama, the necessity of opposing positive elements of character, and the use of naïve or innocent characters as the subjects of drama; these are of perennial interest. There is also a discussion under this head of the difference between major and minor themes. In X (p. 132), speaking of "A London Life," there is a discussion of the use of this theme for secondary rather than primary purposes.

The Literary Life as a Theme (XV) and *The Artist as a Theme* (VII). The long sections of these two Prefaces dealing with these themes form a single essay. XV offers the artist enamoured of perfection, his relation to his art, to his audi-

[1] For possible convenience in reference I append the numbers and titles of those volumes which contain Prefaces. I Roderick Hudson; II The American; III The Portrait of a Lady; V The Princess Casamassima; VII The Tragic Muse; IX The Awkward Age; X The Spoils of Poynton; XI What Maisie Knew; XII The Aspern Papers; XIII The Reverberator; XIV Lady Barbarina; XV The Lesson of the Master; XVI The Author of Beltraffio; XVII The Altar of the Dead; XVIII Daisy Miller; XIX The Wings of the Dove; XXI The Ambassadors; XXIII The Golden Bowl.

ence, and himself. VII presents the artist in relation to society and to himself. In both sections the possibilities and the actualities are worked out with specific reference to the characters in the novels and the tales. The discussion is of practical importance to any writer. Of particular interest is the demonstration in VII that the successful artist as such cannot be a hero in fiction, because he is immersed in his work, while the amateur or the failure remains a person and may have a heroic downfall. The thematic discussion in XVI properly belongs under this head, especially pp. 235–37.

The Use of the Eminent or Great (VII, XII, XV, XVI) and *The Use of Historical Characters* (XII, XV). The separation of these two subjects is artificial, as for James they were two aspects of one problem. Being concerned with the tragedies of the high intelligence and the drama of the socially and intellectually great (much as the old tragedies dealt death to kings and heroes) he argues for using the *type* of the historical and contemporary great and against using the actual historical or contemporary figure. The type of the great gives the artist freedom; actual figures bind him without advantage. If he used in one story or another Shelley, Coleridge, Browning, and (I think) Oscar Wilde, he took them only as types and so far transformed them that they appear as pure fictions. The real argument is this: the novelist is concerned with types and only with the eminent case among the types, and the great man is in a way only the most eminent case of the average type, and is certainly the type that the novelist can do most with. To the charge that his "great" people were such as could never exist, James responded that the world would be better if they did. In short, the novelist's most lucid representation may be only his most ironic gesture.

The Dead as a Theme (XVII). Five pages (242–46) of this Preface present "the permanent appeal to the free intelligence of some image of the lost dead" and describe how this appeal may be worked out in fiction. "The sense of the state of the dead," James felt, "is but part of the sense of the state of living."

On Wonder, Ghosts, and the Supernatural (XII, XVII) and *How to Produce Evil* (XII). These again make two aspects of one theme and the rules for securing one pretty much resemble those for securing the other. They are shown best "by showing almost exclusively the way they are felt, by recognising as their main interest some impression strongly made by them and intensely received." That was why Psychical Research Society Ghosts were unreal; there was no one to apprehend them. The objectively rendered prodigy always ran thin. Thickness is in the human consciousness that records and amplifies. And there is also always necessary, for the reader to feel the ghost, the history of somebody's *normal* relation to it. Thus James felt that the climax of Poe's *Pym* was a failure, because there the horrific was without connections. In both Prefaces the ghost story is put as the modern equivalent of the fairy story; and the one must be as economical of its means as the other. The problem of rendering evil in "The Turn of the Screw" (XII) was slightly different; it had to be represented, like the ghosts who performed it, in the consciousness of it of normal persons, but it could not be described. The particular act when rendered always fell short of being evil, so that the problem seemed rather to make the character *capable* of anything. "Only make the reader's general vision of evil intense enough, I said to myself—and that is already a charming job—and his own experience, his own sympathy (with the children) and horror (of their false friends) will supply him quite sufficiently with all the particulars. Make him *think* the evil, make him think it for himself, and you are released from weak specifications." (XII, 176.)

On the Use of Wonder to Animate a Theme (XI). This is the faculty of wonder on a normal plane and corresponds to freshness, intelligent innocence, and curiosity in the face of life; a faculty which when represented in a character almost of itself alone makes that character live. It is a faculty upon which every novelist depends, both in his books to make them vivid, and in his readers where it is the faculty that drives them to read. It is to be distinguished from the wonder discussed in the paragraph next above.

Romanticism and Reality (II). Eight pages in this Preface (30–37) attempt to answer the question: Why is one picture of life called romantic and another real? After setting aside several answers as false or misleading, James gives his own. "The only *general* attribute of projected romance that I can see, the only one that fits all its cases, is the fact of the kind of experience with which it deals—experience liberated, so to speak; experience disengaged, disembodied, disencumbered, exempt from the conditions that we usually know to attach to it, and if we wish so to put the matter, drag upon it, and operating in a medium which relieves it, in a particular interest, of the inconvenience of a *related,* a measurable state, a state subject to all our vulgar communities." Then James applies his answer to his own novel (*The American*). "The experience here represented is the disconnected and uncontrolled experience—uncontrolled by our general sense of 'the way things happen'—which romance alone more or less successfully palms off on us." Since the reader knows "the way things happen," he must be tactfully drugged for the duration of the novel; and that is part of the art of fiction.

The Time Question (I, 12–14). Although the effects dependent on the superior effect of an adequate lapse of time were consciously important to James, the lapse of time itself was only once discussed by him in the Prefaces, and there to explain or criticise the failure to secure it. Roderick Hudson, he said, falls to pieces too quickly. Even though he is special and eminent, still he must not live, change and disintegrate too rapidly; he loses verisimilitude by so doing. His great capacity for ruin is projected on too small a field. He should have had more adventures and digested more experience be-

INTRODUCTION

fort we can properly believe that he has reached his end. But
James was able to put the whole matter succinctly. "To give
all the sense without all the substance or all the surface, and
so to summarise or foreshorten, so to make values both rich
and sharp, that the mere procession of items and profiles is not
only, for the occasion, superseded, but is, for essential quality,
almost 'compromised'—such a case of delicacy proposes itself
at every turn to the painter of life who wishes both to treat his
chosen subject and to confine his necessary picture." Composition and arrangement must give the *effect* of the lapse of
time. For this purpose elimination was hardly a good enough
device. The construction of a dramatic centre, as a rule in
someone's consciousness, was much better, for the reason that
this device, being acted upon in time, gave in parallel the
positive effect of action, and thus of lapsing time.

Geographical Representation (I, 8–10). These three pages
deal with the question: To what extent should a named place
be rendered on its own account? In *Roderick Hudson* James
named Northampton, Mass. This, he said, he ought not to
have done, since all he required was a humane community
which was yet incapable of providing for "art." For this purpose a mere indication would have been sufficient. His general answer to the question was that a place should be named
if the novelist wanted to make it an effective part of the story,
as Balzac did in his studies of the *ville de province*.

The Commanding Centre as a Principle of Composition (I,
II, VII, X, XI, XIX, XXI, XXIII). This is allied with the
discussion of the use of a Central Intelligence above and with
the three notes immediately below. It is a major consideration
in each of the Prefaces numbered and is to be met with *passim*
elsewhere. The whole question is bound up with James' ex-
ceeding conviction that the art of fiction is an organic form,
and that it can neither be looked at all round nor will it be
able to move on its own account unless it has a solidly posed
centre. Commanding centres are of various descriptions. In I

it is in Rowland Mallet's consciousness of Roderick. In II it is in the image of Newman. In VII it is in the combination of relations between three characters. In X it is in a houseful of beautiful furniture. In XI it is the "ironic" centre of a child's consciousness against or illuminated by which the situations gather meaning. In XIX it is in the title (*The Wings of the Dove*), that is, in the influence of Milly Theale, who is seen by various people from the outside. In XXI it is wholly in Strether's consciousness. In XXIII it is, so to speak, half in the Prince, half in the Princess, and half in the motion with which the act is performed.

The Proportion of Intelligence and Bewilderment (V). Upon the correct proportion depends the verisimilitude of a given character. Omniscience would be incredible; the novelist must not make his "characters too interpretative of the muddle of fate, or in other words too divinely, too priggishly clever." Without bewilderment, as without intelligence, there would be no story to tell. "Experience, as I see it, is our apprehension and our measure of what happens to us as social creatures—any intelligent report of which has to be based on that apprehension." Bewilderment is the subject and someone's intelligent feeling of it the story. The right mixture will depend on the *quality* of the bewilderment, whether it is the vague or the critical. The vague fool is necessary, but the *leading* interest is always in the intensifying, critical consciousness.

The Necessity of Fools (V, X, XI), and *The Use of Muddlement* (XI, XIX). These subjects are evidently related to that of Intelligence and Bewilderment. In themselves nothing, fools are the very agents of action. They represent the stupid force of life and are the cause of trouble to the intelligent consciousness. The general truth for the spectator of life was this: (X, 129)—"The fixed constituents of almost any reproducible action are the fools who minister, at a particular crisis, to the intensity of the free spirit engaged with them." Muddlement is the condition of life which fools promote. "The effort really to see and really to represent is no idle business in face of the *constant* force that makes for muddlement. The great thing is indeed that the muddled state too is one of the very sharpest of the realities, that it also has colour and form and character, has often in fact a broad and rich comicality, many of the signs and values of the appreciable." (XI, 149.)

Intelligence as a Receptive Lucidity (XI, XXI). The first of this pair of Prefaces almost wholly and the second largely deals with the methods of conditioning a sensibility so as to make a subject. In XI James shows how the sensibility of a child, intelligent as may be, can influence and shape and make lucid, people and situations outside as well as within its understanding. She, Maisie, is the presiding receptive intelligence, the sole sensibility, in the book, and is furthermore the sole agent, by her mere existence, determining and changing the moral worth of the other characters. In XXI Strether is outlined as the example of the adult sensibility fulfilling similar functions, with the additional grace of greatly extended understanding.

The Dramatic Scene (III, VII, IX, XI, XIX, XXI, and *passim*). We have already spoken under the same heading of James' general theory of the dramatic scene. It is too much of the whole substance of the technical discussion in many of the Prefaces to make more than a mere outline of its terms here possible. In III, 46 and XIX, 306, there is developed the figure of windows opening on a scene. The eye is the artist, the scene the subject, and the window the limiting form. From each selected window the scene is differently observed. In VII is discussed the theory of alternating scenes in terms of a centre (p. 90). In IX, which is the most purely scenic of all the books, the use of the alternating scene is developed still further. At the end of XI there is a bitter postscript declaring the scenic character of the form. In XXI there is intermittent discussion of how to use the single consciousness to promote scenes, and a comparison with the general scenic method in XIX. It is principally to IX that the reader must resort for a sustained specific discussion of the Scene in fiction and its relation to the Scene in drama, and to XIX, of which pp. 296–306 deal with the scenic structure of that book, where the distinction is made between Scenes and Pictures and it is shown how one partakes of the other, and where it is insisted on that the maximum value is obtained when both weights are felt. Subordinate to this there is, in the same reference, a description of the various reflectors (characters) used to illuminate the subject in terms of the scene.

On Revision (I, XXIII). The Notes on Revision in these Prefaces are mainly of interest with reference to what James actually did in revising his earlier works. He revised, as a rule, only in the sense that he re-envisaged the substance more accurately and more representatively. Revision was responsible re-seeing.

On Illustrations in Fiction (XXIII). This is perhaps the most amusing note in all the Prefaces, and it is impossible to make out whether James did or did not like the frontispieces with which his collected volumes were adorned. He was insistent that no illustration to a book of his should have any direct bearing upon it. The danger was real. "Anything that relieves responsible prose of the duty of being, while placed before us, good enough, interesting enough, and, if the question be of picture, pictorial enough, above all *in itself,* does it the worst of services, and may well inspire in the lover of literature certain lively questions as to the future of that institution."

The Nouvelle as a Form (XV, XVI, XVIII). The nouvelle —the long-short story or the short novel—was perhaps James' favourite form, and the form least likely of appreciation in the Anglo-Saxon reading world, to which it seemed neither one thing nor the other. To James it was a small reflector capable of illuminating or mirroring a great deal of material. To the artist who practised in it the difficulties of its economy were a constant seduction and an exalted delight.

On Rendering Material by its Appearances Alone (V). James had the problem of rendering a character whose whole life centred in the London underworld of socialism, anarchism, and conspiracy, matters of which he personally knew nothing. But, he decided, his wanted effect and value were "precisely those of our not knowing, of society's not knowing, but only guessing and suspecting and trying to ignore, what 'goes on' irreconcilably, subversively, beneath the vast smug surface." Hints and notes and observed appearances were always enough. The real wisdom was this:—that "if you haven't, for fiction, the root of the matter in you, haven't the sense of life and the penetrating imagination, you are a fool in the very presence of the revealed and the assured; but that if you *are* so armed you are not really helpless, not without your resource, even before mysteries abysmal."

And that is a good tone upon which to close our rehearsal of the major subjects James examines in his Prefaces. Other readers and other critics (the two need not be quite the same) might well have found other matters for emphasis; and so too they may reprehend the selection of Minor Notes which follows.

On Development and Continuity (I). Developments are the condition of interest, since the subject is always the related state of figures and things. Hence developments are ridden by the principle of continuity. Actually, relations never end, but the artist must make them appear to do so. Felicity of form and composition depend on knowing to what point a development is *indispensable*.

On Antithesis of Characters (I). The illustration is the antithesis of Mary and Christina in this book. James observes that antitheses rarely come off and that it may pass for a triumph, if taking them together, one of them is strong (p. 18).

INTRODUCTION

On the Emergence of Characters (X, 127). James' view may be summarised in quotation. "A character is interesting as it comes out, and by the process and duration of that emergence, just as a procession is effective by the way it unrolls, turning to a mere mob if it all passes at once."

On Misplaced Middles (VII, XIX). Misplaced Middles are the result of excessive foresight. As the art of the drama is of preparations, that of the novel is only less so. The first half of a fiction is the stage or theatre of the second half, so that too much may be expended on the first. Then the problem is consummately to mask the fault and "confer on the false quantity the brave appearance of the true." James indicates how the middles of VII and XIX were misplaced, and although he believed the fault great, thought that he had in both cases passed it off by craft and dissimulation.

On Improvisation (XII, 172). Nothing was so easy as improvisation, and it usually ran away with the story, e.g., in *The Arabian Nights*. "The thing was to aim at absolute singleness, clearness and roundness, and yet to depend on an imagination working freely, working (call it) with extravagance; by which law it wouldn't be thinkable except as free and wouldn't be amusing except as controlled."

The Anecdote (XIII, 181). "The anecdote consists, ever, of something that has oddly happened to some one, and the first of its duties is to point directly to the person whom it so distinguishes."

The Anecdote and the Developmental (XV, 221, XVI, 232). In the first of these references James observes that whereas the anecdote may come from any source, specifically complicated states must come from the author's own mind. In the second he says that *The Middle Years* is an example of imposed form (he had an order for a short story) and the struggle was to keep compression rich and accretions compressed; to keep the form that of the concise anecdote, whereas the subject would seem one comparatively demanding developments.

INTRODUCTION

James solved the problem by working from the outward edge in rather than from the centre outward; and this was law for the small form. At the end of this Preface, there is a phrase about chemical reductions and compressions making the short story resemble a sonnet.

On Operative Irony (XV, 222). James defended his "super-subtle fry" on the ground that they were ironic, and he found the strength of applied irony "in the sincerities, the lucidities, the utilities that stand behind it." If these characters and these stories were not a campaign for something better than the world offered then they were worthless. "But this is exactly what we mean by operative irony. It implies and projects the possible other case, the case rich and edifying where the actuality is pretentious and vain."

On Foreshortening (VII, XV, XVII, XVIII). This is really a major subject, but the discussions James made of it were never extensive, seldom over two lines at a time. I append samples. In VII, 88, he speaks of foreshortening not by adding or omitting items but by figuring synthetically, by exquisite chemical adjustments. In XVII, 262, the nouvelle *Julia Bride* is considered as a foreshortened novel to the extreme. In XVIII, 278, after defining once again the art of representation and insisting on the excision of the irrelevant, James names Foreshortening as a deep principle and an invaluable device. It conduced, he said, "to the only compactness that has a charm, to the only spareness that has a force, to the only simplicity that has a grace—those, in each order, that produce the *rich* effect."

On Narrative in the First Person (XXI, 320–321). James bore a little heavily against this most familiar of all narrative methods. Whether his general charge will hold is perhaps irrelevant; it holds perfectly with reference to the kinds of fiction he himself wrote, and the injury to unity and composition which he specifies may well be observed in Proust's long novel where every dodge is unavailingly resorted to in the attempt to get round the freedom of the method. The double privilege (in the first person), said James, of being at once subject and object sweeps away difficulties at the expense of discrimination. It prevents the possibility of a centre and prevents real directness of contact. Its best effect, perhaps, is that which in another connection James called the mere "platitude of statement."

On Ficelles (XXI, 322–323). Taking the French theatrical term, James so labeled those characters who belong less to the subject than to the treatment of it. The invention and disposition of *ficelles* is one of the difficulties swept away by the first person narrative.

On Characters as Disponibles (III, 42–44). Here again James adapted a French word, taking it this time from Turgenev. *Disponibles* are the active or passive persons who solicit the author's imagination, appearing as subject to the chances and complications of existence and requiring of the author that he find for them their right relations and build their right fate.

The rule of space forbids extending even so scant a selection from so rich a possible index. But let me add a round dozen with page references alone. On Dialogue (IX, 106); Against Dialect (XVIII, 279); On Authority (XVIII, 281); On Confusion of Forms (IX, 111); On Overtreatment (III, 57; IX, 117); On Writing of the Essence and of the Form (III, 53); On Making Compromises Conformities (XIX, 295); On the Coercive Charm of Form (IX, 111); On Major Themes in Modern Drama (IX, 112); On Sickness as a Theme (XIX, 289); On Reviving Characters (V, 73); On Fiction Read Aloud (XXIII, 346–47); and so on.

The reader may possibly have observed that we have nowhere illustrated the relation which James again and again made eloquently plain between the value or morality of his art and the form in which it appears. It is not easy to select from a multiplicity of choice, and it is impossible, when the matter emerges in a style already so compact, to condense. I should like to quote four sentences from the middle and end of a paragraph in the Preface to *The Portrait of a Lady* (III, 45-46).

There is, I think, no more nutritive or suggestive truth in this connexion than that of the perfect dependence of the "moral" sense of a work of art on the amount of felt life concerned in producing it. The question comes back thus, obviously, to the kind and degree of the artist's prime sensibility, which is the soil out of which his subject springs. The quality and capacity of that soil, its capacity to "grow" with due freshness and straightness any vision of life, represents, strongly or weakly, the projected morality. . . . Here we get exactly the high price of the novel as a literary form—its power not only, while preserving that form with closeness, to range through all the differences of the individual relation to its general subject-matter, all the varieties of outlook on life, of disposition to reflect and project, created by conditions that are never the same from man to man (or, as far as that goes, from woman to woman), but positively to appear more true to its character in proportion as it strains, or tends to burst, with a latent extravagance, its mould.

These sentences represent, I think, the genius and intention of James the novelist, and ought to explain the serious and critical devotion with which he made of his Prefaces a *vade-mecum*—both for himself as the solace of achievement, and for others as a guide and exemplification. We have, by what is really no more than an arbitrary exertion of interest, exhibited a rough scheme of the principal contents; there remain the Prefaces themselves.

III

Although the Prefaces to *The Wings of the Dove* or *The Awkward Age* are more explicitly technical in reference, although that to *What Maisie Knew* more firmly develops the intricacies of a theme, and although that to *The*

INTRODUCTION

Tragic Muse is perhaps in every respect the most useful of all the Prefaces, I think it may be better to fasten our single attention on the Preface to *The Ambassadors*. This was the book of which James wrote most endearingly. It had in his opinion the finest and most intelligent of all his themes, and he thought it the most perfectly rendered of his books. Furthermore in its success it constituted a work thoroughly characteristic of its author and of no one else. There is a contagion and a beautiful desolation before a great triumph of the human mind—before any approach to perfection—which we had best face for what there is in them.

This Preface divides itself about equally between the outline of the story as a story, how it grew in James' mind from the seed of a dropped word (pp. 307–317), and a discussion of the form in which the book was executed with specific examination of the method of presentation through the single consciousness of its hero Lambert Strether (pp. 317–326). If we can expose the substance of these two discussions we shall have been in the process as intimate as it is possible to be with the operation of an artist's mind. In imitating his thought, step by step and image by image, we shall in the end be able to appropriate in a single act of imagination all he has to say.

The situation involved in *The Ambassadors*, James tells us, "is gathered up betimes, that is in the second chapter of Book Fifth . . . planted or 'sunk,' stiffly or saliently, in the centre of the current." Never had he written a story where the seed had grown into so large a plant and yet remained as an independent particle, that is in a single quotable passage. Its intention had been firm throughout.

This independent seed is found in Strether's outburst in Gloriani's Paris garden to little Bilham. "The idea of the tale resides indeed in the very fact that an hour of such unprecedented ease should have been felt by him *as* a crisis." Strether feels that he has missed his life, that he made in his youth a grave mistake about the possibilities of life, and he exhorts Bilham not to repeat his mistake. "Live all you can. Live, live!" And he has the terrible question within him: "*Would* there yet perhaps be time for reparation?" At any rate he sees what he had missed and knows the injury done his character. The story is the demonstration of that vision as it came about, of the vision in process.

The original germ had been the repetition by a friend of words addressed him by a man of distinction similar in burden to those addressed by Strether to little Bilham. This struck James as a theme of great possibilities. Although any theme or subject is absolute once the novelist has accepted it, there are degrees of merit among which he may first choose. "Even among the supremely good—since with such alone is it one's theory of one's honour to be concerned—there is an ideal *beauty* of goodness the invoked action of which is to raise the artistic faith to a maximum. Then, truly, one's theme may be said to shine."

And the theme of *The Ambassadors* shone so for James that it resembled "a monotony of fine weather," in this respect differing much from *The Wings of the Dove*, which gave him continual trouble. "I rejoiced," James said, "in the promise of a hero so mature, who would give me thereby the more to bite into—since it's only into thickened motive and accumulated character, I think, that the painter of life bites more than a little." By maturity James meant character and imagination. But imagination must not be the *predominant* quality in him; for the theme in hand, the *comparatively* imaginative man would do. The predominant imagination could wait for another book, until James should be willing to pay for the privilege of presenting it. (See also on this point the discussion of Intelligence and Bewilderment above.)

There was no question, nevertheless, that *The Ambassadors* had a major theme. There was the "supplement of situation logically involved" in Strether's delivering himself to Bilham. And James proceeds to describe the novelist's thrill

in finding the situation involved by a conceived character.
Once the situations are rightly found the story "assumes the
authenticity of concrete existence"; the labour is to find them.

"Art deals with what we see, it must first contribute full-
handed that ingredient; it plucks its material, otherwise expressed, in the garden of life—which material elsewhere grown
is stale and uneatable." The subject once found, complete
with its situations, must then be submitted to a process. There
is the subject, which is the story of one's hero, and there is the
story of the story itself which is the story of the process of
telling.

Still dealing with the story of his hero, James describes
how he accounted for Strether, how he found what led up to
his outburst in the garden. Where has he come from and
why? What is he doing in Paris? To answer these questions
was to possess Strether. But the answers must follow the
principle of probability. Obviously, by his outburst, he was a
man in a false position. What false position? The most probable would be the right one. Granting that he was American,
he would probably come from New England. If that were
the case, James immediately knew a great deal about him, and
had to sift and sort. He would, presumably, have come to
Paris with a definite view of life which Paris at once assaulted;
and the situation would arise in the interplay or conflict resulting. . . . There was also the energy of the story itself,
which once under way was irresistible, to help its author
along. In the end the story seems to know of itself what it's
about; and its impudence is always there—"there, so to speak,
for grace, and effect, and *allure.*"

These steps taken in finding his story gave it a functional
assurance. "*The* false position, for our belated man of the
world—belated because he had endeavoured so long to escape
being one, and now at last had really to face his doom—the
false position for him, I say, was obviously to have presented
himself at the gate of that boundless menagerie primed with

a moral scheme which was yet framed to break down on any approach to vivid facts; that is to any at all liberal appreciation of them." His note was to be of discrimination and his drama was to "become, under stress, the drama of discrimination."

There follows the question, apparently the only one that troubled James in the whole composition of this book, of whether he should have used Paris as the scene of Strether's outburst and subsequent conversion. Paris had a trivial and vulgar association as the obvious place to be tempted in. The revolution performed by Strether was to have nothing to do with that *bêtise*. He was to be thrown forward rather "upon his lifelong trick of intense reflexion," with Paris a minor matter symbolising the world other than the town of Woolet, Mass., from which he came. Paris was merely the *likely* place for such a drama, and thus saved James much labour of preparation.

Now turning from the story of his hero to the story of his story, James begins by referring to the fact that it appeared in twelve instalments in the *North American Review,* and describes the pleasure he took in making the recurrent breaks and resumptions of serial publication a small compositional law in itself. The book as we have it is in twelve parts. He passes immediately to the considerations which led him to employ only one centre and to keep it entirely in Strether's consciousness. It was Strether's adventure and the only way to make it rigorously his was to have it seen only through his eyes. There were other characters with situations of their own which bore on Strether. "But Strether's sense of these things, and Strether's only, should avail me for showing them; I should know them only through his more or less groping knowledge of them, since his very gropings would figure among his most interesting motions." This rigour of representation would give him both unity and intensity. The difficulties, too, which the rigour imposed, made the best, because the hardest, determinants of effects. Once he adopted his method

he had to be consistent; hence arose his difficulties. For example, there was the problem of making Mrs. Newsome
(whose son Strether had come to Paris to save), actually in
Woolet, Mass., "no less intensely than circuitously present";
that is, to make her influence press on Strether whenever there
was need for it. The advantage of presenting her through
Strether was that only Strether's feeling of her counted for the
story. Any other method would not only have failed but
would have led to positive irrelevance. Hence, "One's work
should have composition, because composition alone is positive beauty."

Next James considers what would have happened to his
story had he endowed Strether with the privilege of the first
person. "Variety, and many other queer matters as well, might
have been smuggled in by the back door." But these could not
have been intensely represented as Strether's experience, but
would have been his only on his own say-so. "Strether, on the
other hand, encaged and provided for as *The Ambassadors*
encages and provides, has to keep in view proprieties much
stiffer and more salutary than our straight and credulous gape
are likely to bring home to him, has exhibitional conditions to
meet, in a word, that forbid the terrible *fluidity* of self-revelation."

Nevertheless, in order to represent Strether James had to
resort to confidants for him, namely Maria Gostrey and Waymarsh, *ficelles* to aid the treatment. It is thanks to the use of
these *ficelles* that James was able to construct the book in a
series of alternating scenes and thus give it an objective air.
Indispensable facts, both of the present and of the past, are
presented dramatically—so the reader can *see* them—only
through their use. But it is necessary, for the *ficelles* to succeed in their function, that their character should be artfully
dissimulated. For example, Maria Gostrey's connection with
the subject is made to carry itself as a real one.

Analogous to the use of *ficelles*, James refers to the final scene in the book as an "artful expedient for mere consistency of form." It gives or adds nothing on its own account but only expresses "as vividly as possible certain things quite other than itself and that are of the already fixed and appointed measure."

Although the general structure of the book is scenic and the specific centre is in Strether's consciousness of the scenes, James was delighted to note that he had dissimulated throughout the book many exquisite treacheries to those principles. He gives as examples Strether's first encounter with Chad Newsome, and Mamie Pocock's hour of suspense in the hotel salon. These are insisted on as instances of the representational which, "for the charm of opposition and renewal," are other than scenic. In short, James mixed his effects without injuring the consistency of his form. "From the equal play of such oppositions the book gathers an intensity that fairly adds to the dramatic." James was willing to argue that this was so "for the sake of the moral involved; which is not that the particular production before us exhausts the interesting questions that it raises, but that the Novel remains still, under the right persuasion, the most independent, most elastic, most prodigious of literary forms."

It is this last sentiment that our analysis of this Preface is meant to exemplify; and it is—such is the sustained ability of James' mind to rehearse the specific in the light of the general—an exemplification which might be repeated in terms of almost any one of these Prefaces.

IV

There is in any day of agonised doubt and exaggerated certainty as to the relation of the artist to society, an unusual attractive force in the image of a man whose doubts are conscientious and whose certainties are all serene. Henry James scrupled relentlessly as to the minor aspects of his art but of its major purpose and essential character his knowledge was calm, full, and ordered. One answer to almost every relevant question will be found, given always in specific terms and flowing from illustrative example, somewhere among his Prefaces; and if the answer he gives is not the only one, nor to some minds necessarily the right one, it has yet the paramount merit that it results from a thoroughly consistent, informed mind operating at its greatest stretch. Since what he gives is always specifically rendered he will even help you disagree with him by clarifying the subject of argument.

He wanted the truth about the important aspects of life as it was experienced, and he wanted to represent that truth with the greatest possible lucidity, beauty, and fineness, not abstractly or in mere statement, but vividly, imposing on it the form of the imagination, the acutest relevant sensibility, which felt it. Life itself—the subject of art—was formless and likely to be a waste, with its situations leading to endless bewilderment; while art, the imaginative representation of life, selected, formed, made lucid and intelligent, gave value and meaning to, the contrasts and oppositions and processions of the society that confronted the artist. The emphases were on intelligence—James was avowedly the novelist of the free spirit, the liberated intelligence—on feeling, and on form.

The subject might be what it would and the feeling of it what it could. When it was once found and known, it should be worked for all it was worth. If it was felt intensely and intelligently enough it would reach, almost of itself, towards adequate form, a prescribed shape and size and density. Then everything must be sacrificed to the exigence of that form, it must never be loose or overflowing but always tight and contained. There was the "coercive charm" of Form, so conceived, which would achieve, dramatise or enact, the moral intent of the theme by making it finely intelligible, better than anything else.

So it is that thinking of the difficulty of representing Isabelle Archer in *The Portrait of a Lady* as a "mere young thing"

INTRODUCTION

who was yet increasingly intelligent, James was able to write these sentences. "Now to see deep difficulty braved is at any time, for the really addicted artist, to feel almost even as a pang, the beautiful incentive, and to feel it verily in such sort as to wish the danger intensified. The difficulty most worth tackling can only be for him, in these conditions, the greatest the case permits of." It is because such sentiments rose out of him like prayers that for James art was enough.

RICHARD P. BLACKMUR.

CONTENTS

The Art of the Novel

I

PREFACE TO "RODERICK HUDSON"

(VOLUME I IN THE NEW YORK EDITION)

"Roderick Hudson" was begun in Florence in the spring of
1874, designed from the first for serial publication in "The
Atlantic Monthly," where it opened in January 1875 and persisted through the year. I yield to the pleasure of placing these
circumstances on record, as I shall place others, and as I have
yielded to the need of renewing acquaintance with the book
after a quarter of a century. This revival of an all but extinct
relation with an early work may often produce for an artist, I
think, more kinds of interest and emotion than he shall find
it easy to express, and yet will light not a little, to his eyes, that
veiled face of his Muse which he is condemned forever and all
anxiously to study. The art of representation bristles with
questions the very terms of which are difficult to apply and to
appreciate; but whatever makes it arduous makes it, for our
refreshment, infinite, causes the practice of it, with experience,
to spread round us in a widening, not in a narrowing circle.
Therefore it is that experience has to organise, for convenience
and cheer, some system of observation—for fear, in the admirable immensity, of losing its way. We see it as pausing from
time to time to consult its notes, to measure, for guidance, as
many aspects and distances as possible, as many steps taken
and obstacles mastered and fruits gathered and beauties enjoyed. Everything counts, nothing is superfluous in such a
survey; the explorer's note-book strikes me here as endlessly
receptive. This accordingly is what I mean by the contributive
value—or put it simply as, to one's own sense, the beguiling

3

charm—of the *accessory* facts in a given artistic case. This is why, as one looks back, the private history of any sincere work, however modest its pretensions, looms with its own completeness in the rich, ambiguous æsthetic air, and seems at once to borrow a dignity and to mark, so to say, a station. This is why, reading over, for revision, correction and republication, the volumes here in hand, I find myself, all attentively, in presence of some such recording scroll or engraved commemorative table—from which the "private" character, moreover, quite insists on dropping out. These notes represent, over a considerable course, the continuity of an artist's endeavour, the growth of his whole operative consciousness and, best of all, perhaps, their own tendency to multiply, with the implication, thereby, of a memory much enriched. Addicted to "stories" and inclined to retrospect, he fondly takes, under this backward view, his whole unfolding, his process of production, for a thrilling tale, almost for a wondrous adventure, only asking himself at what stage of remembrance the mark of the relevant will begin to fail. He frankly proposes to take this mark everywhere for granted.

"Roderick Hudson" was my first attempt at a novel, a long fiction with a "complicated" subject, and I recall again the quite uplifted sense with which my idea, such as it was, permitted me at last to put quite out to sea. I had but hugged the shore on sundry previous small occasions; bumping about, to acquire skill, in the shallow waters and sandy coves of the "short story" and master as yet of no vessel constructed to carry a sail. The subject of "Roderick" figured to me vividly this employment of canvas, and I have not forgotten, even after long years, how the blue southern sea seemed to spread immediately before me and the breath of the spice-islands to be already in the breeze. Yet it must even then have begun for me too, the ache of fear, that was to become so familiar, of being unduly tempted and led on by "developments"; which is but the desperate discipline of the question involved in them. They are of the very essence of the novelist's process, and it is by their aid, fundamentally, that his idea takes form and lives; but they impose on him, through the principle of continuity that rides them, a proportionate anxiety. They are the very condition of interest, which languishes and drops without them; the painter's subject consisting ever, obviously, of the related state, to each other, of certain figures and things. To exhibit these relations, once they have all been recognised, is to "treat" his idea, which involves neglecting none of those that directly minister to interest; the degree of that directness remaining meanwhile a matter of highly difficult appreciation, and one on which felicity of form and composition, as a part of the total effect, mercilessly rests. Up to what point is such and such a development *indispensable* to the interest? What is the point beyond which it ceases to be rigorously so? Where, for the complete expression of one's subject, does a particular relation stop—giving way to some other not concerned in that expression?

Really, universally, relations stop nowhere, and the exquisite problem of the artist is eternally but to draw, by a geometry of his own, the circle within which they shall happily *appear* to do so. He is in the perpetual predicament that the continuity of things is the whole matter, for him, of comedy and tragedy; that this continuity is never, by the space of an instant or an inch, broken, and that, to do anything at all, he has at once intensely to consult and intensely to ignore it. All of which will perhaps pass but for a supersubtle way of pointing the plain moral that a young embroiderer of the canvas of life soon began to work in terror, fairly, of the vast expanse of that surface, of the boundless number of its distinct perforations for the needle, and of the tendency inherent in his many-coloured flowers and figures to cover and consume as many as possible of the little holes. The development of the flower, of the figure, involved thus an immense counting of holes and a careful selection among them. That would have been, it seemed to him, a brave enough process, were it not the very nature of the holes so to invite, to solicit, to persuade, to practise positively a thousand lures and deceits. The prime effect of so sustained a system, so prepared a surface, is to lead on and on; while the fascination of following resides, by the same token, in the presumability *somewhere* of a convenient, of a visibly-appointed stopping-place. Art would be easy indeed if, by a fond power disposed to "patronise" it, such conveniences, such simplifications, had been provided. We have, as the case stands, to invent and establish them, to arrive at them by a difficult, dire process of selection and comparison, of surrender and sacrifice. The very meaning of expertness is acquired courage to brace one's self for the cruel crisis from the moment one sees it grimly loom.

"Roderick Hudson" was further, was earnestly pursued during a summer partly spent in the Black Forest and (as I had returned to America early in September) during three months passed near Boston. It is one of the silver threads of the recoverable texture of that embarrassed phase, however, that the book was not finished when it had to begin appearing in monthly fragments: a fact in the light of which I find myself live over again, and quite with wonderment and tenderness, so intimate an experience of difficulty and delay. To have "liked" so much writing it, to have worked out with such conviction the pale embroidery, and yet not, at the end of so many months, to have come through, was clearly still to have fallen short of any facility and any confidence: though the long-drawn process now most appeals to memory, I confess, by this very quality of shy and groping duration. One fact about it indeed outlives all others; the fact that, as the loved Italy was the scene of my fiction—so much more loved than one has ever been able, even after fifty efforts, to say!—and as having had to leave it persisted as an inward ache, so there was soreness in still contriving, after a fashion, to hang about it and in prolonging, from month to month, the illusion of the

golden air. Little enough of that medium may the novel, read
over today, seem to supply; yet half the actual interest lurks
for me in the earnest, baffled intention of making it felt. A
whole side of the old consciousness, under this mild pressure,
flushes up and prevails again; a reminder, ever so penetrating,
of the quantity of "evocation" involved in my plan, and of the
quantity I must even have supposed myself to achieve. I take
the lingering perception of all this, I may add—that is of the
various admonitions of the whole reminiscence—for a signal
instance of the way a work of art, however small, if but sufficiently sincere, may vivify and even dignify the accidents
and incidents of its growth.

I must that winter (which I again like to put on record
that I spent in New York) have brought up my last instalments in due time, for I recall no haunting anxiety: what I do
recall perfectly is the felt pleasure, during those months—and
in East Twenty-fifth Street!—of trying, on the other side of
the world, still to surround with the appropriate local glow
the characters that had combined, to my vision, the previous
year in Florence. A benediction, a great advantage, as seemed
to me, had so from the first rested on them, and to nurse
them along was really to sit again in the high, charming,
shabby old room which had originally overarched them and
which, in the hot May and June, had looked out, through the
slits of cooling shutters, at the rather dusty but ever-romantic
glare of Piazza Santa Maria Novella. The house formed the
corner (I delight to specify) of Via della Scala, and I fear that
what the early chapters of the book most "render" to me to-
day is not the umbrageous air of their New England town,
but the view of the small cab-stand sleepily disposed—long before the days of strident electric cars—round the rococo obelisk
of the Piazza, which is supported on its pedestal, if I remember rightly, by four delightful little elephants. (That, at any
rate, is how the object in question, deprecating verification,
comes back to me with the clatter of the horse-pails, the dis-

cussions, in the intervals of repose under well-drawn hoods, of the unbuttoned *cocchieri,* sons of the most garrulous of races, and the occasional stillness as of the noonday desert.)

Pathetic, as we say, on the other hand, no doubt, to re-perusal, the manner in which the evocation, so far as attempted, of the small New England town of my first two chapters, fails of intensity—if intensity, in such a connexion, had been indeed to be looked for. *Could* I verily, by the terms of my little plan, have "gone in" for it at the best, and even though one of these terms was the projection, for my fable, at the outset, of some more or less vivid antithesis to a state of civilisation providing for "art"? What I wanted, in essence, was the image of some perfectly humane community which was yet all incapable of providing for it, and I had to take what my scant experience furnished me. I remember feeling meanwhile no drawback in this scantness, but a complete, an exquisite little adequacy, so that the presentation arrived at would quite have served its purpose, I think, had I not misled myself into naming my place. To name a place, in fiction, is to pretend in some degree to represent it—and I speak here of course but of the use of existing names, the only ones that carry weight. I wanted one that carried weight—so at least I supposed; but obviously I was wrong, since my effect lay, so superficially, and could only lie, in the local *type,* as to which I had my handful of impressions. The particular local case was another matter, and I was to see again, after long years, the case into which, all recklessly, the opening passages of "Roderick Hudson" put their foot. I was to have nothing then, on the spot, to sustain me but the rather feeble plea that I had not *pretended* so very much to "do" Northampton, Mass. The plea was charmingly allowed, but nothing could have been more to the point than the way in which, in such a situation, the whole question of the novelist's "doing," with its eternal wealth, or in other words its eternal torment of interest, once more came up. He embarks, rash adventurer, under the star

of "representation," and is pledged thereby to remember that
the art of interesting us in things—once these things are the
right ones for his case—can *only* be the art of representing
them. This relation to them, for invoked interest, involves
his accordingly "doing"; and it is for him to settle with his
intelligence what that variable process shall commit him to.

Its fortune rests primarily, beyond doubt, on somebody's
having, under suggestion, a *sense* for it—even the reader will
do, on occasion, when the writer, as so often happens, completely falls out. The way in which this sense has been, or has
not been, applied constitutes, at all events, in respect to any
fiction, the very ground of critical appreciation. Such appreciation takes account, primarily, of the thing, in the case, to
have *been* done, and I now see what, for the first and second
chapters of "Roderick," that was. It was a peaceful, rural New
England community *quelconque*—it was not, it was under no
necessity of being, Northampton, Mass. But one nestled,
technically, in those days, and with yearning, in the great
shadow of Balzac; his august example, little as the secret
might ever be guessed, towered for me over the scene; so that
what was clearer than anything else was how, if it was a
question of Saumur, of Limoges, of Guérande, he "did"
Saumur, did Limoges, did Guérande. I remember how, in
my feebler fashion, I yearned over the preliminary presentation of my small square patch of the American scene, and yet
was not sufficiently on my guard to see how easily his high
practice might be delusive for my case. Balzac talked of
Nemours and Provins: therefore why should n't one, with
fond fatuity, talk of almost the only small American *ville de
province* of which one had happened to lay up, long before, a
pleased vision? The reason was plain: one was not in the
least, in one's prudence, emulating his systematic closeness. It
didn't confuse the question either that he would verily, after
all, addressed as he was to a due density in his material, have
found little enough in Northampton, Mass. to tackle. He

tackled no group of appearances, no presented face of the social organism (conspicuity thus attending it), *but* to make something of it. To name it simply and not in some degree tackle it would have seemed to him an act reflecting on his general course the deepest dishonour. Therefore it was that, as the moral of these many remarks, I "named," under his contagion, when I was really most conscious of not being held to it; and therefore it was, above all, that for all the effect of representation I was to achieve, I might have let the occasion pass. A "fancy" indication would have served my turn—except that I should so have failed perhaps of a pretext for my present insistence.

Since I do insist, at all events, I find this ghostly interest perhaps even more reasserted for me by the questions begotten within the very covers of the book, those that wander and idle there as in some sweet old overtangled walled garden, a safe paradise of self-criticism. Here it is that if there be air for it to breathe at all, the critical question swarms, and here it is, in particular, that one of the happy hours of the painter's long day may strike. I speak of the painter in general and of his relation to the old picture, the work of his hand, that has been lost to sight and that, when found again, is put back on the easel for measure of what time and the weather may, in the interval, have done to it. Has it too fatally faded, has it blackened or "sunk," or otherwise abdicated, or has it only, blest thought, strengthened, for its allotted duration, and taken up, in its degree, poor dear brave thing, some shade of the all appreciable, yet all indescribable grace that we know as pictorial "tone"? The anxious artist has to wipe it over, in the first place, to see; he has to "clean it up," say, or to varnish it anew, or at the least to place it in a light, for any right judgment of its aspect or its worth. But the very uncertainties themselves yield a thrill, and if subject and treatment, working together, have had their felicity, the artist, the prime creator, may find a strange charm in this stage of the connexion. It helps him to live back into a forgotten state, into convictions, credulities too early spent perhaps, it breathes upon the dead reasons of things, buried as they are in the texture of the work, and makes them revive, so that the actual appearances and the old motives fall together once more, and a lesson and a moral and a consecrating final light are somehow disengaged.

All this, I mean of course, if the case will wonderfully take any such pressure, if the work doesn't break down under even such mild overhauling. The author knows well enough how easily that may happen—which he in fact frequently enough sees it do. The old reasons then are too dead to revive; they were not, it is plain, good enough reasons to live. The only possible relation of the present mind to the thing is to dismiss it altogether. On the other hand, when it is not dismissed—as the only detachment is the detachment of aversion—the creative intimacy is reaffirmed, and appreciation, critical apprehension, insists on becoming as active as it can. Who shall say, granted this, where it shall not begin and where it shall consent to end? The painter who passes over his old sunk canvas the wet sponge that shows him what may still come out again makes his criticism essentially active. When having seen, while his momentary glaze remains, that the canvas *has* kept a few buried secrets, he proceeds to repeat the process with due care and with a bottle of varnish and a brush, he is "living back," as I say, to the top of his bent, is taking up the old relation, so workable apparently, yet, and there is nothing logically to stay him from following it all the way. I have felt myself then, on looking over past productions, the painter making use again and again of the tentative wet sponge. The sunk surface has here and there, beyond doubt, refused to respond: the buried secrets, the intentions, are buried too deep to rise again, and were indeed, it would appear, not much worth the burying. No so, however, when the moistened canvas does obscurely flush and when resort to the varnish-bottle is thereby immediately indicated. The simplest figure for my revision of this present array of earlier, later, larger, smaller, canvases, is to say that I have achieved it by the very aid of the varnish-bottle. It is true of them throughout that, in words I have had occasion to use in another connexion (where too I had revised with a view to "possible amendment of form and enhancement of meaning"), I have "nowhere scrupled to rewrite a sentence or a passage on judging it susceptible of a better turn."

To re-read "Roderick Hudson" was to find one remark so promptly and so urgently prescribed that I could at once only take it as pointing almost too stern a moral. It stared me in the face that the time-scheme of the story is quite inadequate, and positively to that degree that the fault but just fails to wreck it. The thing escapes, I conceive, with its life: the effect sought is fortunately more achieved than missed, since the interest of the subject bears down, auspiciously dissimulates, this particular flaw in the treatment. Everything occurs, none the less, too punctually and moves too fast: Roderick's disintegration, a gradual process, and of which the exhibitional interest is exactly that it *is* gradual and occasional, and thereby traceable and watchable, swallows two years in a mouthful, proceeds quite *not* by years, but by weeks and months, and thus renders the whole view the disservice of appearing to present him as a morbidly special case. The very claim of the fable is naturally that he *is* special, that his great gift makes and keeps him highly exceptional; but that is not for a moment supposed to preclude his appearing typical (of the general type) as well; for the fictive hero successfully appeals to us only as an eminent instance, as eminent as we like, of our own conscious kind. My mistake on Roderick's behalf—and not in the least of conception, but of composition and expression—is that, at the rate at which he falls to pieces, he seems to place himself beyond our understanding and our sympathy. These are not our rates, we say; we ourselves certainly, under like pressure,—for what is it after all?—would make more of a fight. We conceive going to pieces—nothing is easier, since we see people do it, one way or another, all round us; but this young man must either have had less of the principle of development to have had so much of the principle of collapse, or less of the principle of collapse to have had so much of the principle of development. "On the basis of so great a weakness," one hears the reader say, "where was your idea of the interest? On the basis of so great an interest, where is the provision for so much weakness?" One feels indeed, in the light of this challenge, on how much too scantly projected and suggested a field poor Roderick and his large capacity for ruin are made to turn round. It has all begun too soon, as I say, and too simply, and the determinant function attributed to Christina Light, the character of well-nigh sole agent of his catastrophe that this unforunate young woman has forced upon her, fails to commend itself to our sense of truth and proportion.

It was not, however, that I was at ease on this score even in the first fond good faith of composition; I felt too, all the while, how many more ups and downs, how many more adventures and complications my young man would have had to know, how much more experience it would have taken, in short, either to make him go under or to make him triumph. The greater complexity, the superior truth, was all more or less present to me; only the question was, too dreadfully, how make it present to the reader? How boil down so many facts in the alembic, so that the distilled result, the produced appearance, should have intensity, lucidity, brevity, beauty, all the merits required for my effect? How, when it was already so difficult, as I found, to proceed even as I *was* proceeding? It did n't help, alas, it only maddened, to remember that Balzac would have known how, and would have yet asked no additional credit for it.

All the difficulty I could dodge still struck me, at any rate, as leaving more than enough; and yet I was already consciously in presence, here, of the most interesting question the artist has to consider. To give the image and the sense of certain things while still keeping them subordinate to his plan, keeping them in relation to matters more immediate and apparent, to give all the sense, in a word, without all the substance or all the surface, and so to summarise and foreshorten, so to make values both rich and sharp, that the mere procession of items and profiles is not only, for the occasion, superseded, but is, for essential quality, almost "compromised"—such a case of delicacy proposes itself at every turn to the painter of life who wishes both to treat his chosen subject and to confine his necessary picture. It is only by doing such things that art becomes exquisite, and it is only by positively becoming exquisite that it keeps clear of becoming vulgar, repudiates the coarse industries that masquerade in its name. This eternal time-question is accordingly, for the novelist, always there and always formidable; always insisting on the *effect* of the great lapse and passage, of the "dark backward and abysm," by the terms of truth, and on the effect of compression, of composition and form, by the terms of literary arrangement. It is really a business to terrify all but stout hearts into abject omission and mutilation, though the terror would indeed be more general were the general consciousness of the difficulty greater. It is not by consciousness of difficulty, in truth, that the story-teller is mostly ridden; so prodigious a number of stories would otherwise scarce get themselves (shall it be called?) "told." None was ever very well told, I think, under the law of mere elimination—inordinately as that device appears in many quarters to be depended on. I remember doing my best not to be reduced to it for "Roderick," at the same time that I did so helplessly and consciously beg a thousand questions. What I clung to as

my principle of simplification was the precious truth that
I was dealing, after all, essentially with an Action, and that
no action, further, was ever made historically vivid without
a certain factitious compactness; though this logic indeed
opened up horizons and abysses of its own. But into these
we must plunge on some other occasion.

It was at any rate under an admonition or two fished out
of their depths that I must have tightened my hold of the
remedy afforded, such as it was, for the absence of those
more adequate illustrations of Roderick's character and history. Since one was dealing with an Action one might borrow a scrap of the Dramatist's all-in-all, his intensity—
which the novelist so often ruefully envies him as a fortune
in itself. The amount of illustration I could allow to the
grounds of my young man's disaster was unquestionably
meagre, but I might perhaps make it lively; I might produce illusion if I should be able to achieve intensity. It was
for that I must have tried, I now see, with such art as I
could command; but I make out in another quarter above
all what really saved me. My subject, all blissfully, in face
of difficulties, had defined itself—and this in spite of the title
of the book—as not directly, in the least, my young sculp-
tor's adventure. This it had been but indirectly, being all the
while in essence and in final effect another man's, his friend's
and patron's, view and experience of him. One's luck was
to have felt one's subject right—whether instinct or calculation, in those dim days, most served; and the circumstance
even amounts perhaps to a little lesson that when this has
happily occurred faults may show, faults may disfigure, and
yet not upset the work. It remains in equilibrium by having found its centre, the point of command of all the rest.
From this centre the subject has been treated, from this
centre the interest has spread, and so, whatever else it may
do or may not do, the thing has acknowledged a principle of composition and contrives at least to hang together.

We see in such a case why it should so hang; we escape that dreariest displeasure it is open to experiments in this general order to inflict, the sense of any hanging-together precluded as by the very terms of the case.

The centre of interest throughout "Roderick" is in Rowland Mallet's consciousness, and the drama is the very drama of that consciousness—which I had of course to make sufficiently acute in order to enable it, like a set and lighted scene, to hold the play. By making it acute, meanwhile, one made its own movement—or rather, strictly, its movement in the particular connexion—interesting; this movement really being quite the stuff of one's thesis. It had, naturally, Rowland's consciousness, not to be *too* acute —which would have disconnected it and made it superhuman: the beautiful little problem was to keep it connected, connected intimately, with the general human exposure, and thereby bedimmed and befooled and bewildered, anxious, restless, fallible, and yet to endow it with such intelligence that the appearances reflected in it, and constituting together there the situation and the "story," should become by that fact intelligible. Discernible from the first the joy of such a "job" as this making of his relation to everything involved a sufficiently limited, a sufficiently pathetic, tragic, comic, ironic, personal state to be thoroughly natural, and yet at the same time a sufficiently clear medium to represent a whole. This whole was to be the sum of what "happened" to him, or in other words his total adventure; but as what happened to him was above all to feel certain things happening to others, to Roderick, to Christina, to Mary Garland, to Mrs. Hudson, to the Cavaliere, to the Prince, so the beauty of the constructional game was to preserve in everything its especial value for *him*. The ironic effect of his having fallen in love with the girl who is herself in love with Roderick, though he is unwitting, at the time, of that secret—the conception of this last irony, I must add, has remained happier than my execution of it; which should logically have involved the reader's being put into position to take more closely home the impression made by Mary Garland. The ground has not been laid for it, and when that is the case one builds all vainly in the air: one patches up one's superstructure, one paints it in the prettiest colours, one hangs fine old tapestry and rare brocade over its window-sills, one flies emblazoned banners from its roof—the building none the less totters and refuses to stand square.

It is not really *worked-in* that Roderick himself could have pledged his faith in such a quarter, much more at such a crisis, before leaving America: and that weakness, clearly, produces a limp in the whole march of the fable. Just so, though there was no reason on earth (unless I except one, presently to be mentioned) why Rowland should *not*, at Northampton, have conceived a passion, or as near an approach to one as he was capable of, for a remarkable young woman there suddenly dawning on his sight, a particular fundamental care was required for the vivification of that possibility. The care, unfortunately, has not been skilfully enough taken, in spite of the later patching-up of the girl's figure. We fail to accept it, on the actual showing, as that of a young person irresistible at any moment, and above all irresistible at a moment of the liveliest *other* preoccupation, as that of the weaver of (even the highly conditioned) spell that the narrative imputes to her. The spell of attraction is cast upon young men by young women in all sorts of ways, and the novel has no more constant office than to remind us of that. But Mary Garland's way does n't, indubitably, convince us; any more than we are truly convinced, I think, that Rowland's destiny, or say his nature, would have made him accessible at the same hour to two quite distinct commotions, each a very deep one, of his whole personal economy. Rigidly viewed, each of these upheavals of his sensibility must have been exclusive of other upheavals, yet the reader is asked to accept them as working together. They are different vibrations, but the whole sense of the situation depicted is that they should each have been of the strongest, too strong to walk hand in hand. Therefore it is that when, on the ship, under the stars, Roderick suddenly takes his friend into the confidence of his engagement, we instinctively disallow the friend's title to discomfiture. The whole picture presents him as for the time on the mounting wave, exposed highly enough, no doubt, to a hundred discomfitures, but least exposed to that one. The damage to verisimilitude is deep.

The difficulty had been from the first that I required my antithesis—my antithesis to Christina Light, one of the main terms of the subject. One is ridden by the law that antitheses, to be efficient, shall be both direct and complete. Directness seemed to fail unless Mary should be, so to speak, "plain," Christina being essentially so "coloured"; and completeness seemed to fail unless she too should have her potency. She could moreover, by which I mean the antithetic young woman could, perfectly have had it; only success would have been then in the narrator's art to attest it. Christina's own presence and action are, on the other hand, I think, all firm ground; the truth probably being that the ideal antithesis rarely does "come off," and that it has to content itself for the most part with a strong term and a weak term, and even then to feel itself lucky. If one of the terms *is* strong, that perhaps may pass, in the most difficult of the arts, for a triumph. I remember at all events feeling, toward the end of "Roderick," that the Princess Casamassima had been launched, that, wound-up with the right silver key, she would go on a certain time by the motion communicated; thanks to which I knew the pity, the real pang of losing sight of her. I desired as in no other such case I can recall to preserve, to recover the vision; and I have seemed to myself in re-reading the book quite to understand why. The multiplication of touches had produced even more life than the subject required, and that life, in other conditions, in some other prime relation, would still have somehow to be spent. Thus one would watch for her and waylay her at some turn of the road to come—all that was to be needed was to give her time. This I did in fact, meeting her again and taking her up later on.

PREFACE TO "THE AMERICAN"

(VOLUME II IN THE NEW YORK EDITION)

"THE AMERICAN," which I had begun in Paris early in the winter of 1875-76, made its first appearance in "The Atlantic Monthly" in June of the latter year and continued there, from month to month, till May of the next. It started on its course while much was still unwritten, and there again come back to me, with this remembrance, the frequent hauntings and alarms of that comparatively early time; the habit of wondering what would happen if anything *should* "happen," if one should break one's arm by an accident or make a long illness or suffer, in body, mind, fortune, any other visitation involving a loss of time. The habit of apprehension became of course in some degree the habit of confidence that one would pull through, that, with opportunity enough, grave interruption never yet *had* descended, and that a special Providence, in short, despite the sad warning of Thackeray's "Denis Duval" and of Mrs. Gaskell's "Wives and Daughters" (that of Stevenson's "Weir of Hermiston" was yet to come) watches over anxious novelists condemned to the economy of serialisation. I make myself out in memory as having at least for many months and in many places given my Providence much to do: so great a variety of scenes of labour, implying all so much renewal of application, glimmer out of the book as I now read it over. And yet as the faded interest of the whole episode becomes again mildly vivid what I seem most to recover is, in its pale spectrality, a degree of joy, an eagerness on behalf of my recital, that must recklessly enough have overridden anxieties of every sort, including any view of inherent difficulties.

I seem to recall no other like connexion in which the case was met, to my measure, by so fond a complacency, in which my subject can have appeared so apt to take care of itself. I see now that I might all the while have taken much better care of it; yet, as I had at the time no sense of neglecting it, neither acute nor rueful solicitude, I can but speculate all vainly to-day on the oddity of my composure. I ask myself indeed if, possibly, recognising after I was launched the danger of an inordinate leak—since the ship has truly a hole in its side more than sufficient to have sunk it—I may not have managed, as a counsel of mere despair, to stop my ears against the noise of waters and *pretend* to myself I was afloat; being indubitably, in any case, at sea, with no harbour of refuge till the end of my serial voyage. If I succeeded at all in that emulation (in another sphere) of the pursued ostrich I must have succeeded altogether; must have buried my head in the sand and there found beatitude. The explanation of my enjoyment of it, no doubt, is that I was more than commonly enamoured of my idea, and that I believed it, so trusted, so imaginatively fostered, not less capable of limping to its goal on three feet than on one. The lameness might be what it would: I clearly, for myself, felt the thing *go*—which is the most a dramatist can ever ask of his drama; and I shall here accordingly indulge myself in speaking first of how, superficially, it did so proceed; explaining then what I mean by its practical dependence on a miracle.

It had come to me, this happy, halting view of an interesting case, abruptly enough, some years before: I recall sharply the felicity of the first glimpse, though I forget the accident of thought that produced it. I recall that I was seated in an American "horse-car" when I found myself, of a sudden, considering with enthusiasm, as the theme of a "story," the situation, in another country and an aristocratic society, of some robust but insidiously beguiled and betrayed, some cruelly wronged, compatriot: the point being in especial that he should suffer at the hands of persons pretending to represent the highest possible civilisation and to be of an order in every way superior to his own. What would he "do" in that predicament, how would he right himself, or how, failing a remedy, would he conduct himself under his wrong? This would be the question involved, and I remember well how, having entered the horse-car without a dream of it, I was presently to leave that vehicle in full possession of my answer. He would behave in the most interesting manner—it would all depend on that: stricken, smarting, sore, he would arrive at his just vindication and then would fail of all triumphantly and all vulgarly enjoying it. He would hold his revenge and cherish it and feel its sweetness, and then in the very act of forcing it home would sacrifice it in disgust. He would let them go, in short, his haughty contemners, even while feeling them, with joy, in his power, and he would obey, in so doing, one of the large and easy impulses *generally* characteristic of his type. He wouldn't "forgive"—that would have, in the case, no application; he would simply turn, at the supreme moment, away, the bitterness of his personal loss yielding to the very force of his aversion. All he would have at the end would be therefore just the moral convenience, indeed the moral necessity, of his practical, but quite unappreciated, magnanimity; and one's last view of him would be that of a strong man indifferent to his strength and too wrapped in fine, too wrapped above all in *other* and intenser, reflexions for the assertion of his "rights." This last point was of the essence and constituted in fact the subject: there would be no subject at all, obviously,—or simply the commonest of the common,—if my gentleman should enjoy his advantage. I was charmed with my idea, which would take, however, much working out; and pre-

cisely because it had so much to give, I think, must I have
dropped it for the time into the deep well of unconscious
cerebration: not without the hope, doubtless, that it might
eventually emerge from that reservoir, as one had already
known the buried treasure to come to light, with a firm iridescent surface and a notable increase of weight.

This resurrection then took place in Paris, where I was at
the moment living, and in December, 1875; my good fortune
being apparently that Paris had ever so promptly offered
me, and with an immediate directness at which I now marvel (since I had come back there, after earlier visitations,
but a few weeks before), everything that was needed to make
my conception concrete. I seem again at this distant day
to see it become so quickly and easily, quite as if filling
itself with life in that air. The objectivity it had wanted it
promptly put on, and if the questions had been, with the
usual intensity, for my hero and his crisis—the whole formidable list, the who? the what? the where? the when?
the why? the how?—they gathered their answers in the
cold shadow of the Arc de Triomphe, for fine reasons, very
much as if they had been plucking spring flowers for the
weaving of a frolic garland. I saw from one day to another
my particular cluster of circumstances, with the life of the
splendid city playing up in it like a flashing fountain in
a marble basin. The very splendour seemed somehow to
witness and intervene; it was important for the effect of my
friend's discomfiture that it should take place on a high and
lighted stage, and that his original ambition, the project
exposing him, should have sprung from beautiful and noble
suggestions—those that, at certain hours and under certain
impressions, we feel the many-tinted medium by the Seine
irresistibly to communicate. It was all charmingly simple,
this conception, and the current must have gushed, full and
clear, to my imagination, from the moment Christopher Newman rose before me, on a perfect day of the divine Paris

23

spring, in the great gilded Salon Carré of the Louvre. Under this strong contagion of the place he would, by the happiest of hazards, meet his old comrade, now initiated and domiciled; after which the rest would go of itself. If he was to be wronged he would be wronged with just that conspicuity, with his felicity at just that pitch and with the highest aggravation of the general effect of misery mocked at. Great and gilded the whole trap set, in fine, for his wary freshness and into which it would blunder upon its fate. I have, I confess, no memory of a disturbing doubt; once the man himself was imaged to me (and *that* germination is a process almost always untraceable) he must have walked into the situation as by taking a pass-key from his pocket.

But what then meanwhile would be the affront one would see him as most feeling? The affront of course done him as a lover; and yet not that done by his mistress herself, since injuries of this order are the stalest stuff of romance. I was not to have him jilted, any more than I was to have him successfully vindictive: both his wrong and his right would have been in these cases of too vulgar a type. I doubtless even then felt that the conception of Paris as the consecrated scene of rash infatuations and bold bad treacheries belongs, in the Anglo-Saxon imagination, to the infancy of art. The right renovation of any such theme as *that* would place it in Boston or at Cleveland, at Hartford or at Utica—give it some local connexion in which we had not already had so much of it. No, I should make my heroine herself, if heroine there was to be, an equal victim—just as Romeo was not less the sport of fate for not having been interestedly sacrificed by Juliet; and to this end I had but to imagine "great people" again, imagine my hero confronted and involved with them, and impute to them, with a fine free hand, the arrogance and cruelty, the tortuous behaviour, in given conditions, of which great people have been historically so often capable. But as this was the light in which they were to show, so the essence of the matter would be that he should at the right moment find them in his power, and so the situation would reach its highest interest with the question of his utilisation of that knowledge. It would be here, in the possession and application of his power, that he would come out strong and would so deeply appeal to our sympathy. Here above all it really was, however, that my conception unfurled, with the best conscience in the world, the emblazoned flag of romance; which venerable ensign it had, though quite unwittingly, from the first and at every point sported in perfect good faith. I had been plotting arch-romance without knowing it, just as I began to write it that December day without recognising it and just as I all serenely and blissfully pursued the process from month to month and from place to place; just as I now, in short, reading the book over, find it yields me no interest and no reward comparable to the fond perception of this truth.

The thing is consistently, consummately—and I would fain really make bold to say charmingly—romantic; and all without intention, presumption, hesitation, contrition. The effect is equally undesigned and unabashed, and I lose myself, at this late hour, I am bound to add, in a certain sad envy of the free play of so much unchallenged instinct. One would like to woo back such hours of fine precipitation. They represent to the critical sense which the exercise of one's *whole* faculty has, with time, so inevitably and so thoroughly waked up, the happiest season of surrender to the invoked muse and the projected fable: the season of images so free and confident and ready that they brush questions aside and disport themselves, like the artless schoolboys of Gray's beautiful Ode, in all the ecstasy of the ignorance attending them. The time doubtless comes soon enough when questions, as I call them, rule the roost and when the little victim, to adjust Gray's term again to the creature of frolic fancy, does n't dare propose a gambol till they have all (like a board of trustees discussing a new outlay) sat on the possibly scandalous case. I somehow feel, accordingly, that it was lucky to have sacrificed on this particular altar while one still could; though it is perhaps droll—in a yet higher degree—to have done so not simply because one was guileless, but even quite under the conviction, in a general way, that, since no "rendering" of any object and no painting of any picture can take effect without some form of reference and control, so these guarantees could but reside in a high probity of observation. I must decidedly have supposed, all the while, that I was acutely observing—and with a blest absence of wonder at its being so easy. Let me certainly at present rejoice in that absence; for I ask myself how without it I could have written "The American."

Was it indeed meanwhile my excellent conscience that kept the charm as unbroken as it appears to me, in rich retrospect, to have remained?—or is it that I suffer the mere influence of remembered, of associated places and hours, all acute impressions, to palm itself off as the sign of a finer confidence than I could justly claim? It is a pleasure to perceive how again and again the shrunken depths of old work yet permit themselves to be sounded or—even if rather terrible the image—"dragged": the long pole of memory stirs and rummages the bottom, and we fish up such fragments and relics of the submerged life and the extinct consciousness as tempt us to piece them together. My windows looked into the Rue de Luxembourg—since then meagrely re-named Rue Cambon—and the particular light Parisian click of the small cab-horse on the clear asphalt, with its sharpness of detonation between the high houses, makes for the faded page to-day a sort of interlineation of sound. This sound rises to a martial clatter at the moment a troop of cuirassiers charges down the narrow street, each morning, to file, directly opposite my house, through the plain portal of the barracks occupying part of the vast domain at-

tached in a rearward manner to one of the Ministères that
front on the Place Vendôme; an expanse marked, along a
considerable stretch of the street, by one of those high painted
and administratively-placarded garden walls that form deep,
vague, recurrent notes in the organic vastness of the city. I
have but to re-read ten lines to recall my daily effort not to
waste time in hanging over the window-bar for a sight of
the cavalry the hard music of whose hoofs so directly and
thrillingly appealed; an effort that inveterately failed—and a
trivial circumstance now dignified, to my imagination, I may
add, by the fact that the fruits of this weakness, the various
items of the vivid picture, so constantly recaptured, must have
been in themselves suggestive and inspiring, must have been
rich strains, in their way, of the great Paris harmony. I have
ever, in general, found it difficult to write of places under too
immediate an impression—the impression that prevents standing off and allows neither space nor time for perspective. The
image has had for the most part to be dim if the reflexion
was to be, as is proper for a reflexion, both sharp and quiet:
one has a horror, I think, artistically, of agitated reflexions.

Perhaps that is why the novel, after all, was to achieve,
as it went on, no great—certainly no very direct—transfusion of the immense overhanging presence. It had to save
as it could its own life, to keep tight hold of the tenuous
silver thread, the one hope for which was that it should n't
be tangled or clipped. This earnest grasp of the silver thread
was doubtless an easier business in other places—though as
I remount the stream of composition I see it faintly coloured
again: with the bright protection of the Normandy coast
(I worked away a few weeks at Étretat); with the stronger
glow of southernmost France, breaking in during a stay at
Bayonne; then with the fine historic and other "psychic" substance of Saint-Germain-en-Laye, a purple patch of terraced
October before returning to Paris. There comes after that the
memory of a last brief intense invocation of the enclosing

scene, of the pious effort to unwind my tangle, with a firm hand, in the very light (that light of high, narrowish French windows in old rooms, the light somehow, as one always feels, of "style" itself) that had quickened my original vision. I was to pass over to London that autumn; which was a reason the more for considering the matter—the matter of Newman's final predicament—with due intensity: to let a loose end dangle over into alien air would so fix upon the whole, I strenuously felt, the dishonour of piecemeal composition. Therefore I strove to finish—first in a small dusky hotel of the Rive Gauche, where, though the windows again were high, the days were dim and the crepuscular court, domestic, intimate, "quaint," testified to ancient manners almost as if it had been that of Balzac's Maison Vauquer in "Le Père Goriot": and then once more in the Rue de Luxembourg, where a black-framed Empire portrait-medallion, suspended in the centre of each white panel of my almost noble old salon, made the coolest, discreetest, most measured decoration, and where, through casements open to the last mildness of the year, a belated Saint Martin's summer, the tale was taken up afresh by the charming light click and clatter, that sound as of the thin, quick, quite feminine surface-breathing of Paris, the shortest of rhythms for so huge an organism.

I shall not tell whether I did there bring my book to a close—and indeed I shrink, for myself, from putting the question to the test of memory. I follow it so far, the old urgent ingenious business, and then I lose sight of it: from which I infer—all exact recovery of the matter failing—that I did not in the event drag over the Channel a lengthening chain; which would have been detestable. I reduce to the absurd perhaps, however, by that small subjective issue, any undue measure of the interest of this insistent recovery of what I have called attendant facts. There always has been, for the valid work of art, a history—though mainly inviting, doubtless, but to the curious critic, for whom such things grow up and are formed very much in the manner of attaching young lives and characters, those conspicuous cases of happy development as to which evidence and anecdote are always in order. The development indeed must be certain to have been happy, the life sincere, the character fine: the work of art, to create or repay critical curiosity, must in short have been very "valid" indeed. Yet there is on the other hand no mathematical measure of that importance—it may be a matter of widely-varying appreciation; and I am willing to grant, assuredly, that this interest, in a given relation, will nowhere so effectually kindle as on the artist's own part. And I am afraid that after all even his best excuse for it must remain the highly personal plea—the joy of living over, as a chapter of experience, the particular intellectual adventure. Here lurks an immense homage to the general privilege of the artist, to that constructive, that creative passion—portentous words, but they are convenient—the exercise of which finds so many an occasion for appearing to him the highest of human fortunes, the rarest boon of the gods. He values it, all sublimely and perhaps a little fatuously, for itself—as the great extension, great beyond all others, of experience and of consciousness; with the toil and trouble a mere sun-cast shadow that falls, shifts and vanishes, the result of his living in so large a light. On the constant nameless felicity of this Robert Louis Stevenson has, in an admirable passage and as in so many other connexions, said the right word: that the partaker of the "life of art" who repines at the absence of the rewards, as they are called, of the pursuit might surely be better occupied. Much rather should he endlessly wonder at his not having to pay half his substance for his luxurious immersion. He enjoys it, so to speak, without a tax; the effort of labour involved, the torment. of expression, of which we have heard in our time so much, being after all but the last refinement of his privilege. It may leave him weary and worn; but how, after his fashion, he will have lived! As if one were to expect at once freedom and ease! That silly safety is but the sign of bondage and forfeiture. Who can imagine free selection—which is the beautiful, terrible *whole* of art —without free difficulty? This is the very franchise of the city and high ambition of the citizen. The vision of the difficulty, as one looks back, bathes one's course in a golden glow by which the very objects along the road are transfigured and glorified; so that one exhibits them to other eyes with an elation possibly presumptuous.

Since I accuse myself at all events of these complacencies I take advantage of them to repeat that I value, in my retrospect, nothing so much as the lively light on the romantic property of my subject that I had not expected to encounter. If in "The American" I invoked the romantic association without malice prepense, yet with a production of the romantic effect that is for myself unmistakeable, the occasion is of the best perhaps for penetrating a little the obscurity of that principle. By what art or mystery, what craft of selection, omission or commission, does a given picture of life appear to us to surround its theme, its figures and images, with the air of romance while another picture close beside it may affect us as steeping the whole matter in the element of reality? It is a question, no doubt, on the painter's part, very much more of perceived effect, effect *after* the fact, than of conscious design—though indeed I have ever failed to see how a coherent picture of anything is producible save by a complex of fine measurements. The cause of the deflexion, in one pronounced sense or the other, must lie deep, however; so that for the most part we recognise the character of our interest only after the particular magic, as I say, has thoroughly operated—and then in truth but if we be a bit critically minded, if we find our pleasure, that is, in these intimate appreciations (for which, as I am well aware, ninety-nine readers in a hundred have no use whatever). The determining condition would at any rate seem so latent that one may well doubt if the full artistic consciousness ever reaches it; leaving the matter thus a case, ever, not of an author's plotting and planning and calculating, but just of his feeling and seeing, of his conceiving, in a word, and of his thereby inevitably expressing himself, under the influence of one value or the other. These values represent different sorts and degrees of the communicable thrill, and I doubt if any novelist, for instance, ever proposed to commit himself to one kind or the other with as little mitigation as we are sometimes able to find for him. The interest is greatest—the interest of his genius, I mean, and of his general wealth—when he commits himself in both directions; not quite at the same time or to the same effect, of course, but by some need of performing his whole possible revolution, by the law of some rich passion in him for extremes.

Of the men of largest responding imagination before the human scene, of Scott, of Balzac, even of the coarse, comprehensive, prodigious Zola, we feel, I think, that the deflexion toward either quarter has never taken place; that neither the nature of the man's faculty nor the nature of his experience has ever quite determined it. His current remains therefore extraordinarily rich and mixed, washing us successively with the warm wave of the near and familiar and the tonic shock, as may be, of the far and strange. (In making which opposition I suggest not that the strange and the far are at all necessarily romantic: they happen to be simply the unknown, which is quite a different matter. The real represents to my perception the things we cannot possibly *not* know, sooner or later, in one way or another; it being but one of the accidents of our hampered state, and one of the incidents of their quantity and number, that particular instances have not yet come our way. The romantic stands, on the other hand, for the things that, with all the facilties in the world, all the wealth and all the courage and all the wit and all the adventure, we never *can* directly know; the things that can reach us only through the beautiful circuit and subterfuge of our thought and our desire.) There have been, I gather, many definitions of romance, as a matter indispensably of boats, or of caravans, or of tigers, or of "historical characters," or of ghosts, or of forgers, or of detectives, or of beautiful wicked women, or of pistols and knives, but they appear for the most part reducible to the idea of the facing of danger, the acceptance of great risks for the fascination, the very love, of their uncertainty, the joy of success if possible and of battle in any case. This would be a fine formula if it bore examination; but it strikes me as weak and inadequate, as by no means covering the true ground and yet as landing us in strange confusions.

The panting pursuit of danger is the pursuit of life itself, in which danger awaits us possibly at every step and faces us at every turn; so that the dream of an intenser experience easily becomes rather some vision of a sublime security like that enjoyed on the flowery plains of heaven, where we may conceive ourselves proceeding in ecstasy from one prodigious phase and form of it to another. And if it be insisted that the measure of the type is then in the *appreciation* of danger—the sign of our projection of the real being the smallness of its dangers, and that of our projection of the romantic the hugeness, the mark of the distinction being in short, as they say of collars and gloves and shoes, the size and "number" of the danger—this discrimination again surely fails, since it makes our difference not a difference of kind, which is what we want, but a difference only of degree, and subject by that condition to the indignity of a sliding scale and a shifting measure. There are immense and flagrant dangers that are but sordid and squalid ones, as we feel, tainting with their quality the very defiances they provoke; while there are common and covert ones, that "look like nothing" and that can be but inwardly and occultly dealt with, which involve the sharpest hazards to life and honour and the highest instant decisions and intrepidities of action. It is an arbitrary stamp that keeps these latter prosaic and makes the former heroic; and yet I should still less subscribe to a mere "subjective" division—I mean one that would place the difference wholly in the temper of the imperilled agent. It would be impossible to have a more romantic temper than Flaubert's Madame Bovary, and yet nothing less resembles a romance than the record of her adventures. To classify it by that aspect—the definition of the spirit that happens to animate her—is like settling the question (as I have seen it witlessly settled) by the presence or absence of "costume." Where again then does costume begin or end?—save with the "run" of one or another sort of play? We must reserve vague labels for artless mixtures.

The only *general* attribute of projected romance that I can see, the only one that fits all its cases, is the fact of the kind of experience with which it deals—experience liberated, so to speak; experience disengaged, disembroiled, disencumbered, exempt from the conditions that we usually know to attach to it and, if we wish so to put the matter, drag upon it, and operating in a medium which relieves it, in a particular interest, of the inconvenience of a *related,* a measurable state, a state subject to all our vulgar communities. The greatest intensity may so be arrived at evidently —when the sacrifice of community, of the "related" sides of situations, has not been too rash. It must to this end not flagrantly betray itself; we must even be kept if possible, for our illusion, from suspecting any sacrifice at all. The balloon of experience is in fact of course tied to the earth, and under that necessity we swing, thanks to a rope of remarkable length, in the more or less commodious car of the imagination; but it is by the rope we know where

we are, and from the moment that cable is cut we are at
large and unrelated: we only swing apart from the globe
—though remaining as exhilarated, naturally, as we like,
especially when all goes well. The art of the romancer is,
"for the fun of it," insidiously to cut the cable, to cut it
without our detecting him. What I have recognised then
in "The American," much to my surprise and after long
years, is that the experience here represented is the disconnected and uncontrolled experience—uncontrolled by our general sense of "the way things happen"—which romance alone
more or less successfully palms off on us. It is a case of
Newman's own intimate experience all, that being my subject, the thread of which, from beginning to end, is not
once exchanged, however momentarily, for any other thread;
and the experience of others concerning us, and concerning
him, only so far as it touches him and as he recognises,
feels or divines it. There is our general sense of the way
things happen—it abides with us indefeasibly, as readers
of fiction, from the moment we demand that our fiction
shall be intelligible; and there is our particular sense of
the way they don't happen, which is liable to wake up unless reflexion and criticism, in us, have been skilfully and
successfully drugged. There are drugs enough, clearly—it
is all a question of applying them with tact; in which case
the way things don't happen may be artfully made to pass for
the way things do.

Amusing and even touching to me, I profess, at this time
of day, the ingenuity (worthy, with whatever lapses, of
a better cause) with which, on behalf of Newman's adventure, this hocus-pocus is attempted: the value of the instance not being diminished either, surely, by its having been
attempted in such evident good faith. Yes, all is romantic
to my actual vision here, and not least so, I hasten to add,
the fabulous felicity of my candour. The way things happen is frankly not the way in which they are represented

34

as having happened, in Paris, to my hero: the situation
I had conceived only saddled me with that for want of my
invention of something better. The great house of Bellegarde, in a word, would, I now feel, given the circumstances, given the *whole* of the ground, have comported
itself in a manner as different as possible from the manner
to which my narrative commits it; of which truth, moreover, I am by no means sure that, in spite of what I have
called my serenity, I had not all the while an uneasy suspicion. I had dug in my path, alas, a hole into which I
was destined to fall. I was so possessed of my idea that
Newman should be ill-used—which was the essence of my
subject—that I attached too scant an importance to its fashion of coming about. Almost any fashion would serve, I
appear to have assumed, that would give me my main
chance for him; a matter depending not so much on the
particular trick played him as on the interesting face presented by him to *any* damnable trick. So where I part company with *terra-firma* is in making that projected, that
performed outrage so much more showy, dramatically speaking, than sound. Had I patched it up to a greater apparent
soundness my own trick, artistically speaking, would have
been played; I should have cut the cable without my reader's suspecting it. I doubtless at the time, I repeat, believed
I had taken my precautions; but truly they should have
been greater, to impart the air of truth to the attitude—
that is first to the pomp and circumstance, and second to the
queer falsity—of the Bellegardes.

They would positively have jumped then, the Bellegardes,
at my rich and easy American, and not have "minded" in
the least any drawback—especially as, after all, given the
pleasant palette from which I have painted him, there were
few drawbacks to mind. My subject imposed on me a group
of closely-allied persons animated by immense pretensions—
which was all very well, which might be full of the prom-

ise of interest: only of interest felt most of all in the light of comedy and of irony. This, better understood, would have dwelt in the idea not in the least of their not finding Newman good enough for their alliance and thence being ready to sacrifice him, but in that of their taking with alacrity everything he could give them, only asking for more and more, and then adjusting their pretensions and their pride to it with all the comfort in life. Such accommodation of the theory of a noble indifference to the practice of a deep avidity is the real note of policy in forlorn aristocracies—and I meant of course that the Bellegardes should be virtually forlorn. The perversion of truth is by no means, I think, in the displayed acuteness of their remembrance of "who" and "what" they are, or at any rate take themselves for; since it is the misfortune of all insistence on "worldly" advantages— and the situation of such people bristles at the best (by which I mean under whatever invocation of a superficial simplicity) with emphasis, accent, assumption—to produce at times an effect of grossness. The picture of their tergiversation, at all events, however it may originally have seemed to me to hang together, has taken on this rococo appearance precisely because their preferred course, a thousand times preferred, would have been to haul him and his fortune into their boat under cover of night perhaps, in any case as quietly and with as little bumping and splashing as possible, and there accommodate him with the very safest and most convenient seat. Given Newman, given the fact that the thing constitutes itself organically as *his* adventure, that too might very well be a situation and a subject: only it wouldn't have been the theme of "The American" as the book stands, the theme to which I was from so early pledged. Since I had wanted a "wrong" this other turn might even have been arranged to give me *that,* might even have been arranged to meet my requirement that somebody or something should be "in his power" so delightfully; and with the signal effect.

after all, of "defining" everything. (It is as difficult, I said above, to trace the dividing-line between the real and the romantic as to plant a milestone between north and south; but I am not sure an infallible sign of the latter is not this rank vegetation of the "power" of bad people that good get into, or *vice versa*. It is so rarely, alas, into *our* power that any one gets!)

It is difficult for me to-day to believe that I had not, as my work went on, *some* shade of the rueful sense of my affront to verisimilitude; yet I catch the memory at least of no great sharpness, no true critical anguish, of remorse: an anomaly the reason of which in fact now glimmers interestingly out. My concern, as I saw it, was to make and to keep Newman consistent; the picture of his consistency was all my undertaking, and the memory of *that* infatuation perfectly abides with me. He was to be the lighted figure, the others—even doubtless to an excessive degree the woman who is made the agent of his discomfiture—were to be the obscured; by which I should largely get the very effect most to be invoked, that of a generous nature engaged with forces, with difficulties and dangers, that it but half understands. If Newman was attaching enough, I must have argued, his tangle would be sensible enough; for the interest of everything is all that it is *his* vision, *his* conception, *his* interpretation: at the window of his wide, quite sufficiently wide, consciousness we are seated, from that admirable position we "assist." He therefore supremely matters; all the rest matters only as he feels it, treats it, meets it. A beautiful infatuation this, always, I think, the intensity of the creative effort to get into the skin of the creature; the act of personal possession of one being by another at its completest—and with the high enhancement, ever, that it is, by the same stroke, the effort of the artist to preserve for his subject that unity, and for his use of it (in other words for the interest he desires to excite) that effect of a *centre,* which most economise its value. Its value is most discussable when that economy has most operated; the content and the "importance" of a work of art are in fine wholly dependent on its *being* one: outside of which all prate of its representative character, its meaning and its bearing, its morality and humanity, are an impudent thing. Strong in that character, which is the condition of its really bearing witness at all, it is strong every way. So much remains true then on behalf of my instinct of multiplying the fine touches by which Newman should live and communicate life; and yet I still ask myself, I confess, what I can have made of "life," in my picture, at such a juncture as the interval offered as elapsing between my hero's first accepted state and the nuptial rites that are to crown it. Nothing here is in truth "offered"—everything is evaded, and the effect of this, I recognise, is of the oddest. His relation to Madame de Cintré takes a great stride, but the author appears to view that but as a signal for letting it severely alone.

I have been stupefied, in so thoroughly revising the book, to find, on turning a page, that the light in which he is presented immediately after Madame de Bellegarde has conspicuously introduced him to all her circle as her daughter's husband-to-be is that of an evening at the opera quite alone; as if he wouldn't surely spend his leisure, and especially those hours of it, with his intended. Instinctively, from that moment, one would have seen them intimately and, for one's interest, beautifully together; with some illustration of the beauty incumbent on the author. The truth was that at this point the author, all gracelessly, could but hold his breath and pass; lingering was too difficult—he had made for himself a crushing complication. Since Madame de Cintré was after all to "back out" every touch in the picture of her apparent loyalty would add to her eventual shame. She had acted in clear good faith, but how could I give the *detail* of an attitude, on her part, of which the foundation was yet

so weak? I preferred, as the minor evil, to shirk the attempt
—at the cost evidently of a signal loss of "charm"; and with
this lady, altogether, I recognise, a light plank, too light a
plank, is laid for the reader over a dark "psychological" abyss.
The delicate clue to her conduct is never definitely placed in
his hand: I must have liked verily to think it *was* delicate
and to flatter myself it was to be felt with finger-tips rather
than heavily tugged at. Here then, at any rate, is the romantic *tout craché*—the fine flower of Newman's experience
blooming in a medium "cut off" and shut up to itself. I
don't for a moment pronounce any spell proceeding from
it necessarily the less workable, to a rejoicing ingenuity, for
that; beguile the reader's suspicion of *his* being shut up,
transform it for *him* into a positive illusion of the largest
liberty, and the success will ever be proportionate to the
chance. Only all this gave me, I make out, a great deal to
look to, and I was perhaps wrong in thinking that Newman
by himself, and for any occasional extra inch or so I might
smuggle into his measurements, would see me through my
wood. Anything more liberated and disconnected, to repeat
my terms, than his prompt general profession, before the
Tristrams, of aspiring to a "great" marriage, for example,
could surely not well be imagined. I had to take that over
with the rest of him and fit it in—I had indeed to exclude
the outer air. Still, I find on re-perusal that I have been able
to breathe at least in my aching void; so that, clinging to
my hero as to a tall, protective, good-natured elder brother
in a rough place, I leave the record to stand or fall by his
more or less convincing image.

III

PREFACE TO "THE PORTRAIT OF A LADY"

(VOLUME III IN THE NEW YORK EDITION)

"THE PORTRAIT OF A LADY" was, like "Roderick Hudson," begun in Florence, during three months spent there in the spring of 1879. Like "Roderick" and like "The American," it had been designed for publication in "The Atlantic Monthly," where it began to appear in 1880. It differed from its two predecessors, however, in finding a course also open to it, from month to month, in "Macmillan's Magazine"; which was to be for me one of the last occasions of simultaneous "serialisation" in the two countries that the changing conditions of literary intercourse between England and the United States had up to then left unaltered. It is a long novel, and I was long in writing it; I remember being again much occupied with it, the following year, during a stay of several weeks made in Venice. I had rooms on Riva Schiavoni, at the top of a house near the passage leading off to San Zaccaria; the waterside life, the wondrous lagoon spread before me, and the ceaseless human chatter of Venice came in at my windows, to which I seem to myself to have been constantly driven, in the fruitless fidget of composition, as if to see whether, out in the blue channel, the ship of some right suggestion, of some better phrase, of the next happy twist of my subject, the next true touch for my canvas, might n't come into sight. But I recall vividly enough that the response most elicited, in general, to these restless appeals was the rather grim admonition that romantic and historic sites, such as the land of Italy abounds in, offer the artist a questionable aid to concentration when they themselves are not to be the subject of it. They are too rich in their own life and too charged with their own meanings merely to help him out with a lame phrase; they draw him away from his small question to their own greater ones; so that, after a little, he feels, while thus yearning toward them in his difficulty, as if he were asking an army of glorious veterans to help him to arrest a peddler who has given him the wrong change.

There are pages of the book which, in the reading over, have seemed to make me see again the bristling curve of the wide Riva, the large colour-spots of the balconied houses and the repeated undulation of the little hunchbacked bridges, marked by the rise and drop again, with the wave, of fore-shortened clicking pedestrians. The Venetian footfall and the Venetian cry—all talk there, wherever uttered, having the pitch of a call across the water—come in once more at the window, renewing one's old impression of the delighted senses and the divided, frustrated mind. How can places that speak *in general* so to the imagination not give it, at the moment, the particular thing it wants? I recollect again and again, in beautiful places, dropping into that wonderment. The real truth is, I think, that they express, under this appeal, only too much—more than, in the given case, one has use for; so that one finds one's self working less congruously, after all, so far as the surrounding picture is concerned, than in presence of the moderate and the neutral, to which we may lend something of the light of our vision. Such a place as Venice is too proud for such charities; Venice does n't borrow, she but all magnificently gives. We profit by that enormously, but to do so we must either be quite off duty or be on it in her service alone. Such, and so rueful, are these reminiscences; though on the whole, no doubt, one's book, and one's "literary effort" at large, were to be the better for them. Strangely fertilising, in the long run, does a wasted effort of attention often prove. It all depends on *how* the attention has been cheated, has been squandered. There are high-handed insolent frauds, and there are insidious sneaking ones. And there is, I fear, even on the most designing artist's part, always witless enough good faith, always anxious enough desire, to fail to guard him against their deceits.

Trying to recover here, for recognition, the germ of my idea, I see that it must have consisted not at all in any conceit of a "plot," nefarious name, in any flash, upon the fancy, of a set of relations, or in any one of those situations that, by a logic of their own, immediately fall, for the fabulist, into movement, into a march or a rush, a patter of quick steps; but altogether in the sense of a single character, the character and aspect of a particular engaging young woman, to which all the usual elements of a "subject," certainly of a setting, were to need to be super-added. Quite as interesting as the young woman herself, at her best, do I find, I must again repeat, this projection of memory upon the whole matter of the growth, in one's imagination, of some such apology for a motive. These are the fascinations of the fabulist's art, these lurking forces of expansion, these necessities of upspringing in the seed, these beautiful determinations, on the part of the idea entertained, to grow as tall as possible, to push into the light and the air and thickly flower there; and, quite as much, these fine possibilities of recovering, from some good standpoint on the ground gained, the intimate history of the business—of retracing and reconstructing its steps and stages. I have always fondly remembered a remark that I heard fall years ago from the lips of Ivan Turgenieff in regard to his own experience of the usual origin of the fictive picture. It began for him almost always with the vision of some person or persons, who hovered before him, soliciting him, as the active or passive figure, interesting him and appealing to him just as they were and by what they

were. He saw them, in that fashion, as *disponibles,* saw them
subject to the chances, the complications of existence, and
saw them vividly, but then had to find for them the right
relations, those that would most bring them out; to imagine,
to invent and select and piece together the situations most useful and favourable to the sense of the creatures themselves,
the complications they would be most likely to produce and to
feel.

"To arrive at these things is to arrive at my 'story,'" he
said, "and that's the way I look for it. The result is that I'm
often accused of not having 'story' enough. I seem to myself to have as much as I need—to show my people, to
exhibit their relations with each other; for that is all my
measure. If I watch them long enough I see them come
together, I see them *placed,* I see them engaged in this or
that act and in this or that difficulty. How they look and
move and speak and behave, always in the setting I have
found for them, is my account of them—of which I dare
say, alas, *que cela manque souvent d'architecture.* But I would
rather, I think, have too little architecture than too much
—when there's danger of its interfering with my measure
of the truth. The French of course like more of it than
I give—having by their own genius such a hand for it;
and indeed one must give all one can. As for the origin of
one's wind-blown germs themselves, who shall say, as you
ask, where *they* come from? We have to go too far back,
too far behind, to say. Isn't it all we can say that they
come from every quarter of heaven, that they are *there* at
almost any turn of the road? They accumulate, and we are
always picking them over, selecting among them. They
are the breath of life—by which I mean that life, in its
own way, breathes them upon us. They are so, in a manner prescribed and imposed—floated into our minds by the
current of life. That reduces to imbecility the vain critic's
quarrel, so often, with one's subject, when he hasn't the

wit to accept it. Will he point out then which other it should properly have been?—his office being, essentially *to* point out. *Il en serait bien embarrassé*. Ah, when he points out what I've done or failed to do with it, that's another matter: there he's on his ground. I give him up my 'architecture,'" my distinguished friend concluded, "as much as he will."

So this beautiful genius, and I recall with comfort the gratitude I drew from his reference to the intensity of suggestion that may reside in the stray figure, the unattached character, the image *en disponibilité*. It gave me higher warrant than I seemed then to have met for just that blest habit of one's own imagination, the trick of investing some conceived or encountered individual, some brace or group of individuals, with the germinal property and authority. I was myself so much more antecedently conscious of my figures than of their setting—a too preliminary, a preferential interest in which struck me as in general such a putting of the cart before the horse. I might envy, though I couldn't emulate, the imaginative writer so constituted as to see his fable first and to make out its agents afterwards: I could think so little of any fable that it didn't need its agents positively to launch it; I could think so little of any situation that didn't depend for its interest on the nature of the persons situated, and thereby on their way of taking it. There are methods of so-called presentation, I believe— among novelists who have appeared to flourish—that offer the situation as indifferent to that support; but I have not lost the sense of the value for me, at the time, of the admirable Russian's testimony to my not needing, all superstitiously, to try and perform any such gymnastic. Other echoes from the same source linger with me, I confess, as unfadingly—if it be not all indeed one much-embracing echo. It was impossible after that not to read, for one's uses, high lucidity into the tormented and disfigured and bemuddled question of the objective value, and even quite into that of the critical appreciation, of "subject" in the novel.

One had had from an early time, for that matter, the instinct of the right estimate of such values and of its reducing to the inane the dull dispute over the "immoral" subject and the moral. Recognising so promptly the one measure of the worth of a given subject, the question about it that, rightly answered, disposes of all others—is it valid, in a word, is it genuine, is it sincere, the result of some direct impression or perception of life?—I had found small edification, mostly, in a critical pretension that had neglected from the first all delimitation of ground and all definition of terms. The air of my earlier time shows, to memory, as darkened, all round, with that vanity—unless the difference to-day be just in one's own final impatience, the lapse of one's attention. There is, I think, no more nutritive or suggestive truth in this connexion than that of the perfect dependence of the "moral" sense of a work of art on the amount of felt life concerned in producing it. The question comes back thus, obviously, to the kind and the degree of the artist's prime sensibility, which is the soil out of which his subject springs. The quality and capacity of that soil, its ability to "grow" with due freshness and straightness any vision of life, represents, strongly or weakly, the projected morality. That element is but another name for the more or less close connexion of the subject with some mark made on the intelligence, with some sincere experience. By which, at the same time, of course, one is far from contending that this enveloping air of the artist's humanity—which gives the last touch to the worth of the work—is not a widely and wondrously varying element; being on one occasion a rich and magnificent medium and on another a comparatively poor and ungenerous one. Here we get exactly the high price of the novel as a literary form—its power not only, while preserving that form with closeness, to range through all the differences of the individual relation to its general subject-matter, all the varieties of outlook on life, of disposition to reflect and project, created by conditions that are never the same from man to man (or, so far as that goes, from man to woman), but positively to appear more true to its character in proportion as it strains, or tends to burst, with a latent extravagance, its mould.

The house of fiction has in short not one window, but a million—a number of possible windows not to be reckoned, rather; every one of which has been pierced, or is still pierceable, in its vast front, by the need of the individual vision and by the pressure of the individual will. These apertures, of dissimilar shape and size, hang so, all together, over the human scene that we might have expected of them a greater sameness of report than we find. They are but windows at the best, mere holes in a dead wall, disconnected, perched aloft; they are not hinged doors opening straight upon life. But they have this mark of their own that at each of them stands a figure with a pair of eyes, or at least with a field-glass, which forms, again and again, for observation, a unique instrument, insuring to the person making use of it an impression distinct from every other. He and his neighbours are watching the same show, but one seeing more where the other sees less, one seeing black where the other sees white, one seeing big where the other sees small, one seeing coarse where the other sees fine. And so on, and so on; there is fortunately no saying on what, for the particular pair of eyes, the window may *not* open; "fortunately" by reason, precisely, of this incalculability of range. The spreading field, the human scene, is the "choice of subject"; the pierced aperture, either broad or balconied or slit-like and low-browed, is the "literary form"; but they are, singly or together, as nothing without the posted presence of the watcher—without, in other words, the consciousness of the artist. Tell me what the artist is, and I will tell you of what he has *been* conscious.

Thereby I shall express to you at once his boundless freedom and his "moral" reference.

All this is a long way round, however, for my word about my dim first move toward "The Portrait," which was exactly my grasp of a single character—an acquisition I had made, moreover, after a fashion not here to be retraced. Enough that I was, as seemed to me, in complete possession of it, that I had been so for a long time, that this had made it familiar and yet had not blurred its charm, and that, all urgently, all tormentingly, I saw it in motion and, so to speak, in transit. This amounts to saying that I saw it as bent upon its fate—some fate or other; *which,* among the possibilities, being precisely the question. Thus I had my vivid individual —vivid, so strangely, in spite of being still at large, not confined by the conditions, not engaged in the tangle, to which we look for much of the impress that constitutes an identity. If the apparition was still all to be placed how came it to be vivid?—since we puzzle such quantities out, mostly, just by the business of placing them. One could answer such a question beautifully, doubtless, if one could do so subtle, if not so monstrous, a thing as to write the history of the growth of one's imagination. One would describe then what, at a given time, had extraordinarily happened to it, and one would so, for instance, be in a position to tell, with an approach to clearness, how, under favour of occasion, it had been able to take over (take over straight from life) such and such a constituted, animated figure or form. The figure has to that extent, as you see, *been* placed—placed in the imagination that detains it, preserves, protects, enjoys it, conscious of its presence in the dusky, crowded, heterogeneous back-shop of the mind very much as a wary dealer in precious odds and ends, competent to make an "advance" on rare objects confided to him, is conscious of the rare little "piece" left in deposit by the reduced, mysterious lady of title or the speculative amateur, and which is already there to disclose its merit

47

afresh as soon as a key shall have clicked in a cupboard-door.

That may be, I recognise, a somewhat superfine analogy for the particular "value" I here speak of, the image of the young feminine nature that I had had for so considerable a time all curiously at my disposal; but it appears to fond memory quite to fit the fact—with the recall, in addition, of my pious desire but to place my treasure right. I quite remind myself thus of the dealer resigned not to "realise," resigned to keeping the precious object locked up indefinitely rather than commit it, at no matter what price, to vulgar hands. For there *are* dealers in these forms and figures and treasures capable of that refinement. The point is, however, that this single small corner-stone, the conception of a certain young woman affronting her destiny, had begun with being all my outfit for the large building of "The Portrait of a Lady." It came to be a square and spacious house—or has at least seemed so to me in this going over it again; but, such as it is, it had to be put up round my young woman while she stood there in perfect isolation. That is to me, artistically speaking, the circumstance of interest; for I have lost myself once more, I confess, in the curiosity of analysing the structure. By what process of logical accretion was this slight "personality," the mere slim shade of an intelligent but presumptuous girl, to find itself endowed with the high attributes of a Subject?—and indeed by what thinness, at the best, would such a subject not be vitiated? Millions of presumptuous girls, intelligent or not intelligent, daily affront their destiny, and what is it open to their destiny to *be,* at the most, that we should make an ado about it? The novel is of its very nature an "ado," an ado about something, and the larger the form it takes the greater of course the ado. Therefore, consciously, that was what one was in for—for positively organising an ado about Isabel Archer.

One looked it well in the face, I seem to remember, this

extravagance; and with the effect precisely of recognising the charm of the problem. Challenge any such problem with any intelligence, and you immediately see how full it is of substance; the wonder being, all the while, as we look at the world, how absolutely, how inordinately, the Isabel Archers, and even much smaller female fry, insist on mattering. George Eliot has admirably noted it—"In these frail vessels is borne onward through the ages the treasure of human affection." In "Romeo and Juliet" Juliet has to be important, just as, in "Adam Bede" and "The Mill on the Floss" and "Middlemarch" and "Daniel Deronda," Hetty Sorrel and Maggie Tulliver and Rosamond Vincy and Gwendolen Harleth have to be; with that much of firm ground, that much of bracing air, at the disposal all the while of their feet and their lungs. They are typical, none the less, of a class difficult, in the individual case, to make a centre of interest; so difficult in fact that many an expert painter, as for instance Dickens and Walter Scott, as for instance even, in the main, so subtle a hand as that of R. L. Stevenson, has preferred to leave the task unattempted. There are in fact writers as to whom we make out that their refuge from this is to assume it to be not worth their attempting; by which pusillanimity in truth their honour is scantly saved. It is never an attestation of a value, or even of our imperfect sense of one, it is never a tribute to any truth at all, that we shall represent that value badly. It never makes up, artistically, for an artist's dim feeling about a thing that he shall "do" the thing as ill as possible. There are better ways than that, the best of all of which is to begin with less stupidity.

It may be answered meanwhile, in regard to Shakespeare's and to George Eliot's testimony, that their concession to the "importance" of their Juliets and Cleopatras and Portias (even with Portia as the very type and model of the young person intelligent and presumptuous) and to that of their Hettys and Maggies and Rosamonds and Gwendolens, suffers the abatement that these slimnesses are, when figuring as the main props of the theme, never suffered to be sole ministers of its appeal, but have their inadequacy eked out with comic relief and underplots, as the playwrights say, when not with murders and battles and the great mutations of the world. If they are shown as "mattering" as much as they could possibly pretend to, the proof of it is in a hundred other persons, made of much stouter stuff, and each involved moreover in a hundred relations which matter to *them* concomitantly with that one. Cleopatra matters, beyond bounds, to Antony, but his colleagues, his antagonists, the state of Rome and the impending battle also prodigiously matter; Portia matters to Antonio, and to Shylock, and to the Prince of Morocco, to the fifty aspiring princes, but for these gentry there are other lively concerns; for Antonio, notably, there are Shylock and Bassanio and his lost ventures and the extremity of his predicament. This extremity indeed, by the same token, matters to Portia—though its doing so becomes of interest all by the fact that Portia matters to *us*. That she does so, at any rate, and that almost everything comes round to it again, supports my contention as to this fine example of the value recognised in the mere young thing. (I say "mere" young thing because I guess that even Shakespeare, preoccupied mainly though he may have been with the passions of princes, would scarce have pretended to found the best of his appeal for her on her high social position.) It is an example exactly of the deep difficulty braved—the difficulty of making George Eliot's "frail vessel," if not the all-in-all for our attention, at least the clearest of the call.

Now to see deep difficulty braved is at any time, for the really addicted artist, to feel almost even as a pang the beautiful incentive, and to feel it verily in such sort as to wish the danger intensified. The difficulty most worth tackling can only be for him, in these conditions, the greatest the case permits of. So I remember feeling here (in presence, always, that is, of the particular uncertainty of my ground), that there would be one way better than another—oh, ever so much better than any other!—of making it fight out its battle. The frail vessel, that charged with George Eliot's "treasure," and thereby of such importance to those who curiously approach it, has likewise possibilities of importance to itself, possibilities which permit of treatment and in fact peculiarly require it from the moment they are considered at all. There is always the escape from any close account of the weak agent of such spells by using as a bridge for evasion, for retreat and flight, the view of her relation to those surrounding her. Make it predominantly a view of *their* relation and the trick is played: you give the general sense of her effect, and you give it, so far as the raising on it of a superstructure goes, with the maximum of ease. Well, I recall perfectly how little, in my now quite established connexion, the maximum of ease appealed to me, and how I seemed to get rid of it by an honest transposition of the weights in the two scales. "Place the centre of the subject in the young woman's own consciousness," I said to myself, "and you get as interesting and as beautiful a difficulty as you could wish. Stick to *that* —for the centre; put the heaviest weight into *that* scale, which will be so largely the scale of her relation to herself. Make her only interested enough, at the same time, in the things that are not herself, and this relation need n't fear to be too limited. Place meanwhile in the other scale the lighter weight (which is usually the one that tips the balance of interest): press least hard, in short, on the consciousness of your heroine's satellites, especially the male; make it an interest contributive only to the greater one. See, at all events, what can be done in this way. What better field could there be for a due ingenuity? The girl hovers, inextinguishable, as a charming creature, and the job will be to translate her into the highest terms of that formula, and as nearly as possible moreover into *all* of them. To depend upon her and her

little concerns wholly to see you through will necessitate, remember, your really 'doing' her."

So far I reasoned, and it took nothing less than that technical rigour, I now easily see, to inspire me with the right
confidence for erecting on such a plot of ground the neat
and careful and proportioned pile of bricks that arches over
it and that was thus to form, constructionally speaking, a literary monument. Such is the aspect that to-day "The Portrait"
wears for me: a structure reared with an "architectural" com-
petence, as Turgenieff would have said, that makes it, to the
author's own sense, the most proportioned of his productions
after "The Ambassadors"—which was to follow it so many
years later and which has, no doubt, a superior roundness. On
one thing I was determined; that, though I should clearly have
to pile brick upon brick for the creation of an interest, I would
leave no pretext for saying that anything is out of line, scale
or perspective. I would build large—in fine embossed vaults
and painted arches, as who should say, and yet never let it
appear that the chequered pavement, the ground under the
reader's feet, fails to stretch at every point to the base of
the walls. That precautionary spirit, on re-perusal of the
book, is the old note that most touches me: it testifies so, for
my own ear, to the anxiety of my provision for the reader's
amusement. I felt, in view of the possible limitations of my
subject, that no such provision could be excessive, and the
development of the latter was simply the general form of that
earnest quest. And I find indeed that this is the only account
I can give myself of the evolution of the fable: it is all under
the head thus named that I conceive the needful accretion as
having taken place, the right complications as having started.
It was naturally of the essence that the young woman should be
herself complex; that was rudimentary—or was at any rate the
light in which Isabel Archer had originally dawned. It went,
however, but a certain way, and other lights, contending, conflicting lights, and of as many different colours, if possible, as

the rockets, the Roman candles and Catherine-wheels of a "pyrotechnic display," would be employable to attest that she was. I had, no doubt, a groping instinct for the right complications, since I am quite unable to track the footsteps of those that constitute, as the case stands, the general situation exhibited. They are there, for what they are worth, and as numerous as might be; but my memory, I confess, is a blank as to how and whence they came.

I seem to myself to have waked up one morning in possession of them—of Ralph Touchett and his parents, of Madame Merle, of Gilbert Osmond and his daughter and his sister, of Lord Warburton, Caspar Goodwood and Miss Stackpole, the definite array of contributions to Isabel Archer's history. I recognised them, I knew them, they were the numbered pieces of my puzzle, the concrete terms of my "plot." It was as if they had simply, by an impulse of their own, floated into my ken, and all in response to my primary question: "Well, what will she *do?*" Their answer seemed to be that if I would trust them they would show me; on which, with an urgent appeal to them to make it at least as interesting as they could, I trusted them. They were like the group of attendants and entertainers who come down by train when people in the country give a party; they represented the contract for carrying the party on. That was an excellent relation with them—a possible one even with so broken a reed (from her slightness of cohesion) as Henrietta Stackpole. It is a familiar truth to the novelist, at the strenuous hour, that, as certain elements in any work are of the essence, so others are only of the form; that as this or that character, this or that disposition of the material, belongs to the subject directly, so to speak, so this or that other belongs to it but indirectly—belongs intimately to the treatment. This is a truth, however, of which he rarely gets the benefit—since it could be assured to him, really, but by criticism based upon perception, criticism which is too little of this world. He must not think of benefits, moreover, I freely recognise, for that way dishonour lies: he has, that is, but one to think of—the benefit, whatever it may be, involved in his having cast a spell upon the simpler, the very simplest, forms of attention. This is all he is entitled to; he is entitled to nothing, he is bound to admit, that can come to him, from the reader, as a result on the latter's part of any act of reflexion or discrimination. He may *enjoy* this finer tribute—that is another affair, but on condition only of taking it as a gratuity "thrown in," a mere miraculous windfall, the fruit of a tree he may not pretend to have shaken. Against reflexion, against discrimination, in his interest, all earth and air conspire; wherefore it is that, as I say, he must in many a case have schooled himself, from the first, to work but for a "living wage." The living wage is the reader's grant of the least possible quantity of attention required for consciousness of a "spell." The occasional charming "tip" is an act of his intelligence over and beyond this, a golden apple, for the writer's lap, straight from the wind-stirred tree. The artist may of course, in wanton moods, dream of some Paradise (for art) where the direct appeal to the intelligence might be legalised; for to such extravagances as these his yearning mind can scarce hope ever completely to close itself. The most he can do is to remember they *are* extravagances.

All of which is perhaps but a gracefully devious way of saying that Henrietta Stackpole was a good example, in "The Portrait," of the truth to which I just adverted—as good an example as I could name were it not that Maria Gostrey, in "The Ambassadors," then in the bosom of time. may be mentioned as a better. Each of these persons is but wheels to the coach; neither belongs to the body of that vehicle, or is for a moment accommodated with a seat inside. There the subject alone is ensconced, in the form of its "hero and heroine," and of the privileged high officials, say, who ride with the king and queen. There are reasons why one would have liked this to be felt, as in general one would like almost anything to be felt, in one's work, that one has one's self contributively felt. We have seen, however, how idle is that pretension, which I should be sorry to make too much of. Maria Gostrey and Miss Stackpole then are cases, each, of the light *ficelle,* not of the true agent; they may run beside the coach "for all they are worth," they may cling to it till they are out of breath (as poor Miss Stackpole all so vividly does), but neither, all the while, so much as gets her foot on the step, neither ceases for a moment to tread the dusty road. Put it even that they are like the fishwives who helped to bring back to Paris from Versailles, on that most ominous day of the first half of the French Revolution, the carriage of the royal family. The only thing is that I may well be asked, I acknowledge, why then, in the present fiction, I have suffered Henrietta (of whom we have indubitably too much).so officiously, so strangely, so almost inexplicably, to pervade. I will presently say what I can for that anomaly—and in the most conciliatory fashion.

A point I wish still more to make is that if my relation of confidence with the actors in my drama who *were,* unlike Miss Stackpole, true agents, was an excellent one to have arrived at, there still remained my relation with the reader, which was another affair altogether and as to which I felt no one to be trusted but myself. That solicitude was to be accordingly expressed in the artful patience with which, as I have said, I piled brick upon brick. The bricks, for the whole counting-over—putting for bricks little touches and inventions and enhancements by the way—affect me in truth as well-nigh innumerable and as ever so scrupulously fitted together and packed-in. It is an effect of detail, of the minutest; though, if one were in this connexion to say all, one would express the hope that the general, the ampler air of the modest monument still survives. I do at least seem to catch the key to a part of this abundance of small anxious, ingenious illustration as I recollect putting my finger, in my young woman's interest, on the most obvious of her predicates. "What will she 'do'? Why, the first thing she'll do will be to come to Europe; which in fact will form, and all inevitably, no small part of her principal adventure. Coming to Europe is even for the 'frail vessels,' in this wonderful age, a mild adventure; but what is truer than that on one side—the side of their independence of flood and field, of the moving accident, of battle and murder and sudden death—her adventures are to be mild? Without her sense of them, her sense *for* them, as one may say, they are next to nothing at all; but isn't the beauty and the difficulty just in showing their mystic conversion by that sense, conversion into the stuff of drama or, even more delightful word still, of 'story'?" It was all as clear, my contention, as a silver bell. Two very good instances, I think, of this effect of conversion, two cases of the rare chemistry, are the pages in which Isabel, coming into the drawing-room at Gardencourt, coming in from a wet walk or whatever, that rainy afternoon, finds Madame Merle in possession of the place, Madame Merle seated, all absorbed but all serene, at the piano, and deeply recognises, in the striking of such an hour, in the presence there, among the gathering shades, of this personage, of whom a moment before she had never so much as heard, a turning-point in her life. It is dreadful to have too much, for any artistic demonstration, to dot one's i's and insist on one's intentions, and I am not eager to do it now; but the question here was that of producing the maximum of intensity with the minimum of strain.

The interest was to be raised to its pitch and yet the elements to be kept in their key; so that, should the whole thing duly impress, I might show what an "exciting" inward life may do for the person leading it even while it remains perfectly normal. And I cannot think of a more consistent application of that ideal unless it be in the long statement, just beyond the middle of the book, of my young woman's extraordinary meditative vigil on the occasion that was to become for her such a landmark. Reduced to its essence, it is but the vigil of searching criticism; but it throws the action further forward than twenty "incidents" might have done. It was designed to have all the vivacity of incident and all the economy of picture. She sits up, by her dying fire, far into the night, under the spell of recognitions on which she finds the last sharpness suddenly wait. It is a representation simply of her motionlessly *seeing,* and an attempt withal to make the mere still lucidity of her act as "interesting" as the surprise of a caravan or the identification of a pirate. It represents, for that matter, one of the identifications dear to the novelist, and even indispensable to him; but it all goes on without her being approached by another person and without her leaving her chair. It is obviously the best thing in the book, but it is only a supreme illustration of the general plan. As to Henrietta, my apology for whom I just left incomplete, she exemplifies, I fear, in her superabundance, not an element of my plan, but only an excess of my zeal. So early was to begin my tendency to *overtreat,* rather than undertreat (when there was choice or danger) my subject. (Many members of my craft, I gather, are far from agreeing with me, but I have always held over-treating the minor disservice.) "Treating" that of "The Portrait" amounted to never forgetting, by any lapse, that the thing was under a special obligation to be amusing. There was the danger of the noted "thinness"—which was to be averted, tooth and nail, by cultivation of the lively. That is at least how I see it to-day. Henrietta must have been at that time a part of my wonderful notion of the lively. And then there was another matter. I had, within the few preceding years, come to live in London, and the "international" light lay, in those days, to my sense, thick and rich upon the scene. It was the light in which so much of the picture hung. But that *is* another matter. There is really too much to say.

IV

PREFACE TO "THE PRINCESS CASAMASSIMA"

(VOLUME V IN THE NEW YORK EDITION)

THE simplest account of the origin of "The Princess Casamassima" is, I think, that this fiction proceeded quite directly,
during the first year of a long residence in London, from the
habit and the interest of walking the streets. I walked a great
deal—for exercise, for amusement, for acquisition, and above
all I always walked home at the evening's end, when the
evening had been spent elsewhere, as happened more often
than not; and as to do this was to receive many impressions, so the impressions worked and sought an issue, so
the book after a time was born. It is a fact that, as I look
back, the attentive exploration of London, the assault directly
made by the great city upon an imagination quick to react,
fully explains a large part of it. There is a minor element
that refers itself to another source, of which I shall presently
speak; but the prime idea was unmistakeably the ripe round
fruit of perambulation. One walked of course with one's
eyes greatly open, and I hasten to declare that such a practice, carried on for a long time and over a considerable space,
positively provokes, all round, a mystic solicitation, the urgent
appeal, on the part of everything, to be interpreted and, so far
as may be, reproduced. "Subjects" and situations, character
and history, the tragedy and comedy of life, are things of which
the common air, in such conditions, seems pungently to taste;
and to a mind curious, before the human scene, of meanings
and revelations the great grey Babylon easily becomes, on its
face, a garden bristling with an immense illustrative flora.

Possible stories, presentable figures, rise from the thick jungle as the observer moves, fluttering up like startled game, and before he knows it indeed he has fairly to guard himself against the brush of importunate wings. He goes on as with his head in a cloud of humming presences—especially during the younger, the initiatory time, the fresh, the sharply-apprehensive months or years, more or less numerous. We use our material up, we use up even the thick tribute of the London streets—if perception and attention but sufficiently light our steps. But I think of them as lasting, for myself, quite sufficiently long; I think of them as even still—dreadfully changed for the worse in respect to any romantic idea as I find them—breaking out on occasion into eloquence, throwing out deep notes from their vast vague murmur.

There was a moment at any rate when they offered me no image more vivid than that of some individual sensitive nature or fine mind, some small obscure intelligent creature whose education should have been almost wholly derived from them, capable of profiting by all the civilisation, all the accumulations to which they testify, yet condemned to see these things only from outside—in mere quickened consideration, mere wistfulness and envy and despair. It seemed to me I had only to imagine such a spirit intent enough and troubled enough, and to place it in presence of the comings and goings, the great gregarious company, of the more fortunate than himself—all on the scale on which London could show them—to get possession of an interesting theme. I arrived so at the history of little Hyacinth Robinson—he sprang up for me out of the London pavement. To find his possible adventure interesting I had only to conceive his watching the same public show, the same innumerable appearances, I had watched myself, and of his watching very much as I had watched; save indeed for one little difference. This difference would be that so far as all the swarming facts should speak of freedom and ease, knowledge and power, money, oppor-

tunity and satiety, he should be able to revolve round them
but at the most respectful of distances and with every door
of approach shut in his face. For one's self, all conveniently,
there had been doors that opened—opened into light and
warmth and cheer, into good and charming relations; and if
the place as a whole lay heavy on one's consciousness there
was yet always for relief this implication of one's own lucky
share of the freedom and ease, lucky acquaintance with the
number of lurking springs at light pressure of which particular vistas would begin to recede, great lighted, furnished,
peopled galleries, sending forth gusts of agreeable sound.

That main happy sense of the picture was always there
and that retreat from the general grimness never forbidden;
whereby one's own relation to the mere formidable mass
and weight of things was eased off and adjusted. One learned
from an early period what it might be to know London in
such a way as that—an immense and interesting discipline,
an education on terms mostly convenient and delightful. But
what would be the effect of the other way, of having so many
precious things perpetually in one's eyes, yet of missing them
all for any closer knowledge, and of the confinement of closer
knowledge entirely to matters with which a connexion, however intimate, could n't possibly pass for a privilege? Truly,
of course, there are London mysteries (dense categories of
dark arcana) for every spectator, and it's in a degree an exclusion and a state of weakness to be without experience of the
meaner conditions, the lower manners and types, the general
sordid struggle, the weight of the burden of labour, the
ignorance, the misery and the vice. With such matters as
those my tormented young man would have had contact—
they would have formed, fundamentally, from the first, his
natural and immediate London. But the reward of a romantic curiosity would be the question of what the total assault,
that of the world of his work-a-day life and the world of his
divination and his envy together, would have made of him,

and what in especial he would have made of them. As tormented, I say, I thought of him, and that would be the point
—if one could only see him feel enough to be interesting without his feeling so much as not to be natural.

This in fact I have ever found rather terribly the point
—that the figures in any picture, the agents in any drama,
are interesting only in proportion as they feel their respective
situations; since the consciousness, on their part, of the complication exhibited forms for us their link of connexion with
it. But there are degrees of feeling—the muffled, the faint,
the just sufficient, the barely intelligent, as we may say; and
the acute, the intense, the complete, in a word—the power
to be finely aware and richly responsible. It is those moved
in this latter fashion who "get most" out of all that happens
to them and who in so doing enable us, as readers of their
record, as participators by a fond attention, also to get most.
Their being finely aware—as Hamlet and Lear, say, are finely
aware—*makes* absolutely the intensity of their adventure, gives
the maximum of sense to what befalls them. We care, our
curiosity and our sympathy care, comparatively little for what
happens to the stupid, the coarse and the blind; care for it,
and for the effects of it, at the most as helping to precipitate
what happens to the more deeply wondering, to the really
sentient. Hamlet and Lear are surrounded, amid their complications, by the stupid and the blind, who minister in all
sorts of ways to their recorded fate. Persons of markedly
limited sense would, on such a principle as that, play a part
in the career of my tormented youth; but he would n't be of
markedly limited sense himself—he would note as many things
and vibrate to as many occasions as I might venture to make
him.

There would n't moreover simply be the question of his
suffering—of which we might soon get enough; there would
be the question of what, all beset and all perceptive, he should
thus adventurously do, thus dream and hazard and attempt.

The interest of the attitude and the act would be the actor's imagination and vision of them, together with the nature and degree of their felt return upon him. So the intelligent creature would be required and so some picture of his intelligence involved. The picture of an intelligence appears for the most part, it is true, a dead weight for the reader of the English novel to carry, this reader having so often the wondrous property of caring for the displayed tangle of human relations without caring for its intelligibility. The teller of a story is primarily, none the less, the listener to it, the reader of it, too; and, having needed thus to make it out, distinctly, on the crabbed page of life, to disengage it from the rude human character and the more or less Gothic text in which it has been packed away, the very essence of his affair has been the *imputing* of intelligence. The basis of his attention has been that such and such an imbroglio has got started—on the page of life—because of something that some one has felt and more or less understood.

I recognise at the same time, and in planning "The Princess Casamassima" felt it highly important to recognise, the danger of filling too full any supposed and above all any obviously limited vessel of consciousness. If persons either tragically or comically embroiled with life allow us the comic or tragic value of their embroilment in proportion as their struggle is a measured and directed one, it is strangely true, none the less, that beyond a certain point they are spoiled for us by this carrying of a due light. They may carry too much of it for our credence, for our compassion, for our derision. They may be shown as knowing too much and feeling too much—not certainly for their remaining remarkable, but for their remaining "natural" and typical, for their having the needful communities with our own precious liability to fall into traps and be bewildered. It seems probable that if we were never bewildered there would never be a story to tell about us; we should partake of the superior nature of the all-knowing immortals whose annals are dreadfully dull so long as flurried humans are not, for the positive relief of bored Olympians, mixed up with them. Therefore it is that the wary reader for the most part warns the novelist against making his characters too *interpretative* of the muddle of fate, or in other words too divinely, too priggishly clever. "Give us plenty of bewilderment," this monitor seems to say, "so long as there is plenty of slashing out in the bewilderment too. But don't, we beseech you, give us too much intelligence; for intelligence—well, *endangers;* endangers not perhaps the slasher himself, but the very slashing, the subject-matter of any self-respecting story. It opens up too many considerations, possibilities, issues; it *may* lead the slasher into dreary realms where slashing somehow fails and falls to the ground."

That is well reasoned on the part of the reader, who can in spite of it never have an idea—or his earnest discriminations would come to him less easily—of the extreme difficulty, for the painter of the human mixture, of reproducing that mixture aright. "Give us in the persons represented, the subjects of the bewilderment (that bewilderment without which there would be no question of an issue or of the fact of suspense, prime implications in any story) as much experience as possible, but keep down the terms in which you report that experience, because we only understand the very simplest": such in effect are the words in which the novelist constantly hears himself addressed, such the plea made him by the would-be victims of his spell on behalf of that sovereign principle the economy of interest, a principle as to which their instinct is justly strong. He listens anxiously to the charge—nothing can exceed his own solicitude for an economy of interest; but feels himself all in presence of an abyss of ambiguities, the mutual accommodations in which the reader wholly leaves to him. Experience, as I see it, is our apprehension and our measure of what happens to us as social creatures—any intelligent report of which has to be based on that apprehension. The picture of the exposed and entangled state is what is required, and there are certainly always plenty of grounds for keeping down the complexities of a picture. A picture it still has to be, however, and by that condition has to deal effectually with its subject, so that the simple device of more and more keeping down may well not see us quite to our end or even quite to our middle. One suggested way of keeping down, for instance, is not to attribute feeling, or feelings, to persons who would n't in all probability have had any to speak of. The less space, within the frame of the picture, their feelings take up the more space is left for their doings—a fact that may at first seem to make for a refinement of economy.

All of which is charming—yet would be infinitely more so if here at once amibiguity did n't yawn; the unreality of the sharp distinction, where the interest of observation is at stake, between doing and feeling. In the immediate field of life, for action, for application, for getting through a job, nothing may so much matter perhaps as the descent of a suspended weight on this, that or the other spot, with all its subjective concomitants quite secondary and irrelevant. But the affair of the painter is not the immediate, it is the reflected field of life, the realm not of application, but of *appreciation*—a truth that makes our measure of effect altogether different. My report of people's experience—my report as a "story-teller"—is essentially my appreciation of it, and there is no "interest" for me in what my hero, my heroine or any one else does save through that admirable process. As soon as I begin to appreciate simplification is imperilled: the sharply distinguished parts of any adventure, any case of endurance and performance, melt together as an appeal. I then see their "doing," that of the persons just mentioned, as, immensely, their feeling, their feeling as their doing; since I can have none of the conveyed sense and taste of their situation without becoming intimate with them. I can't be intimate without that sense and taste, and I can't appreciate save by intimacy, any more than I can report save by a projected light. Intimacy with a man's specific behaviour, with his given case, is desperately certain to make us see it as a whole—in which event arbitrary limitations of our vision lose whatever beauty they may on occasion have pretended to. What a man thinks and what he feels are the history and the character of what he does; on all of which things the logic of intensity rests. Without intensity where is vividness, and without vividness where is presentability? If I have called the most general state of one's most exposed and assaulted figures the state of bewilderment—the condition for instance on which Thackeray so much insists in the interest of *his* exhibited careers, the condition of a humble heart, a bowed head, a patient wonder, a suspended judgement, before the "awful will" and the mysterious decrees of Providence—so it is rather witless to talk of merely getting rid of that displayed mode of reaction, one of the oft-encountered, one of the highly recommended, categories of feeling.

The whole thing comes to depend thus on the *quality* of bewilderment characteristic of one's creature, the quality involved in the given case or supplied by one's data. There are doubtless many such qualities, ranging from vague and crepuscular to sharpest and most critical; and we have but to imagine one of these latter to see how easily—from the moment it gets its head at all—it may insist on playing a part. There we have then at once a case of feeling, of ever so many possible feelings, stretched across the scene like an attached thread on which the pearls of interest are strung. There are threads shorter and less tense, and I am far from implying that the minor, the coarser and less fruitful forms and degrees of moral reaction, as we may conveniently call it, may not yield lively results. They have their subordinate, comparative, illustrative human value—that appeal of the witless which is often so penetrating. Verily even, I think, no "story" is possible without its fools—as most of the fine painters of life, Shakespeare, Cervantes and Balzac, Fielding, Scott, Thackeray, Dickens, George Meredith, George Eliot, Jane Austen, have abundantly felt. At the same time I confess I never see the *leading* interest of any human hazard but in a consciousness (on the part of the moved and moving creature) subject to fine intensification and wide enlargement. It is as mirrored in that consciousness that the gross fools, the headlong fools, the fatal fools play their part for us—they have much less to show us in themselves. The troubled life mostly at the centre of our subject—whatever our subject, for the artistic hour, happens to be—embraces them and deals with them for its amusement and its anguish: they are apt largely indeed, on a near view, to be all the cause of its trouble. This means, exactly, that the person capable of feeling in the given case more than another of what is to be felt for it, and so serving in the highest degree to *record* it dramatically and objectively, is the only sort of person on whom we can count not to betray, to cheapen or, as we say, give away, the value and beauty of the thing. By so much as the affair matters *for* some such individual, by so much do we get the best there is of it, and by so much as it falls within the scope of a denser and duller, a more vulgar and more shallow capacity, do we get a picture dim and meagre.

The great chroniclers have clearly always been aware of this; they have at least always either placed a mind of some sort—in the sense of a reflecting and colouring medium—in possession of the general adventure (when the latter has not been purely epic, as with Scott, say, as with old Dumas and with Zola); or else paid signally, as to the interest created, for their failure to do so. We may note moreover in passing that this failure is in almost no case intentional or part of a plan, but has sprung from their limited curiosity, their short conception of the particular sensibility projected. Edgar of Ravenswood for instance, visited by the tragic tempest of "The Bride of Lammermoor," has a black cloak and hat and feathers more than he has a mind; just as Hamlet, while equally sabled and draped and plumed, while at least equally romantic, has yet a mind still more than he has a costume. The situation represented is that Ravenswood loves Lucy Ashton through dire difficulty and danger, and that she in the same way loves him; but the relation so created between them is by this neglect of the "feeling" question never shown us as primarily taking place. It is shown only in its secondary, its confused and disfigured aspects—where, however, luckily, it is presented with great romantic good faith. The thing has nevertheless paid for its deviation, as I say, by a sacrifice of intensity; the centre of the subject is empty and the development pushed off, all round, toward the frame—which is, so to speak, beautifully rich and curious. But I mention that relation to each other of the appearances in a particular work only as a striking negative case; there are in the connexion I have glanced at plenty of striking positive ones. It is very true that Fielding's hero in "Tom Jones" is but as "finely," that is but as intimately, bewildered as a young man of great health and spirits may be when he hasn't a grain of imagination: the point to be made is, at all events, that his sense of bewilderment obtains altogether on the comic, never on the tragic plane. He has so much "life" that it amounts, for the effect of comedy and application of satire, almost to his having a mind, that is to his having reactions and a full consciousness; besides which his author—he handsomely possessed of a mind—has such an amplitude of reflexion for him and round him that we see him through the mellow air of Fielding's fine old moralism, fine old humour and fine old style, which somehow really enlarge, make every one and every thing important.

THE PRINCESS CASAMASSIMA

All of which furthers my remarking how much I have
been interested, on reading "The Princess Casamassima"
over, to recognise my sense, sharp from far back, that clearness and concreteness constantly depend, for any pictorial
whole, on some *concentrated* individual notation of them.
That notation goes forward here in the mind of little Hyacinth, immensely quickened by the fact of its so mattering
to his very life what he does make of things: which passion
of intelligence is, as I have already hinted, precisely his
highest value for our curiosity and our sympathy. Yet if
his highest it is not at all his only one, since the truth for
"a young man in a book" by no means entirely resides in
his being either exquisitely sensitive or shiningly clever. It
resides in some such measure of these things as may consort
with the fine measure of other things too—with that of the
other faces of his situation and character. If he's too sensitive and too clever for *them,* if he knows more than is likely
or natural—for *him*—it's as if he weren't at all, as if he were
false and impossible. Extreme and attaching always the difficulty of fixing at a hundred points the place where one's
impelled *bonhomme* may feel enough and "know" enough—
or be in the way of learning enough—for his maximum dramatic value without feeling and knowing too much for his
minimum verisimilitude, his proper fusion with the fable. This
is the charming, the tormenting, the eternal little matter *to
be made right,* in all the weaving of silver threads and tapping
on golden nails; and I should take perhaps too fantastic a
comfort—I mean were not the comforts of the artist just
of the raw essence of fantasy—in any glimpse of such achieved
rightnesses, whether in my own work or that of others. In no
work whatever, doubtless, are they the felicities the most frequent; but they have so inherent a price that even the traceable attempt at them, wherever met, sheds, I think, a fine
influence about.

I have for example a weakness of sympathy with that

constant effort of George Eliot's which plays through Adam Bede and Felix Holt and Tito Melema, through Daniel Deronda and through Lydgate in "Middlemarch," through Maggie Tulliver, through Romola, through Dorothea Brooke and Gwendolen Harleth; the effort to show their adventures and their history—the author's subject-matter all—as determined by their feelings and the nature of their minds. Their emotions, their stirred intelligence, their moral consciousness, become thus, by sufficiently charmed perusal, our own very adventure. The creator of Deronda and of Romola is charged, I know, with having on occasion—as in dealing with those very celebrities themselves—left the figure, the concrete man and woman, too abstract by reason of the quantity of soul employed; but such mischances, where imagination and humour still keep them company, often have an interest that is wanting to agitations of the mere surface or to those that may be only taken for granted. I should even like to give myself the pleasure of retracing from one of my own productions to another the play of a like instinctive disposition, of catching in the fact, at one point after another, from "Roderick Hudson" to "The Golden Bowl," that provision for interest which consists in placing advantageously, placing right in the middle of the light, the most polished of possible mirrors of the subject. Rowland Mallet, in "Roderick Hudson," is exactly such a mirror, not a bit autobiographic or formally "first person" though he be, and I might exemplify the case through a long list, through the nature of such a "mind" even as the all-objective Newman in "The American," through the thickly-peopled imagination of Isabel Archer in "The Portrait of a Lady" (her imagination positively the deepest depth of her imbroglio) down to such unmistakeable examples as that of Merton Densher in "The Wings of the Dove," that of Lambert Strether in "The Ambassadors" (*he* a mirror verily of miraculous silver and quite pre-eminent, I think, for the connexion) and that of the Prince in the first half and that of the Princess in the second half of "The Golden Bowl." I should note the extent to which these persons are, so far as their other passions permit, intense *perceivers,* all, of their respective predicaments, and I should go on from them to fifty other examples; even to the divided Vanderbank of "The Awkward Age," the extreme pinch of whose romance is the vivacity in him, to his positive sorrow and loss, of the state of being aware; even to scanted Fleda Vetch in "The Spoils of Poynton," through whose own delicate vision of everything so little of the human value of her situation is wasted for us; even to the small recording governess confronted with the horrors of "The Turn of the Screw" and to the innocent child patching together all ineffectually those of "What Maisie Knew"; even in short, since I may name so few cases, to the disaffected guardian of an overgrown legend in "The Birthplace," to the luckless fine artist of "The Next Time," trying to despoil himself, for a "hit" and bread and butter, of his fatal fineness, to blunt the tips of his intellectual fingers, and to the hapless butler Brooksmith, ruined by good talk, disqualified for common domestic service by the beautiful growth of his habit of quiet attention, his faculty of appreciation. But though this demonstration of a rooted vice—since a vice it would appear mainly accounted—might yield amusement, the examples referred to must await their turn.

I had had for a long time well before me, at any rate, my small obscure but ardent observer of the "London world," saw him roam and wonder and yearn, saw all the unanswered questions and baffled passions that might ferment in him—once he should be made both sufficiently thoughtful and sufficiently "disinherited"; but this image, however interesting, was of course not by itself a progression, an action, didn't by itself make a drama. I got my action however—failing which one has nothing—under the prompt sense that the state of feeling I was concerned with might develop and beget another state, might return at a given moment, and with the greatest vivacity, on itself. To see this was really to feel one's subject swim into one's ken, especially after a certain other ingenious connexion had been made for it. I find myself again recalling, and with the possible "fun" of it reviving too, how I recognised, as revealed and prescribed, the particular complexion, profession and other conditions of my little presumptuous adventurer, with his combination of intrinsic fineness and fortuitous adversity, his small cluster of "dingy" London associations and the swelling spirit in him which was to be the field of his strange experience. Accessible through his imagination, as I have hinted, to a thousand provocations and intimations, he would become most acquainted with destiny in the form of a lively inward revolution. His being jealous of all the ease of life of which he tastes so little, and, bitten, under this exasperation, with an aggressive, vindictive, destructive social faith, his turning to "treasons, stratagems and spoils" might be as vivid a picture as one chose, but would move to pity and terror only by the aid of some deeper complication, some imposed and formidable issue.

The complication most interesting then would be that he should fall in love with the beauty of the world, actual order and all, at the moment of his most feeling and most hating the famous "iniquity of its social arrangements"; so that his position as an irreconcileable pledged enemy to it, thus rendered false by something more personal than his opinion and his vows, becomes the sharpest of his torments. To make it a torment that really matters, however, he must have got practically involved, specifically committed to the stand he has, under the pressure of more knowledge, found impossible; out of which has come for him the deep dilemma of the disillusioned and repentant conspirator. He has thrown himself into the more than "shady" underworld of militant socialism, he has undertaken to play a part—a part that with the drop of his exasperation and the growth, simply expressed, of his taste, is out of all tune with his passion, at any cost, for life itself, the life, whatever it be, that surrounds him. Dabbling deeply in revolutionary politics of a hole-and-corner sort, he would be "in" up to his neck, and with that precarious part of him particularly involved, so that his tergiversation is the climax of his adventure. What was essential with this was that he should have a social—not less than a socialist—connexion, find a door somehow open to him into the appeased and civilised state, into that warmer glow of things he is precisely to help to undermine. To look for this necessary connexion was for me to meet it suddenly in the form of that extremely *disponible* figure of Christina Light whom I had ten years before found left on my hands at the conclusion of "Roderick Hudson." She had for so long, in the vague limbo of those ghosts we have conjured but not exorcised, been looking for a situation, awaiting a niche and a function.

I shall not pretend to trace the steps and stages by which the imputability of a future to that young woman—which was like the act of clothing her chilled and patient nakedness—had for its prime effect to plant her in my little bookbinder's path. Nothing would doubtless beckon us on further, with a large leisure, than such a chance to study the obscure law under which certain of a novelist's characters, more or less honourably buried, revive for him by a force or a whim of their own and "walk" round his house of art like haunting ghosts, feeling for the old doors they knew, fumbling at stiff latches and pressing their pale faces, in the outer dark, to lighted windows. I mistrust them, I confess, in general; my sense of a really expressed character is that it shall have originally so tasted of the ordeal of service as to feel no disposition to yield again to the strain. Why should the Princess of the climax of "Roderick Hudson" still have made her desire felt, unless in fact to testify that she had not been—for what she was—completely recorded? To continue in evidence, that had struck me from far back as her natural passion; in evidence at any price, not consenting to be laid away with folded hands in the pasteboard tomb, the doll's box, to which we usually relegate the spent puppet after the fashion of a recumbent worthy on the slab of a sepulchral monument. I was to see this, after all, in the event, as the fruit of a restless vanity: Christina had felt herself, known herself, striking, in the earlier connexion, and could n't resign herself not to strike again. Her pressure then was not to be resisted—sharply as the question might come up of why she should pretend to strike just *there*. I shall not attempt to answer it with reasons (one can never tell everything); it was enough that I could recognise her claim to have travelled far —far from where I had last left her: that, one felt, was in character—that was what she naturally *would* have done. Her prime note had been an aversion to the *banal,* and nothing could be of an effect less *banal,* I judged, than her intervention in the life of a dingy little London bookbinder whose sensibility, whose flow of opinions on "public questions" in especial, should have been poisoned at the source.

She would be world-weary—that was another of her notes; and the extravagance of her attitude in these new relations would have its root and its apparent logic in her need to feel freshly about something or other—it might scarce matter what. She can, or she believes she can, feel freshly about the "people" and their wrongs and their sorrows and their perpetual smothered ferment; for these things are furthest removed from those others among which she has hitherto tried to make her life. That was to a certainty where I was to have looked for her— quite *off* and away (once granted the wisdom of listening to her anew at all): therefore Hyacinth's encounter with her could pass for natural, and it was fortunately to be noted that she was to serve for his experience in quite another and a more "leading" sense than any in which he was to serve for hers. I confess I was not averse—such are the possible weaknesses of the artist in face of high difficulties—to feeling that if his appearance of consistency were obtained I might at least try to remain comparatively at my ease about hers. I may add moreover that the resuscitation of Christina (and, on the minor scale, of the Prince and of Madame Grandoni) put in a strong light for me the whole question, for the romancer, of "going on with a character": as Balzac first of all systematically went on, as Thackeray, as Trollope, as Zola all more or less ingeniously went on. I was to find no small savour in the reflexions so precipitated; though I may treat myself here only to this remark about them—that the revivalist impulse on the fond writer's part strikes me as one thing, a charmingly conceivable thing, but the effect of a free indulgence in it (effect, that is, on the nerves of the reader) as, for twenty rather ineffable reasons, quite another.

I remember at any rate feeling myself all in possession of little Hyacinth's consistency, as I have called it, down at Dover during certain weeks that were none too remotely precedent to the autumn of 1885 and the appearance, in "The Atlantic Monthly" again, of the first chapters of the story. There were certain sunny, breezy balconied rooms at the quieter end of the Esplanade of that cheerful castle-crested little town—now infinitely perturbed by gigantic "harbour works," but then only faded and over-soldiered and all pleasantly and humbly submissive to the law that snubs in due course the presumption of flourishing resorts—to which I had already more than once had recourse in hours of quickened industry and which, though much else has been swept away, still archaically exist. To have lately noted this again from the old benched and asphalted walk by the sea, the twinkling Channel beyond which on occasion the opposite coast of France used to gleam as an incident of the charming tendency of the whole prospect (immediate picture and fond design alike) amusingly to *shine,* was somehow to taste afresh, and with a certain surprise, the odd quality of that original confidence that the parts of my plan *would* somehow hang together. I may wonder at my con-

fidence now—given the extreme, the very particular truth and
"authority" required at so many points; but to wonder is to live
back gratefully into the finer reasons of things, with all the
detail of harsh application and friction (that there must have
been) quite happily blurred and dim. The finest of reasons
—I mean for the sublime confidence I speak of—was that I
felt in full *personal* possession of my matter; this really seemed
the fruit of direct experience. My scheme called for the suggested nearness (to all our apparently ordered life) of some
sinister anarchic underworld, heaving in its pain, its power
and its hate; a presentation not of sharp particulars, but of
loose appearances, vague motions and sounds and symptoms,
just perceptible presences and general looming possibilities.
To have adopted the scheme was to have had to meet the
question of one's "notes," over the whole ground, the question
of what, in such directions, one had "gone into" and how
far one had gone; and to have answered that question—to
one's own satisfaction at least—was truly to see one's way.

My notes then, on the much-mixed world of my hero's
both overt and covert consciousness, were exactly my gathered impressions and stirred perceptions, the deposit in my
working imagination of all my visual and all my constructive
sense of London. The very plan of my book had in fact
directly confronted me with the rich principle of the Note,
and was to do much to clear up, once for all, my practical
view of it. If one was to undertake to tell tales and to report with truth on the human scene, it could be but because
"notes" had been from the cradle the ineluctable consequence of one's greatest inward energy: to take them was
as natural as to look, to think, to feel, to recognise, to remember, as to perform any act of understanding. The play of the
energy had been continuous and couldn't change; what
changed was only the objects and situations pressing the
spring of it. Notes had been in other words the things one
couldn't *not* take, and the prime result of all fresh experi-

ence was to remind one of that. I have endeavoured to characterise the peremptory fashion in which my fresh experience of London—the London of the habitual observer, the preoccupied painter, the pedestrian prowler—reminded me; an admonition that represented, I think, the sum of my investigations. I recall pulling no wires, knocking at no closed doors, applying for no "authentic" information; but I recall also on the other hand the practice of never missing an opportunity to add a drop, however small, to the bucket of my impressions or to renew my sense of being able to dip into it. To haunt the great city and by this habit to penetrate it, imaginatively, in as many places as possible—*that* was to be informed, *that* was to pull wires, *that* was to open doors, *that* positively was to groan at times under the weight of one's accumulations.

Face to face with the idea of Hyacinth's subterraneous politics and occult affiliations, I recollect perfectly feeling, in short, that I might well be ashamed if, with my advantages—and there was n't a street, a corner, an hour, of London that was not an advantage—I should n't be able to piece together a proper semblance of those things, as indeed a proper semblance of all the odd parts of his life. There was always of course the chance that the propriety might be challenged— challenged by readers of a knowledge greater than mine. Yet knowledge, after all, of what? My vision of the aspects I more or less fortunately rendered *was,* exactly, my knowledge. If I made my appearances live, what was this but the utmost one could do with them? Let me at the same time not deny that, in answer to probable ironic reflexions on the full license for sketchiness and vagueness and dimness taken indeed by my picture, I had to bethink myself in advance of a defence of my "artistic position." Should n't I find it in the happy contention that the value I wished most to render and the effect I wished most to produce were precisely those of our not knowing, of society's not knowing, but only guessing and suspecting and trying to ignore, what "goes on" irreconcileably, subversively, beneath the vast smug surface? I could n't deal with that positive quantity for itself—my subject had another too exacting side; but I might perhaps show the social ear as on occasion applied to the ground, or catch some gust of the hot breath that I had at many an hour seemed to see escape and hover. What it all came back to was, no doubt, something like *this* wisdom—that if you have n't, for fiction, the root of the matter in you, have n't the sense of *life* and the penetrating imagination, you are a fool in the very presence of the revealed and assured; but that if you *are* so armed you are not really helpless, not without your resource, even before mysteries abysmal.

V

PREFACE TO "THE TRAGIC MUSE"

(VOLUME VII IN THE NEW YORK EDITION)

I PROFESS a certain vagueness of remembrance in respect to the origin and growth of "The Tragic Muse," which appeared in "The Atlantic Monthly" again, beginning January 1889 and running on, inordinately, several months beyond its proper twelve. If it be ever of interest and profit to put one's finger on the productive germ of a work of art, and if in fact a lucid account of any such work involves that prime identification, I can but look on the present fiction as a poor fatherless and motherless, a sort of unregistered and unacknowledged birth. I fail to recover my precious first moment of consciousness of the idea to which it was to give form; to recognise in it—as I like to do in general—the effect of some particular sharp impression or concussion. I call such remembered glimmers always precious, because without them comes no clear vision of what one may have intended, and without that vision no straight measure of what one may have succeeded in doing. What I make out from furthest back is that I must have had from still further back, must in fact practically have always had, the happy thought of some dramatic picture of the "artist-life" and of the difficult terms on which it is at the best secured and enjoyed, the general question of its having to be not altogether easily paid for. To "do something about art"—art, that is, as a human complication and a social stumbling-block—must have been for me early a good deal of a nursed intention, the conflict between art and "the world" striking me thus betimes as one of the half-dozen great primary motives. I remember even having taken for granted with this fond inveteracy that no one of these pregnant themes was likely to prove under the test more full of matter. This being the case, meanwhile, what would all experience have done but enrich one's conviction? —since if on the one hand I had gained a more and more intimate view of the nature of art and the conditions therewith imposed, so the world was a conception that clearly required, and that would for ever continue to take, any amount of filling-in. The happy and fruitful truth, at all events, was that there was opposition—why there *should* be was another matter—and that the opposition would beget an infinity of situations. What had doubtless occurred in fact, moreover, was that just this question of the essence and the reasons of the opposition had shown itself to demand the light of experience; so that to the growth of experience, truly, the treatment of the subject had yielded. It had waited for that advantage.

Yet I continue to see experience giving me its jog mainly in the form of an invitation from the gentle editor of "The Atlantic," the late Thomas Bailey Aldrich, to contribute to his pages a serial that should run through the year. That friendly appeal becomes thus the most definite statement I can make of the "genesis" of the book; though from the moment of its reaching me everything else in the matter seems to live again. What lives not least, to be quite candid, is the fact that I was to see this production make a virtual end, for the time, as by its sinister effect—though for reasons still obscure to me—of the pleasant old custom of the "running" of the novel. Not for many years was I to feel the practice, for my benefit, confidingly revive. The influence of "The Tragic Muse" was thus exactly other than what I had all earnestly (if of course privately enough) invoked for it, and I remember well the particular chill, at last, of the sense of my having launched it in a great grey void from which no echo or message whatever would come back. None, in the event, ever came, and as I now read the book over I find the circumstance make, in its name, for a special tenderness of charity; even for that finer consideration hanging in the parental breast about the maimed or slighted, the disfigured or defeated, the unlucky or unlikely child—with this hapless small mortal thought of further as somehow "compromising." I am thus able to take the thing as having quite wittingly and undisturbedly existed for itself alone, and to liken it to some aromatic bag of gathered herbs of which the string has never been loosed; or, better still, to some jar of potpourri, shaped and overfigured and polished, but of which the lid, never lifted, has provided for the intense accumulation of the fragrance within. The consistent, the sustained, preserved *tone* of "The Tragic Muse," its constant and doubtless rather finedrawn truth to its particular sought pitch and accent, are, critically speaking, its principal merit—the inner harmony that I perhaps presumptuously permit myself to compare to an unevaporated scent.

After which indeed I may well be summoned to say what I mean, in such a business, by an appreciable "tone" and how I can justify my claim to it—a demonstration that will await us later. Suffice it just here that I find the latent historic clue in my hand again with the easy recall of my prompt grasp of such a chance to make a story about art. *There* was my subject this time—all mature with having long waited, and with the blest dignity that my original perception of its value was quite lost in the mists of youth. I must long have carried in my head the notion of a young man who should amid difficulty—the difficulties being the story—have abandoned "public life" for the zealous pursuit of some supposedly minor craft; just as, evidently, there had hovered before me some possible picture (but all comic and ironic) of one of the most salient London "social" passions, the unappeasable curiosity for the things of the theatre; for every one of them, that is, except the drama itself, and for the "personality" of the performer (almost any performer quite sufficiently serving) in particular. This latter, verily, had struck me as an aspect appealing mainly to satiric treatment; the only adequate or effective treatment, I had again and again felt, for most of the distinctively social aspects of London: the general artlessly histrionised air of things caused so many examples to spring from behind any hedge. What came up, however, at once, for my own stretched canvas, was that it would have to be ample, give me really space to turn round, and that a single illustrative case might easily be meagre fare. The young man who should "chuck" admired politics, and of course some other admired object with them, would be all very well; but he would n't be enough—therefore what should one say to some other young man who would chuck something and somebody else, admired in their way too?

There need never, at the worst, be any difficulty about the things advantageously chuckable for art; the question is all but of choosing them in the heap. Yet were I to represent a struggle—an interesting one, indispensably—with the passions of the theatre (as a profession, or at least as an absorption) I should have to place the theatre in another light than the satiric. This, however, would by good luck be perfectly possible too—without a sacrifice of truth; and I should doubtless even be able to make my theatric case as important as I might desire it. It seemed clear that I needed big cases—small ones would practically give my central idea away; and I make out now my still labouring under the illusion that the case of the sacrifice for art *can* ever be, with truth, with taste, with discretion involved, apparently and showily "big." I dare say it glimmered upon me even then that the very sharpest difficulty of the victim of the conflict I should seek to represent, and the very highest interest of his predicament, dwell deep in the fact that his repudiation of the great obvious, great moral or functional or useful character, shall just have to consent to resemble a surrender for absolutely nothing. Those

characters are all large and expansive, seated and established
and endowed; whereas the most charming truth about the
preference for art is that to parade abroad so thoroughly inward and so naturally embarrassed a matter is to falsify and
vulgarise it; that as a preference attended with the honours
of publicity it is indeed nowhere; that in fact, under the
rule of its sincerity, its only honours are those of contraction,
concentration and a seemingly deplorable indifference to
everything but itself. Nothing can well figure as less "big," in
an honest thesis, than a marked instance of somebody's will-
ingness to pass mainly for an ass. Of these things I must, I
say, have been in strictness aware; what I perhaps failed of
was to note that if a certain romantic glamour (even that
of mere eccentricity or of a fine perversity) may be flung over
the act of exchange of a "career" for the æsthetic life in general, the prose and the modesty of the matter yet come in
with any exhibition of the particular branch of æsthetics
selected. Then it is that the attitude of hero or heroine may
look too much—for the romantic effect—like a low crouching over proved trifles. Art indeed has in our day taken on
so many honours and emoluments that the recognition of
its importance is more than a custom, has become on occasion almost a fury: the line is drawn—especially in the English world—only at the importance of heeding what it may
mean.

The more I turn my pieces over, at any rate, the more
I now see I must have found in them, and I remember how,
once well in presence of my three typical examples, my fear
of too ample a canvas quite dropped. The only question was
that if I had marked my political case, from so far back, for
"a story by itself," and then marked my theatrical case for
another, the joining together of these interests, originally
seen as separate, might, all disgracefully, betray the seam,
show for mechanical and superficial. A story was a story,
a picture a picture, and I had a mortal horror of two stories,

two pictures, in one. The reason of this was the clearest —my subject was immediately, under that disadvantage, so cheated of its indispensable centre as to become of no more use for expressing a main intention than a wheel without a hub is of use for moving a cart. It was a fact, apparently, that one *had* on occasion seen two pictures in one; were there not for instance certain sublime Tintorettos at Venice, a measureless Crucifixion in especial, which showed without loss of authority half a dozen actions separately taking place? Yes, that might be, but there had surely been nevertheless a mighty pictorial fusion, so that the virtue of composition had somehow thereby come all mysteriously to its own. Of course the affair would be simple enough if composition could be kept out of the question; yet by what art or process, what bars and bolts, what unmuzzled dogs and pointed guns, perform that feat? I had to know myself utterly inapt for any such valour and recognise that, to make it possible, sundry things should have begun for me much further back than I had felt them even in their dawn. A picture without composition slights its most precious chance for beauty, and is moreover not composed at all unless the painter knows *how* that principle of health and safety, working as an absolutely premeditated art, has prevailed. There may in its absence be life, incontestably, as "The Newcomes" has life, as "Les Trois Mousquetaires," as Tolstoi's "Peace and War," have it; but what do such large loose baggy monsters, with their queer elements of the accidental and the arbitrary, artistically *mean*? We have heard it maintained, we will remember, that such things are "superior to art"; but we understand least of all what *that* may mean, and we look in vain for the artist, the divine explanatory genius, who will come to our aid and tell us. There is life and life, and as waste is only life sacrificed and thereby prevented from "counting," I delight in a deep-breathing economy and an organic form. My business was accordingly to "go in" for complete pictorial fusion, some such common interest between my two first notions as would, in spite of their birth under quite different stars, do them no violence at all.

I recall with this confirmed infatuation of retrospect that through the mild perceptions I here glance at there struck for "The Tragic Muse" the first hour of a season of no small subjective felicity; lighted mainly, I seem to see, by a wide west window that, high aloft, looked over near and far London sunsets, a half-grey, half-flushed expanse of London life. The production of the thing, which yet took a good many months, lives for me again all contemporaneously in that full projection, upon my very table, of the good fog-filtered Kensington mornings; which had a way indeed of seeing the sunset in and which at the very last are merged to memory in a different and a sharper pressure, that of an hotel bedroom in Paris during the autumn of 1889, with the Exposition du Centenaire about to end—and my long story, through the usual difficulties, as well. The usual difficulties—and I fairly cherish the record as some adventurer in another line may hug the sense of his inveterate habit of just saving in time the neck he ever undiscourageably risks —were those bequeathed as a particular vice of the artistic spirit, against which vigilance had been destined from the first to exert itself in vain, and the effect of which was that again and again, perversely, incurably, the centre of my structure would insist on placing itself *not,* so to speak, in the middle. It mattered little that the reader with the idea or the suspicion of a structural centre is the rarest of friends and of critics—a bird, it would seem, as merely fabled as the phœnix: the terminational terror was none the less certain to break in and my work threaten to masquerade for me as an active figure condemned to the disgrace of legs too short, ever so much too short, for its body. I urge myself to the candid confession that in very few of my productions, to my eye, *has* the organic centre succeeded in getting into proper position.

Time after time, then, has the precious waistband or girdle, studded and buckled and placed for brave outward show, practically worked itself, and in spite of desperate remonstrance, or in other words essential counterplotting, to a point perilously near the knees—perilously I mean for the freedom of these parts. In several of my compositions this displacement has so succeeded, at the crisis, in defying and resisting me, has appeared so fraught with probable dishonour, that I still turn upon them, in spite of the greater or less success of final dissimulation, a rueful and wondering eye. These productions have in fact, if I may be so bold about it, specious and spurious centres altogether, to make up for the failure of the true. As to which in my list they are, however, that is another business, not on any terms to be made known. Such at least would seem my resolution so far as I have thus proceeded. Of any attention ever arrested by the pages forming the object of this reference that rigour of discrimination has wholly and consistently failed, I gather, to constitute a part. In which fact there is perhaps after all a rough justice—since the infirmity I speak of, for example, has been always but the direct and immediate fruit of a positive excess of foresight, the overdone desire to provide for future need and lay up heavenly treasure against the demands of my climax. If the art of the drama, as a great French master of it has said, is above all the art of preparations, that is true only to a less extent of the art of the novel, and true exactly in the degree in which the art of the particular novel comes near that of the drama. The first half of a fiction insists ever on figuring to me as the stage or theatre for the second half, and I have in general given so much space to making the theatre propitious that my halves have too often proved strangely unequal. Thereby has arisen with grim regularity the question of artfully, of consummately masking the fault and conferring on the false quantity the brave appearance of the true.

But I am far from pretending that these desperations of

ingenuity have not—as through seeming *most* of the very essence of the problem—their exasperated charm; so far from it that my particular supreme predicament in the Paris hotel, after an undue primary leakage of time, no doubt, over at the great river-spanning museum of the Champ de Mars and the Trocadero, fairly takes on to me now the tender grace of a day that is dead. Re-reading the last chapters of "The Tragic Muse" I catch again the very odour of Paris, which comes up in the rich rumble of the Rue de la Paix—with which my room itself, for that matter, seems impregnated—and which hangs for reminiscence about the embarrassed effort to "finish," not ignobly, within my already exceeded limits; an effort prolonged each day to those late afternoon hours during which the tone of the terrible city seemed to deepen about one to an effect strangely composed at once of the auspicious and the fatal. The "plot" of Paris thickened at such hours beyond any other plot in the world, I think; but there one sat meanwhile with another, on one's hands, absolutely requiring precedence. Not the least imperative of one's conditions was thus that one should have really, should have finely and (given one's scale) concisely treated one's subject, in spite of there being so much of the confounded irreducible quantity still to treat. If I spoke just now, however, of the "exasperated" charm of supreme difficulty, that is because the challenge of economic representation so easily becomes, in any of the arts, intensely interesting to meet. To put all that is possible of one's idea into a form and compass that will contain and express it only by delicate adjustments and an exquisite chemistry, so that there will at the end be neither a drop of one's liquor left nor a hair's breadth of the rim of one's glass to spare—every artist will remember how often that sort of necessity has carried with it its particular inspiration. Therein lies the secret of the appeal, to his mind, of the successfully *foreshortened* thing, where representation is arrived at, as I have already elsewhere had occasion to urge, not by the addition of items (a light that has for its attendant shadow a possible dryness) but by the art of figuring synthetically, a compactness into which the imagination may cut thick, as into the rich density of wedding-cake. The moral of all which indeed, I fear, is, perhaps too trivially, but that the "thick," the false, the dissembling second half of the work before me, associated throughout with the effort to weight my dramatic values as heavily as might be, since they had to be so few, presents that effort as at the very last a quite convulsive, yet in its way highly agreeable, spasm. Of such mild prodigies is the "history" of any specific creative effort composed!

But I have got too much out of the "old" Kensington light of twenty years ago—a lingering oblique ray of which, to-day surely quite extinct, played for a benediction over my canvas. From the moment I made out, at my high-perched west window, my lucky title, that is from the moment Miriam Rooth herself had given it me, so this young woman had given me with it her own position in the book, and so that in turn had given me my precious unity, to which no more than Miriam was either Nick Dormer or Peter Sherringham to be sacrificed. Much of the interest of the matter was immediately therefore in working out the detail of that unity and —always entrancing range of questions—the order, the reason, the relation, of presented aspects. With three *general* aspects, that of Miriam's case, that of Nick's and that of Sherringham's there was work in plenty cut out; since happy as it might be to say "My several actions beautifully become one," the point of the affair would be in *showing* them beautifully become so—without which showing foul failure hovered and pounced. Well, the pleasure of handling an action (or, otherwise expressed, of a "story") is at the worst, for a storyteller, immense, and the interest of such a question as for example keeping Nick Dormer's story his and yet making it also and all effectively in a large part Peter Sherringham's, of keeping Sherringham's his and yet making it in its high degree his kinsman's, too, and Miriam Rooth's into the bargain; just as Miriam Rooth's is by the same token quite operatively his and Nick's, and just as that of each of the young men, by an equal logic, very contributively hers—the interest of such a question, I say, is ever so considerably the interest of the system on which the whole thing is done. I see to-day that it was but half a system to say: "Oh Miriam, a case herself, is the *link* between the two other cases"; that device was to ask for as much help as it gave and to require a good deal more application than it announced on the surface. The sense of a system saves the painter from the baseness of the *arbitrary* stroke, the touch without its reason, but as payment for that service the process insists on being kept impeccably the right one.

These are intimate truths indeed, of which the charm mainly comes out but on experiment and in practice; yet I like to have it well before me here that, after all, "The Tragic Muse" makes it not easy to say which of the situations concerned in it predominates and rules. What has become in that imperfect order, accordingly, of the famous centre of one's subject? It is surely not in Nick's consciousness—since why, if it be, are we treated to such an intolerable dose of Sherringham's? It can't be in Sherringham's—we have for that altogether an excess of Nick's. How on the other hand can it be in Miriam's, given that we have no direct exhibition of hers whatever, that we get at it all inferentially and inductively, seeing it only through a more or less bewildered interpretation of it by others. The emphasis is all on an absolutely objective Miriam, and, this affirmed, how—with such an amount of exposed subjectivity all round her—can so dense a medium be a centre? Such questions as those go straight—thanks to which they are, I profess, delightful; going straight they are of the sort that makes answers possible. Miriam *is* central then to analysis, in spite of being objective; central in virtue of the fact that the whole thing has visibly, from the first, to get itself done in dramatic, or at least in scenic conditions—though scenic conditions which are as near an approach to the dramatic as the novel may permit itself and which have this in common with the latter, that they move in the light of *alternation.* This imposes a consistency other than that of the novel at its loosest, and, for one's subject, a different view and a different placing of the centre. The charm of the scenic consistency, the consistency of the multiplication of *aspects,* that of making them amusingly various, had haunted the author of "The Tragic Muse" from far back, and he was in due course to yield to it all luxuriously, too luxuriously perhaps, in "The Awkward Age," as will doubtless with the extension of these remarks be complacently shown.

To put himself at any rate as much as possible under the protection of it had been ever his practice (he had notably done so in "The Princess Casamassima," so frankly panoramic and processional); and in what case could this protection have had more price than in the one before us? No character in a play (any play not a mere monologue) has, for the right expression of the thing, a *usurping* consciousness; the consciousness of others is exhibited exactly in the same way as that of the "hero"; the prodigious consciousness of Hamlet, the most capacious and most crowded, the moral presence the most asserted, in the whole range of fiction, only takes its turn with that of the other agents of the story, no matter how occasional these may be. It is left in other words to answer for itself equally with theirs: wherefore (by a parity of reasoning if not of example) Miriam's might without inconsequence be placed on the same footing; and all in spite of the fact that the "moral presence" of each of the men most importantly concerned with her—or with the second of whom she at least is importantly concerned—*is* independently answered for. The idea of the book being, as I have said, a picture of some of the personal consequences of the art-appetite raised to intensity, swollen to voracity, the heavy emphasis falls where the symbol of some of the complications so begotten might be made (as I judged, heaven forgive me!) most "amusing": amusing I mean in the blest very modern sense. I never "go behind" Miriam; only poor Sherringham goes, a great deal, and Nick Dormer goes a little, and the author, while they so waste wonderment, goes behind *them:* but none the less she is as thoroughly symbolic, as functional, for illustration of the idea, as either of them, while her image had seemed susceptible of a livelier and "prettier" concretion. I had desired for her, I remember, all manageable vividness—so ineluctable had it long appeared to "do the actress," to touch the theatre, to meet that connexion somehow or other, in any free plunge of the speculative fork into the contemporary social salad.

The late R. L. Stevenson was to write to me, I recall—and precisely on the occasion of "The Tragic Muse"—that he was at a loss to conceive how one could find an interest in anything so vulgar or pretend to gather fruit in so scrubby an orchard; but the view of a creature of the stage, the view of the "histrionic temperament," as suggestive much less, verily, in respect to the poor stage *per se* than in respect to "art" at large, affected me in spite of that as justly tenable. An objection of a more pointed order was forced upon me by an acute friend later on and in another connexion: the challenge of one's right, in any pretended show of social realities, to attach to the image of a "public character," a supposed particular celebrity, a range of interest, of intrinsic distinction, greater than any such display of importance on the part of eminent members of the class as we see them about us. There *was* a nice point if one would—yet only nice enough, after all, to be easily amusing. We shall deal with it later on, however, in a more urgent connexion. What would have worried me much more had it dawned earlier is the light lately thrown by that admirable writer M. Anatole France on the question of any animated view of the histrionic temperament—a light that may well dazzle to distress any ingenuous worker in the same field. In those parts of his brief but inimitable *Histoire Comique* on which he is most to be congratulated—for there are some that prompt to reserves—he has "done the actress," as well as the actor, done above all the mountebank, the mummer and the *cabotin,* and mixed them up with the queer theatric air, in a manner that practically warns all other hands off the material for ever. At the same time I think I saw Miriam, and without a sacrifice of truth, that is of the particular glow of verisimilitude I wished her most to benefit by, in a complexity of relations finer than any that appear possible for the gentry of M. Anatole France.

Her relation to Nick Dormer, for instance, was intended as a superior interest—that of being (while perfectly sincere, sincere for *her,* and therefore perfectly consonant with her impulse perpetually to perform and with her success in performing) the result of a touched imagination, a touched pride for "art," as well as of the charm cast on other sensibilities still. Dormer's relation to herself is a different matter, of which more presently; but the sympathy she, poor young woman, very generously and intelligently offers him where most people have so stinted it, is disclosed largely at the cost of her egotism and her personal pretensions, even though in fact determined by her sense of their together, Nick and she, postponing the "world" to their conception of other and finer decencies. Nick can't on the whole see—for I have represented him as in his day quite sufficiently troubled and anxious—why he should condemn to ugly feebleness his most prized faculty (most prized, at least, by himself) even in order to keep his seat in Parliament, to inherit Mr. Carteret's blessing and money, to gratify his mother and carry out the mission of his father, to marry Julia Dallow in fine, a beautiful imperative woman with a great many thousands a year. It all comes back in the last analysis to the individual vision of decency, the critical as well as the passionate judgment of it under sharp stress; and Nick's vision and judgment, all on the æsthetic ground, have beautifully coincided, to Miriam's imagination, with a now fully marked, an inspired and impenitent, choice of her own: so that, other considerations powerfully aiding indeed, she is ready to see their interest all splendidly as one. She is in the uplifted state to which sacrifices and submissions loom large, but loom so just because they must write sympathy, write passion, large. Her measure of what she would be capable of for him—capable, that is, of *not* asking of him—will depend on what he shall ask of *her,* but she has no fear of not being able to satisfy him, even to the point of "chucking" for him, if need be, that artistic identity of her own which she has begun to build up. It will all be to the glory therefore of their common infatuation with "art": she will doubtless be no less willing to serve his than she was eager to serve her own, purged now of the too great shrillness.

This puts her quite on a different level from that of the vivid monsters of M. France, whose artistic identity is the last thing *they* wish to chuck—their only dismissal is of all material and social overdraping. Nick Dormer in point of fact asks of Miriam nothing but that she shall remain "awfully interesting to paint"; but that is *his* relation, which, as I say, is quite a matter by itself. He at any rate, luckily for both of them it may be, doesn't put her to the test: he is so busy with his own case, busy with testing himself and feeling his reality. He had seen himself as giving up precious things for an object, and that object has somehow not been the young woman in question, nor anything very nearly like her. She on the other hand has asked everything of Peter Sherringham, who has asked everything of *her;* and it is in so doing that she has really most testified for art and invited him to testify. With his professed interest in the theatre—one of those deep subjections that, in men of "taste," the Comédie Française used in old days to conspire for and some such odd and affecting examples of which were to be noted—he yet offers her his hand and an introduction to the very best society if she will leave the stage. The power—and her having the sense of the power—to "shine" in the world is his highest measure of her, the test applied by him to her beautiful human value; just as the manner in which she turns on him is the application of her own standard and touchstone. She is perfectly sure of her own; for—if there were nothing else, and there is much—she has tasted blood, so to speak, in the form of her so prompt and auspicious success with the public, leaving all probations behind (the whole of which, as the book gives it, is too rapid and sudden, though inevitably so: processes, periods, intervals, stages, degrees, connexions, may be easily enough and barely enough named, may be unconvincingly stated, in fiction, to the deep discredit of the writer, but it remains the very deuce to *represent* them, especially represent them under strong compression and in brief and subordinate terms; and this even though the novelist who does n't represent, and represent "all the time," is lost, exactly as much lost as the painter who, at his work and given his intention, does n't paint "all the time").

Turn upon her friend at any rate Miriam does; and one of my main points is missed if it fails to appear that she does so with absolute sincerity and with the cold passion of the high critic who knows, on sight of them together, the more or less dazzling false from the comparatively grey-coloured true. Sherringham's whole profession has been that he rejoices in her as she is, and that the theatre, the organised theatre, will be, as Matthew Arnold was in those very days pronouncing it, irresistible; and it is the promptness with which he sheds his pretended faith as soon as it feels in the air the breath of reality, as soon as it asks of him a proof or a sacrifice, it is this that excites her doubtless sufficiently arrogant scorn. Where is the virtue of his high interest if it has verily never *been* an interest to speak of and if all it has suddenly to suggest is that, in face of a serious call, it shall be unblushingly relinquished? If he and she together, and her great field and future, and the whole cause they had armed and declared for, have not been serious things they have been base make-believes and trivialities—which is what in fact the homage of society to art always turns out so soon as art presumes not to be vulgar and futile. It is immensely the fashion and immensely edifying to listen to, this homage, while it confines its attention to vanities and frauds; but it knows only terror, feels only horror, the moment that, instead of making all the concessions, art proceeds to ask for a few. Miriam is nothing if not strenuous, and evidently nothing if not "cheeky," where Sherringham is concerned at least: these, in the all-egotistical exhibition to which she is condemned, are the very elements of her figure and the very colours of her portrait. But she is mild and inconsequent for Nick Dormer (who demands of her so little); as if gravely and pityingly embracing the truth that *his* sacrifice, on the right side, is probably to have very little of her sort of recompense. I must have had it well before me that she was all aware of the small strain a great sacrifice to Nick would cost her—by reason of the strong effect on her of his own superior logic, in which the very intensity of concentration was so to find its account.

If the man, however, who holds her personally dear yet holds her extremely personal message to the world cheap, so the man capable of a consistency and, as she regards the matter, of an honesty so much higher than Sherringham's, virtually cares, "really" cares, no straw for his fellow struggler. If Nick Dormer attracts and all-indifferently holds her it is because, like herself and unlike Peter, he puts "art" first; but the most he thus does for her in the event is to let her see how she may enjoy, in intimacy, the rigour it has taught him and which he cultivates at her expense. This is the situation in which we leave her, though there would be more still to be said about the difference for her of the two relations—that to each of the men—could I fondly suppose as much of the interest of the book "left over" for the reader as for myself. Sherringham for instance offers Miriam marriage, ever so "handsomely"; but if nothing might lead me on further than the question of what it would have been open to us—us novelists, especially in the old days—to show, "serially," a young man in Nick Dormer's quite different position as offering or a young woman in Miriam's as taking, so for that very reason such an excursion is forbidden me. The trade of the stage-player, and above all of the actress, must have so many detestable sides for the person exercising it that we scarce imagine a full surrender to it without a full surrender, not less, to every immediate compensation, to every freedom and the largest ease within reach: which presentment of the possible case for Miriam would yet have been condemned—and on grounds both various and interesting to trace—to remain very imperfect.

I feel moreover that I might still, with space, abound in remarks about Nick's character and Nick's crisis suggested to my present more reflective vision. It strikes me, alas, that he is not quite so interesting as he was fondly intended to be, and this in spite of the multiplication, within the picture, of his pains and penalties; so that while I turn this slight anomaly over I come upon a reason that affects me as singularly charming and touching and at which indeed I have already glanced. Any presentation of the artist *in triumph* must be flat in proportion as it really sticks to its subject—it can only smuggle in relief and variety. For, to put the matter in an image, all we then—in his triumph—see of the charm-compeller is the back he turns to us as he bends over his work. "His" triumph, decently, is but the triumph of what he produces, and that is another affair. His romance is the romance he himself projects; he eats the cake of the very rarest privilege, the most luscious baked in the oven of the gods—therefore he may n't "have" it, in the form of the privilege of the hero, at the same time. The privilege of the hero—

that is of the martyr or of the interesting and appealing and comparatively floundering *person*—places him in quite a different category, belongs to him only as to the artist deluded, diverted, frustrated or vanquished; when the "amateur" in him gains, for our admiration or compassion or whatever, all that the expert has to do without. Therefore I strove in vain, I feel, to embroil and adorn this young man on whom a hundred ingenious touches are thus lavished: he has insisted in the event on looking as simple and flat as some mere brass check or engraved number, the symbol and guarantee of a stored treasure. The better part of him is locked too much away from us, and the part we see has to pass for—well, what it passes for, so lamentedly, among his friends and relatives. No, accordingly, Nick Dormer isn't "the best thing in the book," as I judge I imagined he would be, and it contains nothing better, I make out, than that preserved and achieved unity and quality of tone, a value in itself, which I referred to at the beginning of these remarks. What I mean by this is that the interest created, and the expression of that interest, are things kept, as to kind, genuine and true to themselves. The appeal, the fidelity to the prime motive, is, with no little art, strained clear (even as silver is polished) in a degree answering—at least by intention—to the air of beauty. There is an awkwardness again in having thus belatedly to point such features out; but in that wrought appearance of animation and harmony, that effect of free movement and yet of recurrent and insistent reference, "The Tragic Muse" has struck me again as conscious of a bright advantage.

VI

PREFACE TO "THE AWKWARD AGE"

(VOLUME IX IN THE NEW YORK EDITION)

I RECALL with perfect ease the idea in which "The Awkward Age" had its origin, but re-perusal gives me pause in respect to naming it. This composition, as it stands, makes, to my vision—and will have made perhaps still more to that of its readers—so considerable a mass beside the germ sunk in it and still possibly distinguishable, that I am half-moved to leave my small secret undivulged. I shall encounter, I think, in the course of this copious commentary, no better example, and none on behalf of which I shall venture to invite more interest, of the quite incalculable tendency of a mere grain of subject-matter to expand and develop and cover the ground when conditions happen to favour it. I say all, surely, when I speak of the thing as planned, in perfect good faith, for brevity, for levity, for simplicity, for jocosity, in fine, and for an accomodating irony. I invoked, for my protection, the spirit of the lightest comedy, but "The Awkward Age" was to belong, in the event, to a group of productions, here re-introduced, which have in common, to their author's eyes, the endearing sign that they asserted in each case an unforeseen principle of growth. They were projected as small things, yet had finally to be provided for as comparative monsters. That is my own title for them, though I should perhaps resent it if applied by another critic—above all in the case of the piece before us, the careful measure of which I have just freshly taken. The result of this consideration has been in the first place to render sharp for me again the interest of the whole process thus illustrated, and in the second quite to place me on unexpectedly good terms with the work itself. As I scan my list I encounter none the "history" of which embodies a greater number of curious truths— or of truths at least by which I find contemplation more enlivened. The thing done and dismissed has ever, at the best, for the ambitious workman, a trick of looking dead, if not buried, so that he almost throbs with ecstasy when, on an anxious review, the flush of life reappears. It is verily on recognising that flush on a whole side of "The Awkward Age" that I brand it all, but ever so tenderly, as monstrous— which is but my way of noting the *quantity* of finish it stows away. Since I speak so undauntedly, when need is, of the value of composition, I shall not beat about the bush to claim for these pages the maximum of that advantage. If such a feat be possible in this field as really taking a lesson from one's own adventure I feel I have now not failed of it—to so much more demonstration of my profit than I can hope to carry through do I find myself urged. Thus it is that, still with a remnant of self-respect, or at least of sanity, one may turn to complacency, one may linger with pride. Let my pride provoke a frown till I justify it; which—though with more matters to be noted here than I have room for—I shall accordingly proceed to do.

Yet I must first make a brave face, no doubt, and present in its native humility my scant but quite ponderable germ. The seed sprouted in that vast nursery of sharp appeals and concrete images which calls itself, for blest convenience, London; it fell even into the order of the minor "social phenomena" with which, as fruit for the observer, that mightiest of the trees of suggestion bristles. It was not, no doubt, a fine purple peach, but it might pass for a round ripe plum, the note one had inevitably had to take of the difference made in certain friendly houses and for certain flourishing mothers by the sometimes dreaded, often delayed, but never fully arrested coming to the forefront of some vague slip of a daughter. For such mild revolutions as these not, to one's imagination, to remain mild one had had, I dare say, to be infinitely addicted to "noticing"; under the rule of that secret vice or that unfair advantage, at any rate, the "sitting downstairs," from a given date, of the merciless maiden previously perched aloft could easily be felt as a crisis. This crisis, and the sense for it in those whom it most concerns, has to confess itself courageously the prime propulsive force of "The Awkward Age." Such a matter might well make a scant show for a "thick book," and no thick book, but just a quite charmingly thin one, was in fact originally dreamt of. For its proposed scale the little idea seemed happy—happy, that is, above all in having come very straight; but its proposed scale was the limit of a small square canvas. One had been present again and again at the exhibition I refer to—which is what I mean by the "coming straight" of this particular London impression; yet one was (and through fallibilities that after all had their sweetness, so that one would on the whole rather have kept them than parted with them) still capable of so false a measurement. When I think indeed of those of my many false measurements that have resulted, after much anguish, in decent symmetries, I find the whole case, I profess, a theme for the philosopher. The little ideas one would n't have treated save for the design of keeping them small, the developed situations that one would never with malice prepense have undertaken, the long stories that had thoroughly meant to be short, the short subjects that had underhandedly plotted to be long, the hypocrisy of modest beginings, the audacity of misplaced middles, the triumph of intentions never entertained—with these patches, as I look about, I see my experience paved: an experience to which nothing is wanting save, I confess, some grasp of its final lesson.

This lesson would, if operative, surely provide some law for the recognition, the determination in advance, of the just limits and the just extent of the situation, *any* situation, that appeals, and that yet, by the presumable, the helpful law of situations. must have its reserves as well as its promises. The storyteller considers it because it promises, and undertakes it, often, just because also making out, as he believes, where the promise conveniently drops. The promise, for instance, of the case I have just named, the case of the account to be taken, in a circle of free talk, of a new and innocent, a wholly un-acclimatised presence, as to which such accommodations have never had to come up, might well have appeared as limited as it was lively; and if these pages were not before us to register my illusion I should never have made a braver claim for it. They themselves admonish me, however, in fifty interesting ways, and they especially emphasise that truth of the vanity of the *a priori* test of what an *idée-mère* may have to give. The truth is that what a happy thought has to give depends immensely on the general turn of the mind capable of it, and on the fact that its loyal entertainer, cultivating fondly its possible relations and extensions, the bright efflorescence latent in it, but having to take other things in their order too, is terribly at the mercy of his mind. That organ has only to exhale, in its degree, a fostering tropic air in order to produce complications almost beyond reckoning. The trap laid for his superficial convenience resides in the fact that, though the relations of a human figure or a social occurrence are what make such objects interesting, they also make them, to the same tune, difficult to isolate, to surround with the sharp black line, to frame in the square, the circle, the charming oval, that helps any arrangement of objects to become a picture. The storyteller has but to have been condemned by nature to a liberally amused and beguiled, a richly sophisticated, view of relations and a fine inquisitive speculative sense for them, to find himself at moments flounder in a deep warm jungle. These are the moments at which he recalls ruefully that the great merit of such and such a small case, the merit for his particular advised use, had been precisely in the smallness.

I may say at once that this had seemed to me, under the

first flush of recognition, the good mark for the pretty notion of the "free circle" put about by having, of a sudden, an ingenuous mind and a pair of limpid searching eyes to count with. Half the attraction was in the current actuality of the thing: repeatedly, right and left, as I have said, one had seen such a drama constituted, and always to the effect of proposing to the interested view one of those questions that are of the essence of drama: what will happen, who suffer, who not suffer, what turn be determined, what crisis created, what issue found? There had of course to be, as a basis, the free circle, but this was material of that admirable order with which the good London never leaves its true lover and believer long unprovided. One could count them on one's fingers (an abundant allowance), the liberal firesides beyond the wide glow of which, in a comparative dimness, female adolescence hovered and waited. The wide glow was bright, was favourable to "real" talk, to play of mind, to an explicit interest in life, a due demonstration of the interest by persons qualified to feel it: all of which meant frankness and ease, the perfection, almost, as it were, of intercourse, and a tone as far as possible removed from that of the nursery and the schoolroom—as far as possible removed even, no doubt, in its appealing "modernity," from that of supposedly privileged scenes of conversation twenty years ago. The charm was, with a hundred other things, in the freedom—the freedom menaced by the inevitable irruption of the ingenuous mind; whereby, if the freedom should be sacrificed, what would truly *become* of the charm? The charm might be figured as dear to members of the circle consciously contributing to it, but it was none the less true that some sacrifice in some quarter would have to be made, and what meditator worth his salt could fail to hold his breath while waiting on the event? The ingenuous mind might, it was true, be suppressed altogether, the general disconcertment averted either by some master-stroke of diplomacy or some rude simplification; yet these were ugly matters, and in the examples before one's eyes nothing ugly, nothing harsh or crude, had flourished. A girl might be married off the day after her irruption, or better still the day before it, to remove her from the sphere of the play of mind; but these were exactly not crudities, and even then, at the worst, an interval had to be bridged. "The Awkward Age" is precisely a study of one of these curtailed or extended periods of tension and apprehension, an account of the manner in which the resented interference with ancient liberties came to be in a particular instance dealt with.

I note once again that I had not escaped seeing it actually and traceably dealt with—after (I admit) a good deal of friendly suspense; also with the nature and degree of the "sacrifice" left very much to one's appreciation. In circles highly civilised the great things, the real things, the hard, the cruel and even the tender things, the true elements of any tension and true facts of any crisis, have ever, for the outsider's, for the critic's use, to be translated into terms—terms in the distinguished name of which, terms for the right employment of which, more than one situation of the type I glance at had struck me as all irresistibly appealing. There appeared in fact at moments no end to the things they said, the suggestions into which they flowered; one of these latter in especial arriving at the highest intensity. Putting vividly before one the perfect system on which the awkward age is handled in most other European societies, it threw again into relief the inveterate English trick of the so morally well-meant and so intellectually helpless compromise. We live notoriously, as I suppose every age lives, in an "epoch of transition"; but it may still be said of the French for instance, I assume, that their social scheme absolutely provides against awkwardness. That is it would be, by this scheme, so infinitely awkward, so awkward beyond any patching-up, for the hovering female young to be conceived as present at "good" talk, that their presence is, theoretically at least, not permitted till their youth has been promptly corrected by marriage—in which case they have ceased to be merely young. The better the talk prevailing in any circle, accordingly, the more organised, the more complete, the element of precaution and exclusion. Talk—giving the term a wide application—is one thing, and a proper inexperience another; and it has never occurred to a logical people that the interest of the greater, the general, need be sacrificed to that of the less, the particular. Such sacrifices strike them as gratuitous and barbarous, as cruel above all to the social intelligence; also as perfectly preventable by wise arrangement. Nothing comes home more, on the other hand, to the observer of English manners than the very moderate degree in which wise arrangement, in the French sense of a scientific economy, has ever been invoked; a fact indeed largely explaining the great interest of their incoherence, their heterogeneity, their wild abundance. The French, all analytically, have conceived of fifty different proprieties, meeting fifty different cases, whereas the English mind, less intensely at work, has never conceived but of one— the grand propriety, for every case, it should in fairness be said, of just being English. As practice, however, has always to be a looser thing than theory, so no application of that rigour has been possible in the London world without a thousand departures from the grim ideal.

The American theory, if I may "drag it in," would be, I think, that talk should never become "better" than the female young, either actually or constructively present, are minded to allow it. *That* system involves as little compromise as the French; it has been absolutely simple, and the beauty of its success shines out in every record of our conditions of intercourse—premising always our "basic" assumption that the female young read the newspapers. The English theory may be in itself almost as simple, but different and much more complex forces have ruled the application of it; so much does the goodness of talk depend on what there may be to talk about. There are more things in London, I think, than anywhere in the world; hence the charm of the dramatic struggle reflected in my book, the struggle somehow to fit propriety into a smooth general case which is really all the while bristling and crumbling into fierce particular ones. The circle surrounding Mrs. Brookenham, in my pages, is of course nothing if not a particular, even a "peculiar" one—and its rather vain effort (the vanity, the real inexpertness, being precisely part of my tale) is toward the courage of that condition. It has cropped up in a social order where individual appreciations of propriety have not been formally alowed for, in spite of their having very often quite rudely and violently and insolently, rather of course than insidiously, flourished; so that as the matter stands, rightly or wrongly, Nanda's retarded, but eventually none the less real, incorporation means virtually Nanda's exposure. It means this, that is, and many things beside—means them for Nanda herself and, with a various intensity, for the other participants in the action; but what it particularly means, surely, is the failure of successful arrangement and the very moral, sharply pointed, of the fruits of compromise. It is compromise that has suffered her to be in question at all, and that has condemned the freedom of the circle to be self-conscious, compunctious, on the whole much more timid than brave—the consequent muddle, if the term be not too gross, representing meanwhile a great inconvenience for life, but, as I found myself feeling, an immense promise, a much greater one than on the "foreign" showing, for the painted picture of life. Beyond which let me add that here immediately is a prime specimen of the way in which the obscurer, the lurking relations of a motive apparently simple, always in wait for their spring, may by seizing their chance for it send simplicity flying. Poor Nanda's little case, and her mother's, and Mr. Longdon's and Vanderbank's and Mitchy's, to say nothing of that of the others, has only to catch a reflected light from over the Channel in order to double at once its appeal to the imagination. (I am considering all these matters, I need scarce say, only as they are concerned with that faculty. With a relation *not* imaginative to his material the storyteller has nothing whatever to do.)

It exactly happened moreover that my own material here was to profit in a particular way by that extension of view. My idea was to be treated with light irony—it would be light and ironical or it would be nothing; so that I asked myself, naturally, what might be the least solemn form to give it, among recognised and familiar forms. The question thus at once arose: What form so familiar, so recognised among alert readers, as that in which the ingenious and inexhaustible, the charming philosophic "Gyp" casts most of her social studies? Gyp had long struck me as mistress, in her levity, of one of the happiest of forms—the only objection to my use of which was a certain extraordinary benightedness on the part of the Anglo-Saxon reader. One had noted this reader as perverse and inconsequent in respect to the absorption of "dialogue" —observed the "public for fiction" consume it, in certain connexions, on the scale and with the smack of lips that mark the consumption of bread-and-jam by a children's school-feast, consume it even at the theatre, so far as our theatre ever vouchsafes it, and yet as flagrantly reject it when served, so to speak, *au naturel*. One had seen good solid slices of fiction, well endued, one might surely have thought, with this easiest of lubrications, deplored by editor and publisher as positively not, for the general gullet as known to *them,* made adequately "slick." " 'Dialogue,' always 'dialogue'!" I had seemed from far back to hear them mostly cry: "We can't have too much of it, we can't have enough of it, and no excess of it, in the form of no matter what savourless dilution, or what boneless dispersion, ever began to injure a book so much as even the very scantest claim put in for form and substance." This wisdom had always been in one's ears; but it had at the same time been equally in one's eyes that really constructive dialogue, dialogue organic and dramatic, speaking for itself, representing and embodying substance and form, is among us an uncanny and abhorrent thing, not to be dealt with on any terms. A comedy or a tragedy may run for a thousand nights without prompting twenty persons in London or in New York to desire that view of its text which is so desired in Paris, as soon as a play begins to loom at all large, that the number of copies of the printed piece in circulation far exceeds at last the number of perform- ances. But as with the printed piece our own public, infatuated as it may be with the theatre, refuses all commerce—though indeed this can't but be, without cynicism, very much through the infirmity the piece, *if* printed, would reveal—so the same horror seems to attach to any typographic hint of the pro- scribed playbook or any insidious plea for it. The immense oddity resides in the almost exclusively typographic order of the offence. An English, an American Gyp would typographi- cally offend, and that would be the end of her. *There* gloomed at me my warning, as well as shone at me my provocation, in respect to the example of this delightful writer. I might emu- late her, since I presumptuously would, but dishonour would await me if, proposing to treat the different faces of my subject in the most completely instituted colloquial form, I should evoke the figure and affirm the presence of participants by the repeated and prefixed name rather than by the recurrent and *af*fixed "said he" and "said she." All I have space to go into here—much as the funny fact I refer to might seem to invite us to dance hand in hand round it—is that I was at any rate duly admonished, that I took my measures accordingly, and that the manner in which I took them has lived again for me ever so arrestingly, so amusingly, on re-examination of the book.

But that I did, positively and seriously—ah so seriously!— emulate the levity of Gyp and, by the same token, of that hardi- est of flowers fostered in her school, M. Henri Lavedan, is a contribution to the history of "The Awkward Age" that I shall obviously have had to brace myself in order to make. Vivid enough to me the expression of face of any kindest of critics, even, moved to declare that he would never in the least have suspected it. Let me say at once, in extenuation of the too respectful distance at which I may thus have appeared to follow my model, that my first care *had* to be the covering of my tracks—lest I truly should be caught in the act of arranging, of organising dialogue to "speak for itself." What I now see to have happened is that I organised and arranged but too well —too well, I mean, for any betrayal of the Gyp taint, however faded and feeble. The trouble appears to have been that while I on the one hand exorcised the baleful association, I succeeded in rousing on nobody's part a sense of any other association whatever, or of my having cast myself into any conceivable or calculable form. My private inspiration had been in the Gyp plan (artfully dissimulated, for dear life, and applied with the very subtlest consistency, but none the less kept in secret view); yet I was to fail to make out in the event that the book succeeded in producing the impression of *any* plan on any person. No hint of that sort of success, or of any critical perception at all in relation to the business, has ever come my way; in spite of which when I speak, as just above, of what was to "happen" under the law of my ingenious labour, I fairly lose myself in the vision of a hundred bright phenomena. Some of these incidents I must treat myself to naming, for they are among the best I shall have on any occasion to retail. But I must first give the measure of the degree in which they were mere matters of the study. This composition had originally appeared in "Harper's Weekly" during the autumn of 1898 and the first weeks of the winter, and the volume containing it was published that spring. I had meanwhile been absent from England, and it was not till my return, some time later, that I had from my publisher any news of our venture. But the news then met at a stroke all my curiosity: "I'm sorry to say the book has done nothing to speak of; I've never in all my experience seen one treated with more general and complete disrespect." There was thus to be nothing left me for fond subsequent reference—of which I doubtless give even now so adequate an illustration—

save the rich reward of the singular interest attaching to the very intimacies of the effort.

It comes back to me, the whole "job," as wonderfully amusing and delightfully difficult from the first; since amusement deeply abides, I think, in any artistic attempt the basis and groundwork of which are conscious of a particular firmness. On that hard fine floor the element of execution feels it may more or less confidently *dance;* in which case puzzling questions, sharp obstacles, dangers of detail, may come up for it by the dozen without breaking its heart or shaking its nerve. It is the difficulty produced by the loose foundation or the vague scheme that breaks the heart—when a luckless fatuity has over-persuaded an author of the "saving" virtue of treatment. Being "treated" is never, in a workable idea, a mere passive condition, and I hold no subject ever susceptible of help that is n't, like the embarrassed man of our proverbial wisdom, first of all able to help itself. I was thus to have here an envious glimpse, in carrying my design through, of that artistic rage and that artistic felicity which I have ever supposed to be intensest and highest, the confidence of the dramatist strong in the sense of his postulate. The dramatist has verily to *build,* is committed to architecture, to construction at any cost; to driving in deep his vertical supports and laying across and firmly fixing his horizontal, his resting pieces—at the risk of no matter what vibration from the tap of his master-hammer. This makes the active value of his basis immense, enabling him, with his flanks protected, to advance undistractedly, even if not at all carelessly, into the comparative fairy-land of the mere minor anxiety. In other words his scheme *holds,* and as he feels this in spite of noted strains and under repeated tests, so he keeps his face to the day. I rejoiced, by that same token, to feel *my* scheme hold, and even a little ruefully watched it give me much more than I had ventured to hope. For I promptly found my conceived arrangement of my material open the door wide to ingenuity. I remember that in sketching my project for the conductors of the periodical I have named I drew on a sheet of paper—and possibly with an effect of the cabalistic, it now comes over me, that even anxious amplification may have but vainly attenuated—the neat figure of a circle consisting of a number of small rounds disposed at equal distance about a central object. The central object was my situation, my subject in itself, to which the thing would owe its title, and the small rounds represented so many distinct lamps, as I liked to call them, the function of each of which would be to light with all due intensity one of its aspects. I had divided it, did n't they see? into aspects—uncanny as the little term might sound (though not for a moment did I suggest we should use it for the public), and by that sign we would conquer.

They "saw," all genially and generously—for I must add that I had made, to the best of my recollection, no morbid scruple of not blabbing about Gyp and her strange incitement. I the more boldly held my tongue over this that the more I, by my intelligence, lived in my arrangement and moved about in it, the more I sank into satisfaction. It was clearly to work to a charm and, during this process—by calling at every step for an exquisite management—"to haunt, to startle and waylay." Each of my "lamps" would be the light of a single "social occasion" in the history and intercourse of the characters concerned, and would bring out to the full the latent colour of the scene in question and cause it to illustrate, to the last drop, its bearing on my theme. I revelled in this notion of the Occasion as a thing by itself, really and completely a scenic thing, and could scarce name it, while crouching amid the thick arcana of my plan, with a large enough O. The beauty of the conception was in this approximation of the respective divisions of my form to the successive Acts of a Play—as to which it was more than ever a case for charmed capitals. The divine distinction of the act of a play—and a greater than any other it easily succeeds in arriving at—was, I reasoned, in its special, its guarded objectivity. This objectivity, in turn, when achieving its ideal, came from the imposed absence of that "going behind," to compass explanations and amplifications, to drag out odds and ends from the "mere" storyteller's great property-shop of aids to illusion: a resource under denial of which it was equally perplexing and delightful, for a change, to proceed. Everything, for that matter, becomes interesting from the moment it has closely to consider, for full effect positively to bestride, the law of its kind. "Kinds" are the very life of literature, and truth and strength come from the complete recognition of them, from abounding to the utmost in their respective senses and sinking deep into their consistency. I myself have scarcely to plead the cause of "going behind," which is right and beautiful and fruitful in its place and order; but as the confusion of kinds is the inelegance of letters and the stultification of values, so to renounce that line utterly and do something quite different instead may become in another connexion the true course and the vehicle of effect. Something in the very nature, in the fine rigour, of this special sacrifice (which is capable of affecting the form-lover, I think, as really more of a projected form than any other) lends it moreover a coercive charm; a charm that grows in proportion as the appeal to it tests and stretches and strains it, puts it powerfully to the touch. To make the presented occasion tell all its story itself, remain shut up in its own presence and yet on that patch of staked-out ground become thoroughly interesting and remain thoroughly clear, is a process not remarkable, no doubt, so long as a very light weight is laid on it, but difficult enough to challenge and inspire great adroitness so soon as the elements to be dealt with begin at all to "size up."

The disdainers of the contemporary drama deny, obviously, with all promptness, that the matter to be expressed by its means—richly and successfully expressed that is—*can* loom with any largeness; since from the moment it does one of the conditions breaks down. The process simply collapses under pressure, they contend, proves its weakness as quickly as the office laid on it ceases to be simple. "Remember," they say to the dramatist, "that you have to be, supremely, three things: you have to be true to your form, you have to be interesting, you have to be clear. You have in other words to prove yourself adequate to taking a heavy weight. But we defy you really to conform to your conditions with any but a light one. Make the thing you have to convey, make the picture you have to paint, at all rich and complex, and you cease to be clear. Remain clear—and with the clearness required by the infantine intelligence of any public consenting to see a play—and what becomes of the 'importance' of your subject? If it's important by any other critical measure than the little foot-rule the 'produced' piece has to conform to, it is predestined to be a muddle. When it has escaped being a muddle the note it has succeeded in striking at the furthest will be recognised as one of those that are called high but by the courtesy, by the intellectual provinciality, of theatrical criticism, which, as we can see for ourselves any morning, is—well, an abyss even deeper than the theatre itself. Don't attempt to crush us with Dumas and Ibsen, for such values are from any informed and enlightened point of view, that is measured by other high values, literary, critical, philosophic, of the most moderate order. Ibsen and Dumas are precisely cases of men, men in their degree, in their poor theatrical straight-jacket, speculative, who have *had* to renounce the finer thing for the coarser, the thick, in short, for the thin and the curious for the self-evident. What earthly intellectual distinction, what 'prestige' of achievement, would have attached to the substance of such things as 'Denise,' as 'Monsieur Alphonse,' as 'Francillon' (and we take the Dumas of the supposedly subtler period) in any other form? What virtues of the same order would have attached to 'The Pillars of Society,' to 'An Enemy of the People,' to 'Ghosts,' to 'Rosmersholm' (or taking also Ibsen's 'subtler period') to 'John Gabriel Borkmann,' to 'The Master-Builder'? Ibsen is in fact wonderfully a case in point, since from the moment he's clear, from the moment he's 'amusing,' it's on the footing of a thesis as simple and superficial as that of 'A Doll's House'—while from the moment he's by apparent intention comprehensive and searching it's on the footing of an effect as confused and obscure as 'The Wild Duck.' From which you easily see *all* the conditions can't be met. The dramatist has to choose but those he's most capable of, and by that choice he's known."

So the objector concludes, and never surely without great profit from his having been "drawn." His apparent triumph —if it be even apparent—still leaves, it will be noted, convenient cover for retort in the riddled face of the opposite stronghold. The last word in these cases is for nobody who can't pretend to an *absolute* test. The terms here used, obviously, are matters of appreciation, and there is no short cut to proof (luckily for us all round) either that "Monsieur Alphonse" develops itself on the highest plane of irony or that "Ghosts" simplifies almost to excruciation. If "John Gabriel Borkmann" is but a pennyworth of effect as to a character we can imagine much more amply presented, and if "Hedda Gabler" makes an appeal enfeebled by remarkable vagueness, there is by the nature of the case no catching the convinced, or call him the deluded, spectator or reader in the act of a mistake. He is to be caught at the worst in the act of attention, of the very greatest attention, and that is all, as a precious preliminary at least, that the playwright asks of him, besides being all the very divinest poet can get. I remember rejoicing as much to remark this, after getting launched in "The Awkward Age," as if I were in fact constructing a play; just as I may doubtless appear now not less anxious to keep the philosophy of the dramatist's course before me than if I belonged to his order. I felt, certainly, the support he feels, I participated in his technical amusement, I tasted to the full the bitter-sweetness of his draught —the beauty and the difficulty (to harp again on that string) of escaping poverty *even though* the references in one's action can only be, with intensity, to each other, to things exactly on the same plane of exhibition with themselves. Exhibition may mean in a "story" twenty different ways, fifty excursions, alternatives, excrescences, and the novel, as largely practised in English, is the perfect paradise of the loose end. The play consents to the logic of but one way, mathematically right, and with the loose end as gross an impertinence on its surface, and as grave a dishonour, as the dangle of a snippet of silk or wool on the right side of a tapestry. We are shut up wholly to cross-relations, relations all within the action itself; no part of which is related to anything but some other part—save of course by the relation of the total to life. And, after invoking the protection of Gyp, I saw the point of my game all in the problem of keeping these conditioned relations. crystalline at the same time that I should, in emulation of life, consent to their being numerous and fine and characteristic of the London world (as the London world was in this quarter and that to be deciphered). All of which was to make in the event for complications.

I see now of course how far, with my complications, I got away from Gyp; but I see to-day so much else too that this particular deflexion from simplicity makes scarce a figure among the others; after having once served its purpose, I mean, of lighting my original imitative innocence. For I recognise in especial, with a waking vibration of that interest in which, as I say, the plan of the book is embalmed for me, that my subject was probably condemned in advance to appreciable, or more exactly perhaps to almost preposterously appreciative, over-treatment. It places itself for me thus in a group of small productions exhibiting this perversity, representations of conceived cases in which my process has been to pump the case gaspingly dry, dry not only of superfluous moisture, but absolutely (for I have encountered the charge) of breatheable air. I may note, in fine, that coming back to the pages before us with a strong impression of their recording, to my shame, that disaster, even to the extent of its disqualifying them for decent reappearance, I have found the adventure taking, to my relief, quite another turn, and have lost myself in the wonder of what "over-treatment" may, in the detail of its desperate ingenuity, consist of. The revived interest I speak of has been therefore that of following critically, from page to page, even as the red Indian tracks in the forest the pale-face, the footsteps of the systematic loyalty I was able to achieve. The amusement of this *constatation* is, as I have hinted, in the detail of the matter, and the detail is so dense, the texture of the figured and smoothed tapestry so close, that the genius of Gyp herself, muse of general looseness, would certainly, once warned, have uttered the first disavowal of my homage. But what has occurred meanwhile is that this high consistency has itself, so to speak, constituted an exhibition, and that an important artistic truth has seemed to me thereby lighted. We brushed against that truth just now in our glance at the denial of expansibility to any idea the mould of the "stage-play" may hope to express without cracking and bursting; and we bear in mind at the same time that the picture of Nanda Brookenham's situation, though perhaps seeming to a careless eye so to wander and sprawl, yet presents itself on absolutely scenic lines, and that each of these scenes in itself, and each as related to each and to all of its companions, abides without a moment's deflexion by the principle of the stage-play.

In doing this then it does more—it helps us ever so happily to see the grave distinction between substance and form in a really wrought work of art signally break down. I hold it impossible to say, before "The Awkward Age," where one of these elements ends and the other begins: I have been unable at least myself, on re-examination, to mark any such joint or seam, to see the two *discharged* offices as separate. They are separate before the fact, but the sacrament of execution indissolubly marries them, and the marriage, like any other marriage, has only to be a "true" one for the scandal of a breach not to show. The thing "done," artistically, is a fusion, or it has not *been* done—in which case of course the artist may be, and all deservedly, pelted with any fragment of his botch the critic shall choose to pick up. But his ground once conquered, in this particular field, he knows nothing of fragments and may say in all security: "Detach one if you can. You can analyse in *your* way, oh yes—to relate, to report, to explain; but you can't disintegrate my synthesis; you can't resolve the elements of my whole into different responsible agents or find your way at all (for your own fell purpose). My mixture has only to be perfect literally to bewilder you—you are lost in the tangle of the forest. Prove this value, this effect, in the air of the whole result, to be of my subject, and that other value, other effect, to be of my treatment, prove that I have n't so shaken them together as the conjurer I profess to be *must* consummately shake, and I consent but to parade as before a booth at the fair." The exemplary closeness of "The Awkward Age" even affects me, on re-perusal, I confess, as treasure quite instinctively and foreseeingly laid up against my present opportunity for these remarks. I have been positively struck by the quantity of meaning and the number of intentions, the extent of *ground for interest,* as I may call it, that I have succeeded in working scenically, yet without loss of sharpness, clearness or "atmosphere," into each of my illuminating Occasions— where, at certain junctures, the due preservation of all these values took, in the familiar phrase, a good deal of doing.

I should have liked just here to re-examine with the reader some of the positively most artful passages I have in mind— such as the hour of Mr. Longdon's beautiful and, as it were, mystic attempt at a compact with Vanderbank, late at night, in the billiard-room of the country-house at which they are staying; such as the other nocturnal passage, under Mr. Longdon's roof, between Vanderbank and Mitchy, where the conduct of so much fine meaning, so many flares of the exhibitory torch through the labyrinth of mere immediate appearances, mere familiar allusions, is successfully and safely effected; such as the whole array of the terms of presentation that are made to serve, all systematically, yet without a gap anywhere, for the presentation, throughout, of a Mitchy "subtle" no less than concrete and concrete no less than deprived of that officious explanation which we know as "going behind"; such as, briefly, the general service of co-ordination and vivification rendered, on lines of ferocious, of really quite heroic compression, by the picture of the assembled group at Mrs. Grendon's, where the "cross-references" of the action are as thick as the green leaves of a garden, but none the less, as they have scenically to be, counted and disposed, weighted with responsibility. Were I minded to use in this connexion a "loud" word—and the critic in general hates loud words as a man of taste may hate loud colours—I should speak of the composition of the chapters entitled "Tishy Grendon," with all the pieces of the game on the table together and each unconfusedly and contributively placed, as triumphantly scientific. I must properly remind myself, rather, that the better lesson of my retrospect would seem to be really a supreme revision of the question of what it may be for a subject to suffer, to call it suffering, by over-treatment. Bowed down so long by the inference that its product had in this case proved such a betrayal, my artistic conscience meets the relief of having to recognise truly here no traces of suffering. The thing carries itself to my maturer and gratified sense as with every symptom of soundness, an insolence of health and joy. And from this precisely I deduce my moral; which is to the effect that, since our only way, in general, of knowing that we have had too much of anything is by *feeling* that too much: so, by the same token, when we don't feel the excess (and I am contending, mind, that in "The Awkward Age" the multiplicity yields to the order) how do we know that the measure not recorded, the notch not reached, does represent adequacy or satiety? The mere feeling helps us for certain degrees of congestion, but for exact science, that is for the criticism of "fine" art, we want the notation. The notation, however, is what we lack, and the verdict of the mere feeling is liable to fluctuate. In other words an imputed defect is never, at the worst, disengageable, or other than matter for appreciation—to come back to my claim for that felicity of the dramatist's case that his synthetic "whole" *is* his form, the only one we have to do with. I like to profit in his company by the fact that if our art has certainly, for the impression it produces, to defer to the rise and fall, in the critical temperature, of the telltale mercury, it still hasn't to reckon with the engraved thermometer-face.

VII

PREFACE TO "THE SPOILS OF POYNTON"

(VOLUME X IN THE NEW YORK EDITION. CONTAINING: "THE SPOILS OF POYNTON," "A LONDON LIFE," "THE CHAPERON")

It was years ago, I remember, one Christmas Eve when I was dining with friends: a lady beside me made in the course of talk one of those allusions that I have always found myself recognising on the spot as "germs." The germ, wherever gathered, has ever been for me the germ of a "story," and most of the stories straining to shape under my hand have sprung from a single small seed, a seed as minute and wind-blown as that casual hint for "The Spoils of Poynton" dropped unwittingly by my neighbour, a mere floating particle in the stream of talk. What above all comes back to me with this reminiscence is the sense of the inveterate minuteness, on such happy occasions, of the precious particle—reduced, that is, to its mere fruitful essence. Such is the interesting truth about the stray suggestion, the wandering word, the vague echo, at touch of which the novelist's imagination winces as at the prick of some sharp point: its virtue is all in its needle-like quality, the power to penetrate as finely as possible. This fineness it is that communicates the virus of suggestion, anything more than the minimum of which spoils the operation. If one is given a hint at all designedly one is sure to be given too much; one's subject is in the merest grain, the speck of truth, of beauty, of reality, scarce visible to the common eye—since, I firmly hold, a good eye for a subject is anything but usual. Strange and attaching, certainly, the consistency with which the first thing to be done for the communicated and seized idea is to reduce almost to nought the form, the air as of a mere disjoined and lacerated lump of life, in which we may have happened to meet it. Life being all inclusion and confusion, and art being all discrimination and selection, the latter, in search of the hard latent *value* with which alone it is concerned, sniffs round the mass as instinctively and unerringly as a dog suspicious of some buried bone. The difference here, however, is that, while the dog desires his bone but to destroy it, the artist finds in *his* tiny nugget, washed free of awkward accretions and hammered into a sacred hardness, the very stuff for a clear affirmation, the happiest chance for the indestructible. It at the same time amuses him again and again to note how, beyond the first step of the actual case, the case that constitutes for him his germ, his vital particle, his grain of gold, life persistently blunders and deviates, loses herself in the sand. The reason is of course that life has no direct sense whatever for the subject and is capable, luckily for us, of nothing but splendid waste. Hence the opportunity for the sublime economy of art, which rescues, which saves, and hoards and "banks," investing and reinvesting these fruits of toil in wondrous useful "works" and thus making up for us, desperate spendthrifts that we all naturally are, the most princely of incomes. It is the subtle secrets of that system, however, that are meanwhile the charming study, with an endless attraction, above all, in the question—endlessly baffling indeed—of the method at the heart of the madness; the madness, I mean, of a zeal, among the reflective sort, so disinterested. If life, presenting us the germ, and left merely to herself in such a business, gives the case away, almost always, before we can stop her, what are the signs for our guidance, what the primary laws for a saving selection, how do we know when and where to intervene, where do we place the beginnings of the wrong or the right deviation? Such would be the elements of an enquiry upon which, I hasten to say, it is quite forbidden me here to embark: I but glance at them in evidence of the rich pasture that at every turn surrounds the ruminant critic. The answer may be after all that mysteries here elude us, that general considerations fail or mislead, and that even the fondest of artists need ask no wider range than the logic of the particular case. The particular case, or in other words his relation to a given subject, once the relation is established, forms in itself a little world of exercise and agitation. Let him hold himself perhaps supremely fortunate if he can meet half the questions with which that air alone may swarm.

So it was, at any rate, that when my amiable friend, on the Christmas Eve, before the table that glowed safe and fair through the brown London night, spoke of such an odd matter as that a good lady in the north, always well looked on, was at daggers drawn with her only son, ever hitherto exemplary, over the ownership of the valuable furniture of a fine old house just accruing to the young man by his father's death, I instantly became aware, with my "sense for the subject," of the prick of inoculation; the *whole* of the virus, as I have called it, being infused by that single touch. There had been but ten words, yet I had recognised in them, as in a flash, all the possibilities of the little drama of my "Spoils," which glimmered then and there into life; so that when in the next breath I began to hear of action taken, on the beautiful ground, by our engaged adversaries, tipped each, from that instant, with the light of the highest distinction, I saw clumsy Life again at her stupid work. For the action taken, and on which my friend, as I knew she would, had already begun all complacently and benightedly further to report, I had absolutely, and could have, no scrap of use; one had been so perfectly qualified to say in advance: "It's the perfect little workable thing, but she'll strangle it in the cradle, even while she pretends, all so cheeringly, to rock it; wherefore I'll stay her hand while yet there's time." I didn't, of course, stay her hand—there never *is* in such cases "time";

and I had once more the full demonstration of the fatal futility of Fact. The turn taken by the excellent situation—excellent, for devlopment, if arrested in the right place, that is in the germ—had the full measure of the classic ineptitude; to which with the full measure of the artistic irony one could once more, and for the thousandth time, but take off one's hat. It was not, however, that this in the least mattered, once the seed had been transplanted to richer soil; and I dwell on that almost inveterate redundancy of the wrong, as opposed to the ideal right, in any free flowering of the actual, by reason only of its approach to calculable regularity.

If there was nothing regular meanwhile, nothing more so than the habit of vigilance, in my quickly feeling where interest would really lie, so I could none the less acknowledge afresh that these small private cheers of recognition made the spirit easy and the temper bland for the confused whole. I "took" in fine, on the spot, to the rich bare little facts of the two related figures, embroiled perhaps all so sordidly; and for reasons of which I could most probably have given at the moment no decent account. Had I been asked why they were, in that stark nudity, to say nothing of that ugliness of attiude, "interesting," I fear I could have said nothing more to the point, even to my own questioning spirit, than "Well, you'll see!" By which of course I should have meant "Well, *I* shall see"—confident meanwhile (as against the appearance or the imputation of poor taste) that interest would spring as soon as one should begin really to see *anything*. That points, I think, to a large part of the very source of interest for the artist: it resides in the srong consciousness of his seeing all for himself. He has to borrow his motive, which is certainly half the battle; and this motive is his ground, his site and his foundation. But after that he only lends and gives, only builds and piles high, lays together the blocks quarried in the deeps of his imagination and on his personal premises. He thus remains all the while in intimate commerce with his

motive, and can say to himself—what really more than anything else inflames and sustains him—that he alone has the
secret of the particular case, he alone can measure the truth of
the direction to be taken by his developed data. There can be
for him, evidently, only one logic for these things; there can be
for him only one truth and one direction—the quarter in which
his subject most completely expresses itself. The careful ascertainment of how it shall do so, and the art of guiding it
with consequent authority—since this sense of "authority"
is for the master-builder the treasure of treasures, or at least the
joy of joys—renews in the modern alchemist something like
the old dream of the secret of life.

Extravagant as the mere statement sounds, one seemed accordingly to handle the secret of life in drawing the positive
right truth out of the so easy muddle of wrong truths in
which the interesting possibilities of that "row," so to call
it, between mother and son over their household gods might
have been stifled. I find it odd to consider, as I thus revert,
that I could have had none but the most general warrant for
"seeing anything in it," as the phrase would have been; that
I could n't in the least, on the spot, as I have already hinted,
have justified my faith. One thing was "in it," in the sordid
situation, on the first blush, and one thing only—though this,
in its limited way, no doubt, a curious enough value: the
sharp light it might project on that most modern of our current passions, the fierce appetite for the upholsterer's and join-
er's and brazier's work, the chairs and tables, the cabinets and
presses, the material odds and ends, of the more labouring
ages. A lively mark of our manners indeed the diffusion of
this curiosity and this avidity, and full of suggestion, clearly,
as to their possible influence on other passions and other relations. On the face of it the "things" themselves would form
the very centre of such a crisis; these grouped objects, all conscious of their eminence and their price, would enjoy, in any
picture of a conflict, the heroic importance. They would have

to be presented, they would have to be painted—arduous and desperate thought; something would have to be done for them not too ignobly unlike the great array in which Balzac, say, would have marshalled them: *that* amount of workable interest at least would evidently be "in it."

It would be wrapped in the silver tissue of some such conviction, at any rate, that I must have laid away my prime impression for a rest not disturbed till long afterwards, till the year 1896, I make out, when there arose a question of my contributing three "short stories" to "The Atlantic Monthly"; or supplying rather perhaps a third to complete a trio two members of which had appeared. The echo of the situation mentioned to me at our Christmas Eve dinner awoke again, I recall, at that touch—I recall, no doubt, with true humility, in view of my renewed mismeasurement of my charge. Painfully associated for me had "The Spoils of Poynton" remained, until recent re-perusal, with the awkward consequence of that fond error. The subject had emerged from cool reclusion all suffused with a flush of meaning; thanks to which irresistible air, as I could but plead in the event, I found myself—as against a mere commercial austerity—beguiled and led on. The thing had "come," the flower of conception had bloomed—all in the happy dusk of indifference and neglect; yet, strongly and frankly as it might now appeal, my idea would n't surely overstrain a *natural* brevity. A story that could n't possibly be long would have inevitably to be "short," and out of the depths of that delusion it accordingly began to struggle. To my own view, after the "first number," this composition (which in the magazine bore another title) conformed but to its nature, which was not to transcend a modest amplitude; but, dispatched in instalments, it felt itself eyed, from month to month, I seem to remember, with an editorial ruefulness excellently well founded—from the moment such differences of sense could exist, that is, as to the short and the long. The sole impression it made, I woefully gathered, was that of length, and it has till lately, as I say, been present to me but as the poor little "long" thing.

It began to appear in April 1896, and, as is apt blessedly to occur for me throughout this process of revision, the old, the shrunken concomitants muster again as I turn the pages. They lurk between the lines; these serve for them as the barred seraglio-windows behind which, to the outsider in the glare of the Eastern street, forms indistinguishable seem to move and peer; "association" in fine bears upon them with its infinite magic. Peering through the lattice from without inward I recapture a cottage on a cliff-side, to which, at the earliest approach of the summer-time, redoubtable in London through the luxuriance of still other than "natural" forces, I had betaken myself to finish a book in quiet and to begin another in fear. The cottage was, in its kind, perfection; mainly by reason of a small paved terrace which, curving forward from the cliff-edge like the prow of a ship, overhung a view as level, as purple, as full of rich change, as the expanse of the sea. The horizon was in fact a band of sea; a small red-roofed town, of great antiquity, perched on its sea-rock, clustered within the picture off to the right; while above one's head rustled a dense summer shade, that of a trained and arching ash, rising from the middle of the terrace, brushing the parapet with a heavy fringe and covering the place like a vast umbrella. Beneath this umbrella and really under exquisite protection "The Spoils of Poynton" managed more or less symmetrically to grow.

I recall that I was committed to begin, the day I finished it, short of dire penalties, "The Other House"; with which work, however, of whatever high profit the considerations springing from it might be too, we have nothing to do here —and to the felt jealousy of which, as that of a grudging neighbour, I allude only for sweet recovery of the fact, mainly interesting to myself I admit, that the rhythm of the earlier book shows no flurry of hand. I "liked" it—the ear-

lier book: I venture now, after years, to welcome the sense
of that amenity as well; so immensely refreshing is it to be
moved, in any case, toward these retrospective simplicities.
Painters and writers, I gather, are, when easily accessible to
such appeals, frequently questioned as to those of their productions they may most have delighted in; but the profession
of delight has always struck me as the last to consort, for
the artist, with any candid account of his troubled effort—
ever the sum, for the most part, of so many lapses and compromises, simplifications and surrenders. Which is the work
in which he has n't surrendered, under dire difficulty, the best
thing he meant to have kept? In which indeed, before the
dreadful *done,* does n't he ask himself what has become of
the thing all for the sweet sake of which it was to proceed
to that extremity? Preference and complacency, on these
terms, riot in general as they best may; not disputing, however, a grain of which weighty truth, I still make out, between my reconsidered lines, as it were, that I must—my
opera-box of a terrace and my great green umbrella indeed
aiding—have assisted at the growth and predominance of
Fleda Vetch.

For something like Fleda Vetch had surely been latent in
one's first apprehension of the theme; it wanted, for treatment, a centre, and, the most obvious centre being "barred,"
this image, while I still wondered, had, with all the assurance
in the world, sprung up in its place. The real centre, as I
say, the citadel of the interest, with the fight waged round it,
would have been the felt beauty and value of the prize of
battle, the Things, always the splendid Things, placed in the
middle light, figured and constituted, with each identity made
vivid, each character discriminated, and their common consciousness of their great dramatic part established. The rendered tribute of these honours, however, no vigilant editor, as
I have intimated, could be conceived as allowing room for;
since, by so much as the general glittering presence should

spread, by so much as it should suggest the gleam of brazen idols and precious metals and inserted gems in the tempered light of some arching place of worship, by just so much would the muse of "dialogue," most usurping influence of all the romancingly invoked, be routed without ceremony, to lay her grievance at the feet of her gods. The spoils of Poynton were not directly articulate, and though they might have, and constantly did have, wondrous things to say, their message fostered about them a certain hush of cheaper sound—as a consequence of which, in fine, they would have been costly to keep up. In this manner Fleda Vetch, maintainable at less expense—though even she, I make out, less expert in spreading chatter thin than the readers of romance mainly like their heroines to-day—marked her place in my foreground at one ingratiating stroke. She planted herself centrally, and the stroke, as I call it, the demonstration after which she could n't be gainsaid, was the simple act of letting it be seen she had character.

For somehow—that was the way interest broke out, once the germ had been transferred to the sunny south window-sill of one's fonder attention—character, the question of what my agitated friends should individually, and all intimately and at the core, show themselves, would unmistakeably be the key to my modest drama, and would indeed alone make a drama of any sort possible. Yes, it is a story of cabinets and chairs and tables; they formed the bone of contention, but what would merely "become" of them, magnificently passive, seemed to represent a comparatively vulgar issue. The passions, the faculties, the forces their beauty would, like that of antique Helen of Troy, set in motion, was what, as a painter, one had really wanted of them, was the power in them that one had from the first appreciated. Emphatically, by that truth, there would have to be moral developments—dreadful as such a prospect might loom for a poor interpreter committed to brevity. A character is interesting as it comes out, and by the process and duration of that emergence; just as a procession is effective by the way it unrolls, turning to a mere mob if all of it passes at once. My little procession, I foresaw then from an early stage, would refuse to pass at once; though I could keep it more or less down, of course, by reducing it to three or four persons. Practically, in "The Spoils," the reduction is to four, though indeed—and I clung to that as to my plea for simplicity—the main agents, with the others all dependent, are Mrs. Gereth and Fleda. Fleda's ingratiating stroke, for importance, on the threshold, had been that she would understand; and positively, from that moment, the progress and march of my tale became and remained that of her understanding.

Absolutely, with this, I committed myself to making the affirmation and the penetration of it my action and my "story"; once more, too, with the re-entertained perception that a subject so lighted, a subject residing in somebody's excited and concentrated feeling about something—both the something and the somebody being of course as important as possible—has more beauty to give out than under any other style of pressure. One is confronted obviously thus with the question of the importances; with that in particular, no doubt, of the weight of intelligent consciousness, consciousness of the whole, or of something ominously like it, that one may decently permit a represented figure to appear to throw. Some plea for this cause, that of the intelligence of the moved mannikin, I have already had occasion to make, and can scarce hope too often to evade it. This intelligence, an honourable amount of it, on the part of the person to whom one most invites attention, has but to play with sufficient freedom and ease, or call it with the right grace, to guarantee us that quantum of the impression of beauty which is the most fixed of the possible advantages of our producible effect. It may fail, as a positive presence, on other sides and in other connexions; but more or less of the treasure is stored safe from the moment such a quality of inward life is distilled, or in other words from the moment so fine an interpretation and criticism as that of Fleda Vetch's—to cite the present case—is applied without waste to the surrounding tangle.

It is easy to object of course "Why the deuce then Fleda Vetch, why a mere little flurried bundle of petticoats, why not Hamlet or Milton's Satan at once, if you're going in for a superior display of 'mind'?" To which I fear I can only reply that in pedestrian prose, and in the "short story," one is, for the best reasons, no less on one's guard than on the stretch; and also that I have ever recognised, even in the midst of the curiosity that such displays may quicken, the rule of an exquisite economy. The thing is to lodge somewhere at the heart of one's complexity an irrepressible *appreciation,* but where a light lamp will carry all the flame I incline to look askance at a heavy. From beginning to end, in "The Spoils of Poynton," appreciation, even to that of the very whole, lives in Fleda; which is precisely why, as a consequence rather grandly imposed, every one else shows for comparatively stupid; the tangle, the drama, the tragedy and comedy of those who appreciate consisting so much of their relation with those who don't. From the presented reflexion of this truth my story draws, I think, a certain assured appearance of roundness and felicity. The "things" are radiant, shedding afar, with a merciless monotony, all their light, exerting their ravage without remorse; and Fleda almost demonically both sees and feels, while the others but feel without seeing. Thus we get perhaps a vivid enough little example, in the concrete, of the general truth, for the spectator of life, that the fixed constitutents of almost any reproducible action are the fools who minister, at a particular crisis, to the intensity of the free spirit engaged with them. The fools are interesting by contrast, by the salience they acquire, and by a hundred other of their advantages; and the free spirit, always much tormented, and by no means always triumphant, is heroic, ironic, pathetic or whatever, and, as exemplified in the record of Fleda Vetch, for instance, "successful," only through having remained free.

I recognise that the novelist with a weakness for that ground of appeal is foredoomed to a well-nigh extravagant insistence on the free spirit, seeing the possibility of one in every bush; I may perhaps speak of it as noteworthy that this very volume happens to exhibit in two other cases my disposition to let the interest stand or fall by the tried spontaneity and vivacity of the freedom. It is in fact for that respectable reason that I enclose "A London Life" and "The Chaperon" between these covers; my purpose having been here to class my reprintable productions as far as possible according to their kinds. The two tales I have just named are of the same "kind" as "The Spoils," to the extent of their each dealing with a human predicament in the light, for the charm of the thing, of the amount of "appreciation" to be plausibly imputed to the subject of it. They are each—and truly there are more of such to come—"stories about women," very young women, who, affected with a certain high lucidity, thereby become characters; in consequence of which their doings, their sufferings or whatever, take on, I assume, an importance. Laura Wing, in "A London Life," has, like Fleda Vetch, acuteness and intensity, reflexion and passion, has above all a contributive and participant view of her situation; just as Rose Tramore, in "The Chaperon," rejoices, almost to insolence, very much in the same cluster of attributes and advantages. They are thus of a family—which shall have also for us, we seem forewarned, more members, and of each sex.

As to our young woman of "The Spoils," meanwhile, I briefly come back to my claim for a certain definiteness of beauty in the special effect wrought by her aid. My problem had decently to be met—that of establishing for the other persons the vividness of their appearance of comparative stupidity, that of exposing them to the full thick wash of the penumbra surrounding the central light, and yet keeping their motions, within it, distinct, coherent and "amusing." But these are exactly of course the most "amusing" things to do; nothing, for example, being of a higher reward artistically than the shade of success aimed at in such a figure as Mrs. Gereth. A character she too, absolutely, yet the very reverse of a free spirit. I have found myself so pleased with Mrs. Gereth, I confess, on resuming acquaintance with her, that, complete and in all equilibrium as she seems to me to stand and move there, I shrink from breathing upon her any breath of qualification; without which, however, I fail of my point that, thanks to the "value" represented by Fleda, and to the position to which the elder woman is confined by that irradiation, the latter is at the best a "false" character, floundering as she does in the dusk of disproportionate passion. She is a *figure,* oh definitely—which is a very different matter; for you may be a figure with all the blinding, with all the hampering passion in life, and may have the grand air in what shall yet prove to the finer view (which Fleda again, *e. g.,* could at any time strike off) but a perfect rage of awkwardness. Mrs. Gereth was, obviously, with her pride and her pluck, of an admirable fine paste; but she was not intelligent, was only clever, and therefore would have been no use to us at all as centre of our subject—compared with Fleda, who was only intelligent, not distinctively able. The little drama confirms at all events excellently, I think, the contention of the old wisdom that the question of the personal will has more than all else to say to the verisimilitude of these exhibitions. The will that rides the crisis quite most triumphantly is that of the awful Mona Brigstock, who is *all* will, without the smallest leak of force into taste or tenderness or vision, into any sense of shades or relations or proportions. She loses no minute in that perception of incongruities in which half Fleda's passion is wasted and misled, and into which Mrs. Gereth, to her practical loss, that is by the fatal grace of a sense of comedy, occasionally and disinterestedly strays. Every one, every thing, in the story is accordingly sterile *but* the so thriftily constructed Mona, able at any moment to bear the whole of her dead weight at once on any given inch of a resisting surface. Fleda, obliged to neglect inches, sees and feels but in acres and expanses and blue perspectives; Mrs. Gereth too, in comparison, while her imagination broods, drops half the stitches of the web she seeks to weave.

If I speak of classifying I hasten to recognise that there are other marks for the purpose still and that, failing other considerations, "A London Life" would properly consort, in this series, with a dozen of the tales by which I at one period sought to illustrate and enliven the supposed "international" conflict of manners; a general theme dealing for the most part with the bewilderment of the good American, of either sex and of almost any age, in presence of the "European" order. This group of data might possibly have shown, for the reverse of its medal, the more or less desperate contortions of the European under American social pressure. Three or four tried glances in that direction seemed to suggest, however, no great harvest to be gathered; so that the pictorial value of the general opposition was practically confined to one phase. More reasons are here involved than I can begin to go into—as indeed I confess that the reflexions set in motion by the international fallacy at large, as I am now moved to regard it, quite crowd upon me; I simply note therefore, on one corner of the ground, the scant results, above all for interesting detail, promised by confronting the fruits of a constituted order with the fruits of no order at all. We may strike lights by opposing order to order, one sort to another sort; for in that case we get the correspondences and equivalents that make differences mean something; we get the interest and the tension of disparity where a certain parity may have been in question. Where it may *not* have been in question, where the dramatic encounter is but the poor concussion of positives on one side with negatives on the other, we get little beyond a consideration of the differences between fishes and fowls.

By which I don't mean to say that the appeal of the fallacy, as I call it, was not at one time quite inevitably irresistible; had it nothing else to recommend it to the imagination it would always have had the advantage of its showy surface, of suggesting situations as to which assurance seemed easy, founded, as it felt itself, on constant observation. The attraction was thus not a little, I judge, the attraction of facility; the international was easy to do, because, as one's wayside bloomed with it, one had but to put forth one's hand and pluck the frequent flower. Add to this that the flower *was,* so often, quite positively a flower—that of the young American innocence transplanted to European air. The general subject had, in fine, a charm while it lasted; but I shall have much more to say about it on another occasion. What here concerns us is that "A London Life" breaks down altogether, I have had to recognise, as a contribution to my comprehensive picture of bewildered Americanism. I fail to make out to-day why I need have conceived my three principal persons as sharers in that particular bewilderment. There was enough of the general human and social sort for them without it; poor young Wendover in especial, I think, fails on any such ground to attest himself—I need n't, surely, have been at costs to bring him all the way from New York. Laura Wing, touching creature as she was designed to appear, strikes me as a rare little person who would have been a rare little person anywhere, and who, in that character, must have felt and judged and suffered and acted as she did, whatever her producing clime.

The great anomaly, however, is Mrs. Lionel; a study of a type quite sufficiently to be accounted for on the very scene of her development, and with her signs and marks easily mistakeable, in London, for the notes of a native luxuriance. I recall the emphasis, quite the derison, with which a remarkably wise old friend, not American, a trenchant judge who had observed manners in many countries and had done me the honour to read my tale, put to me: "What on earth possessed you to make of your Selina an American, or to make one of your two or three Americans a Selina?—resembling so to the life something quite else, something which hereabouts one need n't go far to seek, but failing of any felicity for a creature engendered *lá-bas,*" And I think my friend conveyed, or desired to convey, that the wicked woman of my story was falsified above all, as an imported product, by something distinctly other than so engendered in the superficial "form" of her perversity, a high stiff-backed angular action which is, or was then, beyond any American "faking." The truth is, no doubt, that, though Mrs. Lionel, on my page, does n't in the least achieve character, she yet passes before us as a sufficiently vivid image, which was to be the effect designed for her—an image the hard rustle of whose long steps and the sinister tinkle of whose multiplied trinkets belie the association invoked for them and positively operate for another. Not perhaps, moreover, as I am moved to subjoin, that the point greatly matters. What matters, for one's appreciation of a work of art, however modest, is that the prime intention shall have been justified—for any judgment of which we must be clear as to what it was. It was n't after all of the prime, the very most prime, intention of the tale in question that the persons concerned in them should have had this, that or the other land of birth; but that the central situation should really be rendered—that of a charming and decent young thing, from wheresoever proceeding, who has her decision and her action to take, horribly and unexpectedly, in face of a squalid "scandal' the main agent of which is her nearest relative, and who, at the dreadful crisis, to guard against personal bespattering, is moved, with a miserable want of effect, to a wild vague frantic gesture, an appeal for protection that virtually proves a precipitation of her disgrace.

Nobody concerned need, as I say, have come from New York for that; though, as I have likewise intimated, I must have seen the creation of my heroine, in 1888, and the representation of the differences I wished to establish between her own known world and the world from which she finds herself recoiling, facilitated in a high degree by assured reference to the simpler social order across the sea. I had my vision (as I recover the happy spell) of her having "come over" to find, to her dismay, what "London" had made of the person in the world hitherto most akin to her; in addition to which I was during those years infinitely interested in almost any demonstration of the effect of London. This was a form of response to the incessant appeal of the great city, one's grateful, one's devoted recognition of which fairly broke out from day to day. It was material ever to one's hand; and the impression was always there that no one so much as the candid outsider, caught up and involved in the sweep of the machine, could measure the values revealed. Laura Wing must have figured for me thus as the necessary candid outsider—from the moment some received impression of the elements about me was to be projected and embodied. In fact as I remount the stream it is the particular freshness of that enjoyed relation I seem to taste again; the positive fond belief that I had my right oppositions. They seemed to ensure somehow the perfect march of my tolerably simple action; the straightness, the artful economy of which—save that of a particular point where my ingenuity shows to so small advantage that, to anticipate opprobrium, I can but hold it up to derision—has n't ceased to be appreciable. The thing made its first appearance in "Scribner's Magazine" during the summer of 1888, and I remember being not long before at work upon it, remember in fact beginning it, in one of the wonderful faded back rooms of an old Venetian palace, a room with a pompous Tiepolo ceiling and walls of ancient pale-green damask, slightly shredded and patched, which, on the warm mornings, looked into the shade of a court where a high outer staircase, strikingly bold, yet strikingly relaxed, held together one scarce knew how; where Gothic windows broke out, on discoloured blanks of wall, at quite arbitrary levels, and where above all the strong Venetian voice, full of history and humanity and waking perpetual echoes, seemed to say more in ten warm words, of whatever tone, than any twenty pages of one's cold pale prose.

In spite of all of which, I may add, I do penance here only for the awkwardness of that departure from the adopted form of my recital which resides in the picture of the interview with young Wendover contrived by Lady Davenant in the interest of some better provision for their poor young friend. Here indeed is a lapse from artistic dignity, a confession of want of resource, which I may not pretend to explain to-day, and on behalf of which I have nothing to urge save a consciousness of my dereliction presumably too vague at the time. I had seen my elements presented in a certain way, settled the little law under which my story was to be told, and with this consistency, as any reader of the tale may easily make out for himself, interviews to which my central figure was not a party, scenes revolving on an improvised pivot of their own, had nothing to do with the affair. I might of course have adopted another plan—the artist is free, surely, to adopt any he fancies, provided it *be* a plan and he adopt it intelligently; and to that scheme of composition the independent picture of a passage between Lady Davenant and young Wendover might perfectly have conformed. As the case stands it conforms to nothing; whereas the beauty of a thing of this order really done as a whole is ever, certainly, that its parts are in abject dependence, and that even any great charm they may individually and capriciously put forth is infirm so far as it does n't measurably contribute to a harmony. My momentary helplessness sprang, no doubt, from my failure to devise in time some way of giving the value of Lady Davenant's appeal to the young man, of making it play its part in my heroine's history and consciousness, without so awkwardly thrusting the lump sum on the reader.

Circumventions of difficulty of this degree are precisely the finest privilege of the craftsman, who, to be worth his salt, and master of *any* contrived harmony, must take no tough technical problem for insoluble. These technical subterfuges and subtleties, these indirectly-expressed values, kept indirect in a higher interest, made subordinate to some general beauty, some artistic intention that can give an account of itself, what are they after all but one of the nobler parts of our amusement? Superficially, in "A London Life," it might well have seemed that the only way to picture the intervention on Laura Wing's behalf of the couple just named was to break the chain of the girl's own consciousness and report the matter quite straight and quite shamelessly; this course had indeed every merit but that of its playing the particular game to which I had addressed myself. My prime loyalty was to the interest of the game, and the honour to be won the more desirable by that fact. Any muddle-headed designer can beg the question of perspective, but science is required for making it rule the scene. If it be asked how then we were to have assisted at the copious passage I thus incriminate without our privilege of presence, I can only say that my discovery of the right way should—and would—have been the very flower of the performance. The real "fun" of the thing would have been exactly to sacrifice my comparative platitude of statement—a deplorable depth at any time, I have attempted elsewhere to signify, for any pretending master of representation to sink to—without sacrificing a grain of what was to be conveyed. The real fun, in other words, would have been in not, by an exceptional collapse of other ingenuity, making my attack on the spectator's consciousness a call as immediate as a postman's knock. This attack, at every other point, reaches that objective only through the medium of the interesting girl's own vision, own experience, with which all the facts are richly charged and coloured. That saturates our sense of them with the savour of Laura's sense—thanks to which enhancement we get intensity. But from the chapter to which I have called attention, so that it may serve perhaps as a lesson, intensity ruefully drops. I can't say worse for it—and have been the more concerned to say what I do that without this flaw the execution might have appeared from beginning to end close and exemplary.

It is with all that better confidence, I think, that the last of my three tales here carries itself. I recapture perfectly again, in respect to "The Chaperon," both the first jog of my imagination and the particular local influence that presided at its birth—the latter a ramshackle inn on the Irish coast, where the table at which I wrote was of an equilibrium so vague that I wonder to-day how any object constructed on it should stand so firm. The strange sad charm of the tearful Irish light hangs about the memory of the labour of which this small fiction—first published in two numbers of "The Atlantic Monthly" of 1891—was one of the fruits; but the subject had glimmered upon me, two or three years before, in an air of comedy comparatively free from sharp under-tastes. Once more, as in the case of its companions here, the single spoken word, in London, had said all—after the manner of that clear ring of the electric bell that the barest touch of the button may produce. The talk being of a certain lady who, in consequence of early passages, had lived for years apart from her husband and in no affluence of good company, it was mentioned of her that her situation had improved, and the desert around her been more or less brought under cultivation, by the fact of her having at last made acquaintance with her young unmarried daughter, a charming girl just introduced to the world and thereby qualified for "taking her out," floating her in spite of whatever past damage. Here in truth, it seemed to me, *was* a morsel of queer comedy to play with, and my tale

embodies the neat experiment. Fortunately in this case the
principle of composition adopted is loyally observed; the
values gathered are, without exception, gathered by the light
of the intense little personal consciousness, invoked from the
first, that shines over my field and the predominance of which
is usurped by none other. That is the main note to be made
about "The Chaperon"; except this further, which I must
reserve, however—as I shall find excellent occasion—for an
ampler development. A short story, to my sense and as the
term is used in magazines, has to choose between being either
an anecdote or a picture and can but play its part strictly according to its kind. I rejoice in the anecdote, but I revel in
the picture; though having doubtless at times to note that a
given attempt may place itself near the dividing-line. This is
in some degree the case with "The Chaperon," in which, none
the less, on the whole, picture ingeniously prevails; picture
aiming at those richly summarised and foreshortened effects—
the opposite pole again from expansion inorganic and thin—
that refer their terms of production, for which the magician
has ever to don his best cap and gown, to the inner compartment of our box of tricks. From *them* comes the true grave
close consistency in which parts hang together even as the
interweavings of a tapestry. "The Chaperon" has perhaps, so
far as it goes, something of that texture. Yet I shall be able,
I think, to cite examples with still more.

VIII

PREFACE TO "WHAT MAISIE KNEW"

(VOLUME XI IN THE NEW YORK EDITION. CONTAINING: "WHAT MAISIE KNEW," "IN THE CAGE," "THE PUPIL")

I RECOGNISE again, for the first of these three Tales, another instance of the growth of the "great oak" from the little acorn; since "What Maisie Knew" is at least a tree that spreads beyond any provision its small germ might on a first handling have appeared likely to make for it. The accidental mention had been made to me of the manner in which the situation of some luckless child of a divorced couple was affected, under my informant's eyes, by the re-marriage of one of its parents—I forget which; so that, thanks to the limited desire for its company expressed by the step-parent, the law of its little life, its being entertained in rotation by its father and its mother, wouldn't easily prevail. Whereas each of these persons had at first vindictively desired to keep it from the other, so at present the re-married relative sought now rather to be rid of it—that is to leave it as much as possible, and beyond the appointed times and seasons, on the hands of the adversary; which malpractice, resented by the latter as bad faith, would of course be repaid and avenged by an equal treachery. The wretched infant was thus to find itself practically disowned, rebounding from racquet to racquet like a tennis-ball or a shuttlecock. This figure could but touch the fancy to the quick and strike one as the beginning of a story—a story commanding a great choice of developments. I recollect, however, promptly thinking that for a proper symmetry the second parent should marry too—which in the case named to me indeed would probably soon occur, and was in any case what the ideal of the situation required. The second step-parent would have but to be correspondingly incommoded by obligations to the offspring of a hated predecessor for the misfortune of the little victim to become altogether exemplary. The business would accordingly be sad enough, yet I am not sure its possibility of interest would so much have appealed to me had I not soon felt that the ugly facts, so stated or conceived, by no means constituted the whole appeal.

The light of an imagination touched by them couldn't help therefore projecting a further ray, thanks to which it became rather quaintly clear that, not less than the chance of misery and of a degraded state, the chance of happiness and of an improved state might be here involved for the child, round about whom the complexity of life would thus turn to fineness, to richness—and indeed would have but so to turn for the small creature to be steeped in security and ease. Sketchily clustered even, these elements gave out that vague pictorial glow which forms the first appeal of a living "subject" to the painter's consciousness; but the glimmer became intense as I proceeded to a further analysis. The further analysis is for that matter almost always the torch of rapture and victory, as the artist's firm hand grasps and plays it—I mean, naturally, of the smothered rapture and the obscure victory, enjoyed and celebrated not in the street but before some innnermost shrine; the odds being a hundred to one, in almost any connexion, that it doesn't arrive by any easy first process at the *best* residuum of truth. That was the charm, sensibly, of the picture thus at first confusedly showing; the elements so couldn't but flush, to their very surface, with some deeper depth of irony than the mere obvious. It lurked in the crude postulate like a buried scent; the more the attention hovered the more aware it become of the fragrance. To which I may add that the more I scratched the surface and penetrated, the more potent, to the intellectual nostril, became this virtue. At last, accordingly, the residuum, as I have called it, reached, I was in presence of the red dramatic spark that glowed at the core of my vision and that, as I gently blew upon it, burned higher and clearer. This precious particle was the *full* ironic truth—the most interesting item to be read into the child's situation. For satisfaction of the mind, in other words, the small expanding consciousness would have to be saved, have to become presentable as a register of impressions; and saved by the experience of certain advantages, by some enjoyed profit and some achieved confidence, rather than coarsened, blurred, sterilised, by ignorance and pain. This better state, in the young life, would reside in the exercise of a function other than that of disconcerting the selfishness of its parents—which was all that had on the face of the matter seemed reserved to it in the way of criticism applied to their rupture. The early relation would be exchanged for a later; instead of simply submitting to the inherited tie and the imposed complication, of suffering from them, our little wonder-working agent would create, without design, quite fresh elements of this order—contribute, that is, to the formation of a fresh tie, from which it would then (and for all the world as if through a small demonic foresight) proceed to derive great profit.

This is but to say that the light in which the vision so readily grew to a wholeness was that of a second marriage on both sides; the father having, in the freedom of divorce, but to take another wife, as well as the mother, under a like licence, another husband, for the case to begin, at least, to stand beautifully on its feet. There would be thus a perfect logic for what might come—come even with the mere attribution of a certain sensibility (if but a mere relative fineness) to either of the new parties. Say the prime cause making for the ultimate attempt to shirk on one side or the other, and better still if on both, a due share of the decreed burden should have been, after all, in each progenitor, a constitutional inaptitude for *any* burden, and a base intolerance of it: we should thus get a motive not requiring, but happily dispensing with, too particular a perversity in the step-parents. The child seen as creating by the fact of its forlornness a relation between its step-parents, the more intimate the better, dramatically speaking; the child, by the mere appeal of neglectedness and the mere consciousness of relief, weaving about, with the best faith in the world, the close web of sophistication; the child becoming a centre and pretext for a fresh system of misbehaviour, a system moreover of a nature to spread and ramify: *there* would be the "full" irony, there the promising theme into which the hint I had originally picked up would logically flower. No themes are so human as those that reflect for us, out of the confusion of life, the close connexion of bliss and bale, of the things that help with the things that hurt, so dangling before us for ever that bright hard medal, of so strange an alloy, one face of which is somebody's right and ease and the other somebody's pain and wrong. To live with all intensity and perplexity and felicity in its terribly mixed little world would thus be the part of my interesting small mortal; bringing people together who would be at least more correctly separate; keeping people separate who would be at least more correctly together; flourishing, to a degree, at the cost of many conventions and proprieties, even decencies, really keeping the torch of virtue alive in an air tending infinitely to smother it; really in short making confusion worse confounded by drawing some stray fragrance of an ideal across the scent of selfishness, by sowing on barren strands, through the mere fact of presence, the seed of the moral life.

All this would be to say, I at once recognised, that my light vessel of consciousness, swaying in such a draught, could n't be with verisimilitude a rude little boy; since, beyond the fact that little boys are never so "present," the sensibility of the female young is indubitably, for early youth,

the greater, and my plan would call, on the part of my protagonist, for "no end" of sensibility. I might impute that
amount of it without extravagance to a slip of a girl whose
faculties should have been well shaken up; but I should have
so to depend on its action to keep my story clear that I must be
able to show it in all assurance as naturally intense. To this
end I should have of course to suppose for my heroine dispositions originally promising, but above all I should have to invest
her with perceptions easily and almost infinitely quickened. So
handsomely fitted out, yet not in a manner too grossly to
affront probability, she might well see me through the whole
course of my design; which design, more and more attractive
as I turned it over, and dignified by the most delightful difficulty, would be to make and to keep her so limited consciousness the very field of my picture while at the same time guard-
ing with care the integrity of the objects represented. With the
charm of this possibility, therefore, the project for "Maisie"
rounded itself and loomed large—any subject looming large, for
that matter, I am bound to add, from the moment one is ridden
by the law of entire expression. I have already elsewhere noted,
I think, that the memory of my own work preserves for me
no theme that, at some moment or other of its development,
and always only waiting for the right connexion or chance,
has n't signally refused to remain humble, even (or perhaps all
the more resentfully) when fondly selected for its conscious
and hopeless humility. Once "out," like a house-dog of a temper above confinement, it defies the mere whistle, it roams, it
hunts, it seeks out and "sees" life; it can be brought back but
by hand and then only to take its futile thrashing. It was n't
at any rate for an idea seen in the light I here glance at not to
have due warrant of its value—how could the value of a scheme
so finely workable *not* be great? The one presented register of
the whole complexity would be the play of the child's confused
and obscure notation of it, and yet the whole, as I say, should
be unmistakeably, should be honourably there, seen through

the faint intelligence, or at the least attested by the imponderable presence, and still advertising its sense.

I recall that my first view of this neat possibility was as the attaching problem of the picture restricted (while yet achieving, as I say, completeness and coherency) to what the child might be conceived to have *understood*—to have been able to interpret and appreciate. Further reflexion and experiment showed me my subject strangled in that extreme of rigour. The infant mind would at the best leave great gaps and voids; so that with a systematic surface possibly beyond reproach we should nevertheless fail of clearness of sense. I should have to stretch the matter to what my wondering witness materially and inevitably *saw;* a great deal of which quantity she either would n't understand at all or would quite misunderstand—and on those lines, only on those, my task would be prettily cut out. To that then I settled—to the question of giving it *all,* the whole situation surrounding her, but of giving it only through the occasions and connexions of her proximity and her attention; only as it might pass before her and appeal to her, as it might touch her and affect her, for better or worse, for perceptive gain or perceptive loss: so that we fellow witnesses, we not more invited but only more expert critics, should feel in strong possession of it. This would be, to begin with, a plan of absolutely definite and measurable application—that in itself always a mark of beauty; and I have been interested to find on re-perusal of the work that some such controlling grace successfully rules it. Nothing could be more "done," I think, in the light of its happiest intention; and this in spite of an appearance that at moments obscures my consistency. Small children have many more perceptions than they have terms to translate them; their vision is at any moment much richer, their apprehension even constantly stronger, than their prompt, their at all producible, vocabulary. Amusing therefore as it might at the first blush have seemed to restrict myself in this case to the terms as well as to the experience, it became at once plain that such an attempt would fail. Maisie's terms accordingly play their part—since her simpler conclusions quite depend on them; but our own commentary constantly attends and amplifies. This it is that on occasion, doubtless, seems to represent us as going so "behind" the facts of her spectacle as to exaggerate the activity of her relation to them. The difference here is but of a shade: it is her relation, her activity of spirit, that determines all our own concern—we simply take advantage of these things better than she herself. Only, even though it is her interest that mainly makes matters interesting for us, we inevitably note this in figures that are not yet at her command and that are nevertheless required whenever those aspects about her and those parts of her experience that she understands darken off into others that she rather tormentedly misses. All of which gave me a high firm logic to observe; supplied the force for which the straightener of almost any tangle is grateful while he labours, the sense of pulling at threads intrinsically worth it—strong enough and fine enough and entire enough.

Of course, beyond this, was another and well-nigh equal charm—equal in spite of its being almost independent of the acute constructional, the endless expressional question. This was the quite different question of the particular kind of truth of resistance I might be able to impute to my central figure—*some* intensity, some continuity of resistance being naturally of the essence of the subject. Successfully to resist (to resist, that is, the strain of observation and the assault of experience) what would that be, on the part of so young a person, but to remain fresh, and still fresh, and to have even a freshness to communicate?—the case being with Maisie to the end that she treats her friends to the rich little spectacle of objects embalmed in her wonder. She wonders, in other words, to the end, to the death—the death of her childhood, properly speaking; after which (with the inevitable shift, sooner or later, of her point of view) her situation will change and become another affair, subject to other measurements and with a new centre altogether. The particular reaction that will have led her to that point, and that it has been of an exquisite interest to study in her, will have spent itself; there will be another scale, another perspective, another horizon. Our business meanwhile therefore is to extract from her current reaction whatever it may be worth; and for that matter we recognise in it the highest exhibitional virtue. Truly, I reflect, if the theme had had no other beauty it would still have had this rare and distinguished one of its so expressing the variety of the child's values. She is not only the extraordinary "ironic centre" I have already noted; she has the wonderful importance of shedding a light far beyond any reach of her comprehension; of lending to poorer persons and things, by the mere fact of their being involved with her and by the special scale she creates for them, a precious element of dignity. I lose myself, truly, in appreciation of my theme on noting what she does by her "freshness" for appearances in themselves vulgar and empty enough. They become, as she deals with them, the stuff of poetry and tragedy and art; she has simply to wonder, as I say, about them, and they begin to have meanings, aspects, solidities, connexions—connexions with the "universal!"—that they could scarce have hoped for. Ida Farange alone, so to speak, or Beale alone, that is either of them otherwise connected—what intensity, what "objectivity" (the most developed degree of *being* anyhow thinkable for them) would they have? How would they repay at all the favour of our attention?

Maisie makes them portentous all by the play of her good faith, makes her mother above all, to my vision—unless I have wholly failed to render it—concrete, immense and awful; so that we get, for our profit, and get by an economy of process interesting in itself, the thoroughly pictured creature, the striking figured symbol. At two points in particular, I seem to recognise, we enjoy at its maximum this effect of associational magic. The passage in which her father's terms of intercourse

with the insinuating but so strange and unattractive lady whom
he has had the detestable levity to whisk her off to see late at
night, is a signal example of the all but incalculable way in
which interest may be constituted. The facts involved are that
Beale Farange is ignoble, that the friend to whom he introduces
his daughter is deplorable, and that from the commerce of the
two, *as* the two merely, we would fain avert our heads. Yet
the thing has but to become a part of the child's bewilderment
for these small sterilities to drop from it and for the *scene* to
emerge and prevail—vivid, special, wrought hard, to the hardness of the unforgettable; the scene that is exactly what Beale
and Ida and Mrs. Cuddon, and even Sir Claude and Mrs. Beale,
would never for a moment have succeeded in making their
scant unredeemed importances—namely *appreciable*. I find another instance in the episode of Maisie's unprepared encounter,
while walking in the Park with Sir Claude, of her mother and
that beguiled attendant of her mother, the encouraging, the
appealing "Captain," to whom this lady contrives to commit her for twenty minutes while she herself deals with the
second husband. The human substance here would have
seemed in advance well-nigh too poor for conversion, the
three "mature" figures of too short a radiation, too stupid
(*so* stupid it was for Sir Claude to have married Ida!) too
vain, too thin, for any clear application; but promptly, immediately, the child's own importance, spreading and con-
tagiously acting, has determined the *total* value otherwise.
Nothing of course, meanwhile, is an older story to the observer of manners and the painter of life than the grotesque
finality with which such terms as "painful," "unpleasant"
and "disgusting" are often applied to his results; to that
degree, in truth, that the free use of them as weightily conclusive again and again re-enforces his estimate of the critical
sense of circles in which they artlessly flourish. Of course
under that superstition I was punctually to have had read to
me the lesson that the "mixing-up" of a child with anything

unpleasant confessed itself an aggravation of the unpleasantness, and that nothing could well be more disgusting than to attribute to Maisie so intimate an "acquaintance" with the gross immoralities surrounding her.

The only thing to say of such lucidities is that, however one may have "discounted" in advance, and as once for all, their general radiance, one is disappointed if the hour for them, in the particular connexion, does n't strike—they so keep before us elements with which even the most sedate philosopher must always reckon. The painter of life has indeed work cut out for him when a considerable part of life offers itself in the guise of that sapience. The effort really to see and really to represent is no idle business in face of the *constant* force that makes for muddlement. The great thing is indeed that the muddled state too is one of the very sharpest of the realities, that it also has colour and form and character, has often in fact a broad and rich comicality, many of the signs and values of the appreciable. Thus it was to be, for example, I might gather, that the very principle of Maisie's appeal, her undestroyed freshness, in other words that vivacity of intelligence by which she indeed does vibrate in the infected air, indeed does flourish in her immoral world, may pass for a barren and senseless thing, or at best a negligible one. For nobody to whom life at large is *easily* interesting do the finer, the shyer, the more anxious small vibrations, fine and shy and anxious with the passion that precedes knowledge, succeed in being negligible: which is doubtless one of many reasons why the passage between the child and the kindly, friendly, ugly gentleman who, seated with her in Kensington Gardens under a spreading tree, positively answers to her for her mother as no one has ever answered, and so stirs her, filially and morally, as she has never been stirred, throws into highest relief, to my sense at least, the side on which the subject is strong, and becomes the type-passage—other advantages certainly aiding, as I may say—for the expression of its beauty. The active, contributive close-circling won-

der, as I have called it, in which the child's identity is guarded
and preserved, and which makes her case remarkable exactly
by the weight of the tax on it, provides distinction for her, provides vitality and variety, through the operation of the tax
—which would have done comparatively little for us had n't
it been monstrous. A pity for us surely to have been deprived
of this just reflexion. "Maisie" is of 1907.

I pass by, for the moment, the second of these compositions,
finding in the third, which again deals with the experience of
a very young person, a connexion more immediate; and this
even at the risk of seeming to undermine my remark of a
few pages back as to the comparative sensibility of the sexes.
My urchin of "The Pupil" (1891) has sensibility in abundance,
it would seem—and yet preserves in spite of it, I judge, his
strong little male quality. But there are fifty things to say
here; which indeed rush upon me within my present close
limits in such a cloud as to demand much clearance. This is
perhaps indeed but the aftersense of the assault made on my
mind, as I perfectly recall, by every aspect of the original vision,
which struck me as abounding in aspects. It lives again for me,
this vision, as it first alighted; though the inimitable prime
flutter, the air as of an ineffable sign made by the immediate
beat of the wings of the poised figure of fancy that has just settled, is one of those guarantees of value that can never be re-
captured. The sign has been made to the seer only—it is *his*
queer affair; of which any report to others, not as yet involved,
has but the same effect of flatness as attends, amid a group
gathered under the canopy of night, any stray allusion to a
shooting star. The miracle, since miracle it seems, is all for the
candid exclaimer. The miracle for the author of "The Pupil,"
at any rate, was when, years ago, one summer day, in a very
hot Italian railway-carriage, which stopped and dawdled everywhere, favouring conversation, a friend with whom I shared it,
a doctor of medicine who had come from a far country to
settle in Florence, happened to speak to me of a wonderful

American family, an odd adventurous, extravagant band, of
high but rather unauthenticated pretensions, the most interesting member of which was a small boy, acute and pre-
cocious, afflicted with a heart of weak action, but beautifully
intelligent, who saw their prowling precarious life exactly as
it was, and measured and judged it, and measured and judged
them, all round, ever so quaintly; presenting himself in short
as an extraordinary little person. Here was more than enough
for a summer's day even in old Italy—here was a thump-
ing windfall. No process and no steps intervened: I *saw,* on
the spot, little Morgan Moreen, I saw all the rest of the
Moreens; I felt, to the last delicacy, the nature of my young
friend's relation with them (he had become at once my young
friend) and, by the same stroke, to its uttermost fine throb,
the subjection to *him* of the beguiled, bewildered, defrauded,
unremunerated, yet after all richly repaid youth who would
to a certainty, under stress of compassion, embark with the
tribe on tutorship, and whose edifying connexion with it
would be my leading document.

This must serve as my account of the origin of "The Pupil":
it will commend itself, I feel, to all imaginative and projective
persons who have had—and what imaginative and projective
person has n't?—any like experience of the suddenly-determined
absolute of perception. The whole cluster of items forming
the image is on these occasions born at once; the parts are not
pieced together, they conspire and interdepend; but what it
really comes to, no doubt, is that at a simple touch an old
latent and dormant impression, a buried germ, implanted by
experience and then forgotten, flashes to the surface as a fish,
with a single "squirm," rises to the baited hook, and there
meets instantly the vivifying ray. I remember at all events
having no doubt of anything or anyone here; the vision kept
to the end its ease and its charm; it worked itself out with
confidence. These are minor matters when the question is of
minor results; yet almost any assured and downright imagina-

tive act is—granted the sort of record in which I here indulge—worth fondly commemorating. One cherishes, after
the fact, any proved case of the independent life of the imagination; above all if by that faculty one has been appointed
mainly to live. We are then *never* detached from the question
of what it may out of simple charity do for us. Besides which,
in relation to the poor Moreens, innumerable notes, as I
have intimated, all equally urging their relevance, press here
to the front. The general adventure of the little composition itself—for singular things were to happen to it, though
among such importunities not the most worth noting now
—would be, occasion favouring, a thing to live over; moving
as one did, roundabout it, in I scarce know what thick and
coloured air of slightly tarnished anecdote, of dim association,
of casual confused romance; a compound defying analysis,
but truly, for the social chronicler, any student in especial
of the copious "cosmopolite" legend, a boundless and tangled,
but highly explorable, garden. Why, somehow—these were
the intensifying questions—did one see the Moreens, whom I
place at Nice, at Venice, in Paris, as of the special essence of
the little old miscellaneous cosmopolite Florence, the Florence
of other, of irrecoverable years, the restless yet withal so convenient scene of a society that has passed away for ever with
all its faded ghosts and fragile relics; immaterial presences that
have quite ceased to revisit (trust an old romancer's, an old
pious observer's fine sense to have made sure of it!) walks
and prospects once sacred and shaded, but now laid bare, gaping wide, despoiled of their past and unfriendly to any appreciation of it?—through which the unconscious Barbarians troop
with the regularity and passivity of "supplies," or other promiscuous goods, prepaid and forwarded.

They had nothing to do, the dear Moreens, with this dreadful period, any more than I, as occupied and charmed with
them, was humiliatingly subject to it; we were, all together,
of a better romantic age and faith; we referred ourselves, with

our highest complacency, to the classic years of the great Americo-European legend; the years of limited communication, of monstrous and unattenuated contrast, of prodigious and unrecorded adventure. The comparatively brief but infinitely rich "cycle" of romance embedded in the earlier, the very early American reactions and returns (mediæval in the sense of being, at most, of the mid-century), what does it resemble today but a gold-mine overgrown and smothered, dislocated, and no longer workable?—all for want of the right indications for sounding, the right implements for digging, doubtless even of the right workmen, those with the right tradition and "feeling" for the job. The most extraordinary things appear to have happened, during that golden age, in the "old" countries—in Asia and Africa as well as in Europe—to the candid children of the West, things admirably incongruous and incredible; but no story of all the list was to find its just interpreter, and nothing is now more probable than that every key to interpretation has been lost. The modern reporter's big brushes, attached to broom-handles that match the height of his sky-scrapers, would sadly besmear the fine parchment of our missing record. We were to lose, clearly, at any rate, a vast body of precious anecdotes, a long gallery of wonderful portraits, an array of the oddest possible figures in the oddest possible attitudes. The Moreens were of the family then of the great unstudied precursors—poor and shabby members, no doubt; dim and superseded types. I must add indeed that, such as they were, or as they may at present incoherently appear, I don't pretend really to have "done" them; all I have given in "The Pupil" is little Morgan's troubled vision of them as reflected in the vision, also troubled enough, of his devoted friend. The manner of the thing may thus illustrate the author's incorrigible taste for gradations and superpositions of effect; his love, when it is a question of a picture, of anything that makes for proportion and perspective, that contributes to a view of *all* the dimensions. Addicted to seeing "through"—one thing through another, accordingly, and still other things through *that*—he takes, too greedily perhaps, on any errand, as many things as possible by the way. It is after this fashion that he incurs the stigma of labouring uncannily for a certain fulness of truth—truth diffused, distributed and, as it were, atmospheric.

The second in order of these fictions speaks for itself, I think, so frankly as scarce to suffer further expatiation. Its origin is written upon it large, and the idea it puts into play so abides in one of the commonest and most taken-for-granted of London impressions that some such experimentally-figured situation as that of "In the Cage" must again and again have flowered (granted the grain of observation) in generous minds. It had become for me, at any rate, an old story by the time (1898) I cast it into this particular form. The postal-telegraph office in general, and above all the small local office of one's immediate neighbourhood, scene of the transaction of so much of one's daily business, haunt of one's needs and one's duties, of one's labours and one's patiences, almost of one's rewards and one's disappointments, one's joys and one's sorrows, had ever had, to my sense, so much of London to give out, so much of its huge perpetual story to tell, that any momentary wait there seemed to take place in a strong social draught, the stiffest possible breeze of the human comedy. One had of course in these connexions one's especial resort, the office nearest one's own door, where one had come to enjoy in a manner the fruits of frequentation and the amenities of intercourse. So had grown up, for speculation—prone as one's mind had ever been to that form of waste—the question of what it might "mean," wherever the admirable service was installed, for confined and cramped and yet considerably tutored young officials of either sex to be made so free, intellectually, of a range of experience otherwise quite closed to them. This wonderment, once the spark was kindled, became an amusement, or an obsession, like another; though falling indeed, at the best, no doubt, but into that deepest abyss of all the wonderments that break out for the student of great cities. From the moment that he *is* a student, this most beset of critics, his danger is inevitably of imputing to too many others, right and left, the critical impulse and the acuter vision— so very long may it take him to learn that the mass of mankind are banded, probably by the sanest of instincts, to defend themselves to the death against any such vitiation of their simplicity. To criticise is to appreciate, to appropriate, to take intellectual possession, to establish in fine a relation with the criticised thing and make it one's own. The large intellectual appetite projects itself thus on many things, while the small—not better advised, but unconscious of need for advice—projects itself on few.

Admirable thus its economic instinct; it is curious of nothing that it has n't vital use for. You may starve in London, it is clear, without discovering a use for any theory of the more equal division of victuals—which is moreover exactly what it would appear that thousands of the non-speculative annually do. Their example is much to the point, in the light of all the barren trouble they are saved; but somehow, after all, it gives no pause to the "artist," to the morbid imagination. That rash, that idle faculty continues to abound in questions, and to supply answers to as many of them as possible; all of which makes a great occupation for idleness. To the fantastic scale on which this last-named state may, in favouring conditions, organise itself, to the activities it may practise when the favouring conditions happen to crop up in Mayfair or in Kensington, our portrayal of the caged telegraphist may well appear a proper little monument. The composition before us tells in fact clearly enough, it seems to me, the story of its growth; and relevance will probably be found in any moral it may pluck—by which I mean any moral the impulse to have framed it may pluck—from the vice of reading rank subtleties into simple souls and reckless expenditure into thrifty ones. The matter comes back again, I fear, but to the author's irrepressible and insatiable, his extravagant and immoral, interest in personal character and in the "nature" of a mind, of almost any mind the heaving little sea of his subject may cast up—as to which these remarks have already, in other connexions, recorded his apology: all without prejudice to such shrines and stations of penance as still shall enliven our way. The range of wonderment attributed in our tale to the young woman employed at Cocker's differs little in essence from the speculative thread on which the pearls of Maisie's experience, in this same volume—pearls of so strange an iridescence—are mostly strung. She wonders, putting it simply, very much as Morgan Moreen wonders; and they all wonder, for that matter, very much after the fashion of our portentous little Hyacinth of "The Princess Casamassima," tainted to the core, as we have seen him, with the trick of mental reaction on the things about him and fairly staggering under the appropriations, as I have called them, that he owes to the critical spirit. He collapses, poor Hyacinth, like a thief at night, overcharged with treasures of reflexion and spoils of passion of which he can give, in his poverty and obscurity, no honest account.

It is much in this manner, we see on analysis, that Morgan Moreen breaks down—his burden indeed not so heavy, but his strength so much less formed. The two little spirits of maidens, in the group, bear up, oddly enough, beyond those of their brothers; but the just remark for each of these small exhibited lives is of course that, in the longer or the shorter piece, they are actively, are luxuriously, lived. The luxury is that of the number of their moral vibrations, well-nigh unrestricted—not that of an account at the grocer's: whatever it be, at any rate, it makes them, as examples and "cases," rare. My brooding telegraphist may be in fact, on her ground of ingenuity, scarcely more thinkable than desirable; yet if I have made her but a libel, up and down the city, on an estimable class, I feel it still something to have admonished that class, even though obscurely enough, of neglected interests and undivined occasions. My central spirit, in the anecdote, is, for verisimilitude, I grant, too ardent a focus of divination; but without this excess the phenomena detailed would have lacked their principle of cohesion. The action of the drama is simply the girl's "subjective" adventure—that of her quite definitely winged intelligence; just as the catastrophe, just as the solution, depends on her winged wit. Why, however, should I explain further—for a case that, modestly as it would seem to present itself, has yet already whirled us so far? A course of incident complicated by the intervention of winged wit—which is here, as I say, confessed to—would be generally expected, I judge, to commit me to the explanation of everything. But from that undertaking I shrink, and take refuge instead, for an instant, in a much looser privilege.

If I speak, as just above, of the *action* embodied, each time, in these so "quiet" recitals, it is under renewed recognition of the inveterate instinct with which they keep conforming to the "scenic" law. They demean themselves for all the world—they quite insist on it, that is, whenever they have a chance—as little constituted dramas, little exhibitions founded on the logic of the "scene," the unit of the scene, the general scenic consistency, and knowing little more than that. To read them over has been to find them on this ground never at fault. The process repeats and renews itself, moving in the light it has once for all adopted. These finer idiosyncracies of a literary form seem to be regarded as outside the scope of criticism—small reference to them do I remember ever to have met; such surprises of re-perusal, such recoveries of old fundamental intention, such moments of almost ruefully independent discrimination, would doubtless in that case not have waylaid my steps. Going over the pages here placed together has been for me, at all events, quite to watch the scenic system at play. The treatment by "scene," regularly, quite rhythmically recurs; the intervals between, the massing of the elements to a different effect and by a quite other law, remain, in this fashion, all preparative, just as the scenic occasions in themselves become, at a given moment, illustrative, each of the agents, true to its function, taking up the theme from the other very much as the fiddles, in an orchestra, may take it up from the cornets and flutes, or the wind-instruments take it up from the violins. The point, however, is that the scenic passages are *wholly* and logically scenic, having for their rule of beauty the principle of the "conduct," the organic development, of a scene—the entire succession of values that flower and bear fruit on ground solidly laid for them. The great advantage for the total effect is that we feel, with the definite alternation, how the theme *is* being treated. That is we feel it when, in such tangled connexions, we happen to care. I should n't really go on as if this were the case with many readers.

IX

PREFACE TO "THE ASPERN PAPERS"

(VOLUME XII IN THE NEW YORK EDITION. CONTAINING: "THE ASPERN PAPERS," "THE TURN OF THE SCREW," "THE LIAR," "THE TWO FACES")

I NOT only recover with ease, but I delight to recall, the first impulse given to the idea of "The Aspern Papers." It is at the same time true that my present mention of it may per haps too effectually dispose of any complacent claim to my having "found" the situation. Not that I quite know indeed what situations the seeking fabulist does "find"; he seeks them enough assuredly, but his discoveries are, like those of the navigator, the chemist, the biologist, scarce more than alert recognitions. He *comes upon* the interesting thing as Columbus came upon the isle of San Salvador, because he had moved in the right direction for it—also because he knew, with the encounter, what "making land" then and there represented. Nature had so placed it, to profit—if as profit we may measure the matter!—by his fine unrest, just as history, "literary history" we in this connexion call it, had in an out-of-the-way corner of the great garden of life thrown off a curious flower that I was to feel worth gathering as soon as I saw it. I got wind of my positive fact, I followed the scent. It was in Florence years ago; which is precisely, of the whole matter, what I like most to remember. The air of the old-time Italy invests it, a mixture that on the faintest invitation I rejoice again to inhale—and this in spite of the mere cold renewal, ever, of the infirm side of that felicity, the sense, in the whole element, of things too numerous, too deep, too obscure, too strange, or even simply too beautiful, for any ease of intellectual relation. One must pay one's self largely with words, I think, one must induce almost any "Italian subject" *to make believe* it gives up its secret, in order to keep at all on working—or call them perhaps rather playing—terms with the general impression. We entertain it thus, the impression, by the aid of a merciful convention which resembles the fashion of our intercourse with Iberians or Orientals whose form of courtesy places everything they have at our disposal. We thank them and call upon them, but without acting on their professions. The offer has been too large and our assurance is too small; we peep at most into two or three of the chambers of their hospitality, with the rest of the case stretching beyond our ken and escaping our penetration. The pious fiction suffices; we have entered, we have seen, we are charmed. So, right and left, in Italy—before the great historic complexity at least—penetration fails; we scratch at the extensive surface, we meet the perfunctory smile, we hang about in the golden air. But we exaggerate our gathered values only if we are eminently witless. It is fortunately the exhibition in all the world before which, as admirers, we can most remain superficial without feeling silly.

All of which I note, however, perhaps with too scant relevance to the inexhaustible charm of Roman and Florentine memories. Off the ground, at a distance, our fond indifference to being "silly" grows fonder still; the working convention, as I have called it—the convention of the real revelations and surrenders on one side and the real immersions and appreciations on the other—has not only nothing to keep it down, but every glimpse of contrast, every pang of exile and every nostalgic twinge to keep it up. These latter haunting presences in fact, let me note, almost reduce at first to a mere blurred, sad, scarcely consolable vision this present revisiting, re-appropriating impulse. There are parts of one's past, evidently, that bask consentingly and serenely enough in the light of other days—which is but the intensity of thought; and there are other parts that take it as with agitation and pain, a troubled consciousness that heaves as with the disorder of drinking it deeply in. So it is at any rate, fairly in too thick and rich a retrospect, that I see my old Venice of "The Aspern Papers," that I see the still earlier one of Jeffrey Aspern himself, and that I see even the comparatively recent Florence that was to drop into my ear the solicitation of these things. I would fain "lay it on" thick for the very love of them—that at least I may profess; and, with the ground of this desire frankly admitted, something that somehow makes, in the whole story, for a romantic harmony. I have had occasion in the course of these remarks to define my sense of the romantic, and am glad to encounter again here an instance of that virtue as I understand it. I shall presently say why this small case so ranges itself, but must first refer more exactly to the thrill of appreciation it was immediately to excite in me. I saw it somehow at the very first blush as romantic—for the use, of course I mean, I should certainly have had to make of it—that Jane Clairmont, the half-sister of Mary Godwin, Shelley's second wife and for a while the intimate friend of Byron and the mother of his daughter Allegra, should have been living on in Florence, where she had long lived, up to our own day, and that in fact, had I happened to hear of her but a little sooner, I might have seen her in the flesh. The question of whether I should have wished to do so was another matter—the question of whether I should n't have preferred to keep her preciously unseen, to run no risk, in other words, by too rude a choice, of depreciating that romance-value which, as I say, it was instantly inevitable to attach (through association above all, with another signal circumstance) to her long survival.

I had luckily not had to deal with the difficult option; difficult in such a case by reason of that odd law which somehow always makes the minimum of valid suggestion serve the man of imagination better than the maximum. The historian, essentially, wants more documents than he can really use; the dramatist only wants more liberties than he can really take. Nothing, fortunately, however, had, as the case stood, depended on my delicacy; I might have "looked up" Miss Clairmont in previous years had I been earlier informed—the silence about her seemed full of the "irony of fate"; but I felt myself more concerned with the mere strong fact of her having testified for the reality and the closeness of our relation to the past than with any question of the particular sort of person I might have flattered myself I "found." I had certainly at the very least been saved the undue simplicity of pretending to read meanings into things absolutely sealed and beyond test or proof—to tap a fount of waters that could n't possibly not have run dry. The thrill of learning that she had "overlapped," and by so much, and the wonder of my having doubtless at several earlier seasons passed again and again, all unknowing, the door of her house, where she sat above, within call and in her habit as she lived, these things gave me all I wanted; I seem to remember in fact that my more or less immediately recognising that I positively ought n't—"for anything to come of it"—to have wanted more. I saw, quickly, how something might come of it *thus;* whereas a fine instinct told me that the effect of a nearer view of the case (the case of the overlapping) would probably have had to be quite differently calculable. It was really with another item of knowledge, however, that I measured the mistake I should have made in waking up sooner to the question of opportunity. That item consisted of the action taken on the premises by a person who *had* waked up in time, and the legend of whose consequent adventure, as a few spoken words put it before me, at once kindled a flame. This gentleman, an American of long ago, an ardent Shelleyite, a singularly marked figure and himself in the highest degree a subject for a free sketch—I had known him a little, but there is not a reflected glint of him in "The Aspern Papers"—was named to me as having made interest with Miss Clairmont to be accepted as a lodger on the calculation that she would have Shelley documents for which, in the possibly not remote event of her death, he would thus enjoy priority of chance to treat with her representatives. He had at any rate, according to the legend, become, on earnest Shelley grounds, her yearning, though also her highly diplomatic, *pensionnaire*—but without gathering, as was to befall, the fruit of his design.

Legend here dropped to another key; it remained in a manner interesting, but became to my ear a trifle coarse, or at least rather vague and obscure. It mentioned a younger female relative of the ancient woman as a person who, for a queer climax, had had to be dealt with; it flickered so for a moment and then, as a light, to my great relief, quite went out. It had flickered indeed but at the best—yet had flickered enough to give me my "facts," bare facts of intimation; which, scant handful though they were, were more distinct and more numerous than I mostly *like* facts: like them, that is, as we say of an etcher's progressive subject, in an early "state." Nine tenths of the artist's interest in them is that of what he shall add to them and how he shall turn them. Mine, however, in the connexion I speak of, had fortunately got away from me, and quite of their own movement, in time not to crush me. So it was, at all events, that my imagination preserved power to react under the mere essential charm—that, I mean, of a final scene of the rich dim Shelley drama played out in the very theatre of our own "modernity." This was the beauty that appealed to me; there had been, so to speak, a forward continuity, from the actual man, the divine poet, on; and the curious, the ingenious, the admirable thing would be to throw it backward again, to compress—squeezing it hard!—the connexion that had drawn itself out, and convert so the stretched relation into a value of nearness on our own part. In short I saw my chance as admirable, and one reason, when the direction is right, may serve as well as fifty; but if I "took over," as I say, everything that was of the essence, I stayed my hand for the rest. The Italian side of the legend closely clung; if only because the so possible terms of my Juliana's life in the Italy of other days could make conceivable for her the fortunate privacy, the long uninvaded and uninterviewed state on which I represent her situation as founded. Yes, a surviving unexploited unparagraphed Juliana was up to a quarter of a century since still supposeable—as much so as any such buried treasure, any such grave unprofaned, would defy probability now. And then the case had the air of the past just in the degree in which that air, I confess, most appeals to me—when the region over which it hangs is far enough away without being too far.

I delight in a palpable imaginable *visitable* past—in the nearer distances and the clearer mysteries, the marks and signs of a world we may reach over to as by making a long arm we grasp an object at the other end of our own table. The table is the one, the common expanse, and where we lean, so stretching, we find it firm and continuous. That, to my imagination, is the past fragrant of all, or of almost all, the poetry of the thing outlived and lost and gone, and yet in which the precious element of closeness, telling so of connexions but tasting so of differences, remains appreciable. With more moves back the element of the appreciable shrinks—just as the charm of looking over a garden-wall into another garden breaks down when successions of walls appear. The other gardens, those still beyond, may be there, but even by use of our longest ladder we are baffled and bewildered—the view is mainly a view of barriers. The one partition makes the place we have wondered about *other,* both richly and recogniseably so; but who shall pretend to impute an effect of composition to the twenty? We are divided of course between liking to feel the past strange and liking to feel it familiar; the difficulty is, for intensity, to catch it at the moment when the scales of the balance hang with the right evenness. I say for intensity, for we may profit by them in other aspects enough if we are content to measure or to feel loosely. It would take me too far, however, to tell why the particular afternoon light that I thus call intense rests clearer to my sense on the Byronic age, as I conveniently name it, than on periods more protected by the "dignity" of history. With the times beyond, intrinsically more "strange," the tender grace, for the backward vision, has faded, the afternoon darkened; for any time nearer to us the special effect has n't begun. So there, to put the matter crudely, is the appeal I fondly recognise, an appeal residing doubtless more in the "special effect," in some deep associational force, than in a virtue more intrinsic. I am afraid I must add, since I allow myself so much to fantasticate, that the impulse had more than once taken me to project the Byronic age and the afternoon light across the great sea, to see in short whether association would carry so far and what the young century might pass for on that side of the modern world where it was not only itself so irremediably youngest, but was bound up with youth in everything else. There was a refinement of curiosity in this imputation of a golden strangeness to American social facts—though I cannot pretend, I fear, that there was any greater wisdom.

Since what it had come to then was, harmlessly enough, cultivating a sense of the past under that close protection, it was natural, it was fond and filial, to wonder if a few of the distilled drops might n't be gathered from some vision of, say, "old" New York. Would that human congeries, to aid obligingly in the production of a fable, be conceivable as "taking" the afternoon light with the right happy slant?—or could a recogniseable reflexion of the Byronic age, in other words, be picked up on the banks of the Hudson? (Only just there, beyond the great sea, if anywhere: in no other connexion would the question so much as raise its head. I admit that Jeffrey Aspern is n't even feebly localised, but I *thought* New York as I projected him.) It was "amusing," in any case, always, to try experiments; and the experiment for the right *transposition* of my Juliana would be to fit her out with an immortalising poet as transposed as herself. Delicacy had demanded, I felt, that my appropriation of the Florentine legend should purge it, first of all, of references too obvious; so that, to begin with, I shifted the scene of the adventure. Juliana, as I saw her, was thinkable only in Byronic and more or less immediately post-Byronic Italy; but there were conditions in which she was ideally arrangeable, as happened, especially in respect to the later time and the long undetected survival; there being absolutely no refinement of the mouldy rococo, in human or whatever other form, that you may not disembark at the dislocated water-steps of almost any decayed monument of Venetian greatness in auspicious quest of. It was a question, in fine, of covering one's tracks—though with no great elaboration I am bound to admit; and I felt I could n't cover mine more than in postulating a comparative American Byron to match an American Miss Clairmont—she as absolute as she would. I scarce know whether best to say for this device to-day that it cost me little or that it cost me much; it was "cheap" or expensive according to the degree of verisimilitude artfully obtained. If that degree appears *nil* the "art," such as it was, is wasted, and my remembrance of the contention, on the part of a highly critical friend who at that time and later on often had my ear, that it had been simply foredoomed to be wasted, puts before me the passage in the private history of "The Aspern Papers," that I now find, I confess, most interesting. I comfort myself for the needful brevity of a present glance at it by the sense that the general question involved, under criticism, can't but come up for us again at higher pressure.

My friend's argument bore then—at the time and afterward—on my vicious practice, as he maintained, of postulating for the purpose of my fable celebrities who not only *had n't* existed in the conditions I imputed to them, but who for the most part (and in no case more markedly than in that of Jeffrey Aspern) could n't possibly have done so. The stricture was to apply itself to a whole group of short fictions in which I had, with whatver ingenuity, assigned to several so-called eminent figures positions absolutely unthinkable in our actual encompassing air, an air definitely unfavourable to certain forms of eminence. It was vicious, my critic contended, to flourish forth on one's page "great people," public persons, who should n't more or less square with our quite definite and calculable array of such notabilities; and by this rule I was heavily incriminated. The rule demanded that the "public person" portrayed should be at least of the tradition, of the general complexion, of the face-value, exactly, of some past or present producible counterfoil. Mere private figures, under one's hand, might correspond with nobody, it being of their essence to be but narrowly known; the represented state of being conspicuous, on the other hand, involved before anything else a recognition—and none of my eminent folk were recogniseable. It was all very well for instance to have put one's self at such pains for Miriam Rooth in "The Tragic Muse"; but *there* was misapplied zeal, there a case of pitiful waste, crying aloud to be denounced. Miriam is offered not as a young person passing unnoticed by her age —like the Biddy Dormers and Julia Dallows, say, of the same book, but as a high rarity, a time-figure of the scope inevitably attended by other commemorations. Where on earth would be then Miriam's inscribed "counterfoil," and in what conditions of the contemporary English theatre, in what conditions of criticism, of appreciation, under what conceivable Anglo-Saxon star, might we take an artistic value of this order either for produced or for recognised? We are, as a "public," chalk-marked by nothing, more unmistakeably, than by the truth that we know nothing of such values—any more than, as my friend was to impress on me, we are susceptible of consciousness of such others (these in the sphere of literary eminence) as my Neil Paraday in "The Death of the Lion," as my Hugh Vereker in "The Figure in the Carpet," as my Ralph Limbert, above all, in "The Next Time," as sundry unprecedented and unmatched heroes and martyrs of the artistic ideal, in short, elsewhere exemplified in my pages.

We shall come to these objects of animadversion in another hour, when I shall have no difficulty in producing the defence I found for them—since, obviously, I hadn't cast them into the world *all* naked and ashamed; and I deal for the moment but with the stigma in general as Jeffrey Aspern carries it.

The charge being that I foist upon our early American annals a distinguished presence for which they yield me absolutely no warrant—"Where, within them, gracious heaven, were we to look for so much as an approach to the social elements of habitat and climate of birds of that note and plumage?"—I find his link with reality then just in the tone of the picture wrought round him. What was that tone but exactly, but exquisitely, calculated, the harmless hocus-pocus under cover of which we might suppose him to have existed? This tone is the tone, artistically speaking of "amusement," the current floating that precious influence home quite as one of those high tides watched by the smugglers of old might, in case of their boat's being boarded, be trusted to wash far up the strand the cask of foreign liquor expertly committed to it. If through our lean prime Western period no dim and charming ghost of an adventurous lyric genius might by a stretch of fancy flit, if the time was really too hard to "take," in the light form proposed, the elegant reflexion, then so much the worse for the time—it was all one could say! The retort to that of course was that such a plea represented no "link" with reality—which was what was under discussion—but only a link, and flimsy enough too, with the deepest depths of the artificial: the restrictive truth exactly contended for, which may embody my critic's last word rather of course than my own. My own, so far as I shall pretend in that especial connexion to report it, was that one's warrant, in such a case, hangs essentially on the question of whether or no the false element imputed would have borne that test of further development which so exposes the wrong and so consecrates the right. My last word was, heaven forgive me, that, occasion favouring, I could have perfectly "worked out" Jeffrey Aspern. The boast remains indeed to be verified when we shall arrive at the other challenged cases.

That particular challenge at least "The Turn of the Screw" does n't incur; and this perfectly independent and irresponsible little fiction rejoices, beyond any rival on a like ground, in a conscious provision of prompt retort to the sharpest question that may be addressed to it. For it has the small strength— if I should n't say rather the unattackable ease—of a perfect homogeneity, of being, to the very last grain of its virtue, all of a kind; the very kind, as happens, least apt to be baited by earnest criticism, the only sort of criticism of which account need be taken. To have handled again this so full-blown flower of high fancy is to be led back by it to easy and happy recognitions. Let the first of these be that of the starting-point itself —the sense, all charming again, of the circle, one winter afternoon, round the hall-fire of a grave old country-house where (for all the world as if to resolve itself promptly and obligingly into convertible, into "literary" stuff) the talk turned, on I forget what homely pretext, to apparitions and night-fears, to the marked and sad drop in the general supply, and still more in the general quality, of such commodities. The good, the really effective and heart-shaking ghost-stories (roughly so to term them) appeared all to have been told, and neither new crop nor new type in any quarter awaited us. The new type indeed, the mere modern "psychical" case, washed clean of all queerness as by exposure to a flowing laboratory tap, and equipped with credentials vouching for this—the new type clearly promised little, for the more it was respectably certified the less it seemed of a nature to rouse the dear old sacred terror. Thus it was, I remember, that amid our lament for a beautiful lost form, our distinguished host expressed the wish that he might but have recovered for us one of the scantest of fragments of this form at its best. He had never forgotten the impression made on him as a young man by the withheld glimpse, as it were, of a dreadful matter that had been reported years before, and with as few particulars, to a lady with whom he had youthfully talked. The story would have been thrilling could she but have found herself in better possession of it, dealing as it did with a couple of small children in an out-of-the way place, to whom the spirits of certain "bad" servants, dead in the employ of the house, were believed to have appeared with the design of "getting hold" of them. This was all, but there had been more, which my friend's old converser had lost the thread of: she could only assure him of the wonder of the allegations as she had anciently heard them made. He himself could give us but this shadow of a shadow—my own appreciation of which, I need scarcely say, was exactly wrapped up in that thinness. On the surface there wasn't much, but another grain, none the less, would have spoiled the precious pinch addressed to its end as neatly as some modicum extracted from an old silver snuff-box and held between finger and thumb. I was to remember the haunted children and the prowling servile spirits as a "value," of the disquieting sort, in all conscience sufficient; so that when, after an interval, I was asked for something seasonable by the promoters of a periodical dealing in the time-honoured Christmas-tide toy, I bethought myself at once of the vividest little note for sinister romance that I had ever jotted down.

Such was the private source of "The Turn of the Screw"; and I wondered, I confess, why so fine a germ, gleaming there in the wayside dust of life, had never been deftly picked up. The thing had for me the immense merit of allowing the imagination absolute freedom of hand, of inviting it to act on a perfectly clear field, with no "outside" control involved, no pattern of the usual or the true or the terrible "pleasant" (save always of course the high pleasantry of one's very form) to consort with. This makes in fact the charm of my second reference, that I find here a perfect example of an exercise of the imagination unassisted, unassociated—playing the game, making the score, in the phrase ot our sporting day, off its own bat. To what degree the game was worth playing, I need n't attempt to say: the exercise I have noted strikes me now, I confess, as the interesting thing, the imaginative faculty acting with the *whole* of the case on its hands. The exhibition involved is in other words a fairy-tale pure and simple—save indeed as to its springing not from an artless and measureless, but from a conscious and cultivated credulity. Yet the fairy-tale belongs mainly to either of two classes, the short and sharp and single, charged more or less with the compactness of anecdote (as to which let the familiars of our childhood, Cinderella and Blue-Beard and Hop o' my Thumb and Little Red Riding Hood and many of the gems of the Brothers Grimm directly testify), or else the long and loose, the copious, the various, the endless, where, dramatically speaking, roundness is quite sacrificed—sacrificed to fulness, sacrificed to exuberance, if one will: witness at hazard almost any one of the Arabian Nights. The charm of all these things for the distracted modern mind is in the clear field of experience, as I call it, over which we are thus led to roam; an annexed but independent world in which nothing is right save as we rightly imagine it. We have to do *that,* and we do it happily for the short spurt and in the smaller piece, achieving so perhaps beauty and lucidity; we flounder, we lose breath, on the other hand—that is we fail, not of continuity, but of an agreeable unity, of the "roundness" in which beauty and lucidity largely reside—when we go in, as they say, for great lengths and breadths. And this, oddly enough, not because "keeping it up" is n't abundantly within the compass of the imagination appealed to in certain conditions, but because the finer interest depends just on *how* it is kept up.

Nothing is so easy as improvisation, the running on and

on of invention; it is sadly compromised, however, from the moment its stream breaks bounds and gets into flood. Then the waters may spread indeed, gathering houses and herds and crops and cities into their arms and wrenching off, for our amusement, the whole face of the land—only violating by the same stroke our sense of the course and the channel, which is our sense of the uses of a stream and the virtue of a story. Improvisation, as in the Arabian Nights, may keep on terms with encountered objects by sweeping them in and floating them on its breast; but the great effect it so loses —that of keeping on terms with itself. This is ever, I intimate, the hard thing for the fairy-tale; but by just so much as it struck me as hard did it in "The Turn of the Screw" affect me as irresistibly prescribed. To improvise with extreme freedom and yet at the same time without the possibility of ravage, without the hint of a flood; to keep the stream, in a word, on something like ideal terms with itself: that was here my definite business. The thing was to aim at absolute singleness, clearness and roundness, and yet to depend on an imagination working freely, working (call it) with extravagance; by which law it wouldn't be thinkable except as free and wouldn't be amusing except as controlled. The merit of the tale, as it stands, is accordingly, I judge, that it has struggled successfully with its dangers. It is an excursion into chaos while remaining, like Blue-Beard and Cinderella, but an anecdote—though an anecdote amplified and highly emphasised and returning upon itself; as, for that matter, Cinderella and Blue-Beard return. I need scarcely add after this that it is a piece of ingenuity pure and simple, of cold artistic calculation, an *amusette* to catch those not easily caught (the "fun" of the capture of the merely witless being ever but small), the jaded, the disillusioned, the fastidious. Otherwise expressed, the study is of a conceived "tone," the tone of suspected and felt trouble, of an inordinate and incalculable sort—the tone of tragic, yet of exquisite, mystification. To knead the subject of my young friend's, the supposititious narrator's, mystification thick, and yet strain the expression of it so clear and fine that beauty would result: no side of the matter so revives for me as that endeavour. Indeed if the artistic value of such an experiment be measured by the intellectual echoes it may again, long after, set in motion, the case would make in favour of this little firm fantasy—which I seem to see draw behind it to-day a train of associations. I ought doubtless to blush for thus confessing them so numerous that I can but pick among them for reference. I recall for instance a reproach made me by a reader capable evidently, for the time, of some attention, but not quite capable of enough, who complained that I had n't sufficiently "characterised" my young woman engaged in her labyrinth; had n't endowed her with signs and marks, features and humours, had n't in a word invited her to deal with her own mystery as well as with that of Peter Quint, Miss Jessel and the hapless children. I remember well, whatever the absurdity of its now coming back to me, my reply to that criticism—under which one's artistic, one's ironic heart shook for the instant almost to breaking. "You indulge in that stricture at your ease, and I don't mind confiding to you that—strange as it may appear!—one has to choose ever so delicately among one's difficulties, attaching one's self to the greatest, bearing hard on those and intelligently neglecting the others. If one attempts to tackle them all one is certain to deal completely with none; whereas the effectual dealing with a few casts a blest golden haze under cover of which, like wanton mocking goddesses in clouds, the others find prudent to retire. It was 'déjà très-joli,' in 'The Turn of the Screw,' please believe, the general proposition of our young woman's keeping crystalline her record of so many intense anomalies and obscurities—by which I don't of course mean her explanation of them, a different matter; and I saw no way, I feebly grant (fighting, at the best too, periodically, for every grudged inch of my space) to exhibit her in relations other than those; one of which, precisely, would have been her relation to her own nature. We have surely as much of her own nature as we can swallow in watching it reflect her anxieties and inductions. It constitutes no little of a character indeed, in such conditions, for a young person, as she says, 'privately bred,' that she is able to make her particular credible statement of such strange matters. She has 'authority,' which is a good deal to have given her, and I could n't have arrived at so much had I clumsily tried for more."

For which truth I claim part of the charm latent on occasion in the extracted reasons of beautiful things—putting for the beautiful always, in a work of art, the close, the curious, the deep. Let me place above all, however, under the protection of that presence the side by which this fiction appeals most to consideration: its choice of its way of meeting its gravest difficulty. There were difficulties not so grave: I had for instance simply to renounce all attempt to keep the kind and degree of impression I wished to produce on terms with the to-day so copious psychical record of cases of apparitions. Different signs and circumstances, in the reports, mark these cases; different things are done—though on the whole very little appears to be—by the persons appearing; the point is, however, that some things are never done at all: this negative quantity is large—certain reserves and properties and immobilities consistently impose themselves. Recorded and attested "ghosts" are in other words as little expressive, as little dramatic, above all as little continuous and conscious and responsive, as is consistent with their taking the trouble—and an immense trouble they find it, we gather—to appear at all. Wonderful and interesting therefore at a given moment, they are inconceivable figures in an *action*—and "The Turn of the Screw" was an action, desperately, or it was nothing. I had to decide in fine between having my apparitions correct and having my story "good"- -that is producing my im-

pression of the dreadful, my designed horror. Good ghosts,
speaking by book, make poor subjects, and it was clear that
from the first my hovering prowling blighting presences, my
pair of abnormal agents, would have to depart altogether from
the rules. They would be agents in fact; there would be laid
on them the dire duty of causing the situation to reek with the
air of Evil. Their desire and their ability to do so, visibly meas-
uring meanwhile their effect, together with their observed and
described success—this was exactly my central idea; so that,
briefly, I cast my lot with pure romance, the appearances conforming to the true type being so little romantic.

This is to say, I recognise again, that Peter Quint and Miss
Jessel are not "ghosts" at all, as we now know the ghost, but
goblins, elves, imps, demons as loosely constructed as those of
the old trials for witchcraft; if not, more pleasingly, fairies of
the legendary order, wooing their victims forth to see them
dance under the moon. Not indeed that I suggest their reduci-
bility to any form of the pleasing pure and simple; they please
at the best but through having helped me to express my subject all directly and intensely. Here it was—in the use made of
them—that I felt a high degree of art really required; and here
it is that, on reading the tale over, I find my precautions justified. The essence of the matter was the villainy of motive in
the evoked predatory creatures; so that the result would be
ignoble—by which I mean would be trivial—were this element of evil but feebly or inanely suggested. Thus arose on
behalf of my idea the lively interest of a possible suggestion
and process of *adumbration;* the question of how best to convey that sense of the depths of the sinister without which my
fable would so woefully limp. Portentous evil—how was I
to save that, as an intention on the part of my demon-spirits,
from the drop, the comparative vulgarity, inevitably attending,
throughout the whole range of possible brief illustration, the
offered example, the imputed vice, the cited act, the limited
deplorable presentable instance? To bring the bad dead back

to life for a second round of badness is to warrant them as indeed prodigious, and to become hence as shy of specifications as of a waiting anti-climax. One had seen, in fiction, some grand form of wrong-doing, or better still of wrong-being, imputed, seen it promised and announced as by the hot breath of the Pit—and then, all lamentably, shrink to the compass of some particular brutality, some particular immorality, some particular infamy portrayed: with the result, alas, of the demonstration's falling sadly short. If *my* bad things, for "The Turn of the Screw," I felt, should succumb to this danger, if they should n't seem sufficiently bad, there would be nothing for me but to hang my artistic head lower than I had ever known occasion to do.

The view of that discomfort and the fear of that dishonour, it accordingly must have been, that struck the proper light for my right, though by no means easy, short cut. What, in the last analysis, had I to give the sense of? Of their being, the haunting pair, capable, as the phrase is, of everything—that is of exerting, in respect to the children, the very worst action small victims so conditioned might be conceived as subject to. What would *be* then, on reflexion, this utmost conceivability? —a question to which the answer all admirably came. There is for such a case no eligible *absolute* of the wrong; it remains relative to fifty other elements, a matter of appreciation, speculation, imagination—these things moreover quite exactly in the light of the spectator's, the critic's, the reader's experience. Only make the reader's general vision of evil intense enough, I said to myself—and that already is a charming job—and his own experience, his own imagination, his own sympathy (with the children) and horror (of their false friends) will supply him quite sufficiently with all the particulars. Make him *think* the evil, make him think it for himself, and you are released from weak specifications. This ingenuity I took pains—as indeed great pains were required—to apply; and with a success apparently beyond my liveliest hope. Droll enough at the same

time, I must add, some of the evidence—even when most convincing—of this success. How can I feel my calculation to
have failed, my wrought suggestion not to have worked, that is,
on my being assailed, as has befallen me, with the charge of a
monstrous emphasis, the charge of all indecently expatiating?
There is not only from beginning to end of the matter not an
inch of expatiation, but my values are positively all blanks save
so far as an excited horror, a promoted pity, a created expertness—on which punctual effects of strong causes no writer
can ever fail to plume himself—proceed to read into them
more or less fantastic figures. Of high interest to the author
meanwhile—and by the same stroke a theme for the moralist
—the artless resentful reaction of the entertained person who
has abounded in the sense of the situation. He visits his
abundance, morally, on the artist—who has but clung to an
ideal of faultlessness. Such indeed, for this latter, are some
of the observations by which the prolonged strain of that clinging may be enlivened!

I arrive with "The Liar" (1888) and "The Two Faces"
(1900) at the first members of the considerable group of
shorter, of shortest tales here republished; though I should perhaps place quite in the forefront "The Chaperon" and "The
Pupil," at which we have already glanced. I am conscious
of much to say of these numerous small productions as a
family—a family indeed quite organised as such, with its
proper representatives, its "heads," its subdivisions and its
branches, its poor relations perhaps not least: its unmistakeable train of poor relations in fact, the very poorer, the poorest
of whom I am, in family parlance, for this formal appearance
in society, "cutting" without a scruple. These repudiated members, some of them, for that matter, well-nourished and sub-
stantial presences enough, with their compromising rustiness
plausibly, almost touchingly dissimulated, I fondly figure as
standing wistful but excluded, after the fashion of the outer
fringe of the connected whom there are not carriages enough

to convey from the church—whether (for we have our choice of similes) to the wedding-feast or to the interment! Great tor me from far back had been the interest of the whole "question of the short story," roundabout which our age has, for lamentable reasons, heard so vain a babble; but I foresee occasions yet to come when it will abundantly waylay me. Then it will insist on presenting itself but in too many lights. Little else perhaps meanwhile is more relevant as to "The Liar" than the small fact of its having, when its hour came, quite especially conformed to that custom of shooting straight from the planted seed, of responding at once to the touched spring, of which my fond appeal here to "origins" and evolutions so depicts the sway. When it shall come to fitting, historically, anything like *all* my small children of fancy with their pair of progenitors, and all my reproductive unions with their inevitable fruit, I shall seem to offer my backward consciousness in the image of a shell charged and recharged by the Fates with some patent and infallible explosive. Never would there seem to have been a pretense to such economy of ammunition!

However this may be, I come back, for "The Liar," as for so many of its fellows, to holding my personal experience, poor thing though it may have been, immediately accountable. For by what else in the world but by fatal design had I been placed at dinner one autumn evening of old London days face to face with a gentleman, met for the first time, though favourably known to me by name and fame, in whom I recognised the most unbridled colloquial romancer the "joy of life" had ever found occasion to envy? Under what other conceivable coercion had I been invited to reckon, through the evening, with the type, with the character, with the countenance, of this magnificent master's wife, who, veracious, serene and charming, yet not once meeting straight the eyes of one of us, did her duty by each, and by her husband most of all, without so much as, in the vulgar phrase, turning a hair? It was long ago. but

I have never, to this hour, forgotten the evening itself—embalmed for me now in an old-time sweetness beyond any aspect of my reproduction. I made but a fifth person, the other couple our host and hostess; between whom and one of the company, while we listened to the woven wonders of a summer holiday, the exploits of a salamander, among Mediterranean isles, were exchanged, dimly and discreetly, ever so guardedly, but all expressively, imperceptible lingering looks. It was exquisite, it *could* but become, inevitably, some "short story" or other, which it clearly pre-fitted as the hand the glove. I must reserve "The Two Faces" till I come to speak of the thrilling question of the poor painter's tormented acceptance, in advance, of the scanted canvas; of the writer's rueful hopeful assent to the conditions known to him as "too little room to turn round." Of the liveliest interest then— or so at least I could luckily always project the case—to see how he may nevertheless, in the event, effectively manœuvre. The value of "The Two Faces"—by reason of which I have not hesitated to gather it in—is thus peculiarly an economic one. It may conceal rather than exhale its intense little principle of calculation; but the neat evolution, as I call it, the example of the turn of the *whole* coach and pair in the contracted court, without the "spill" of a single passenger or the derangement of a single parcel, is only in three or four cases (where the coach is fuller still) more appreciable.

X

PREFACE TO "THE REVERBERATOR"

(VOLUME XIII IN THE NEW YORK EDITION. CONTAINING: "THE REVERBERATOR," "MADAME DE MAUVES," "A PASSIONATE PILGRIM," "THE MADONNA OF THE FUTURE," "LOUISA PALLANT")

I HAVE gathered into this volume some early brevities, the third in order of which dates from further back than any tale comprised in the Edition. The first in order appeared considerably later, but I have given it precedence in this group by reason of its greatest length. It is the most recent in the list, but, as having originally (in the good old days, though they are as yet none so remote, of "pleasant" publication) enjoyed the honour of two pretty little volumes "all to itself," it falls into the category of Shorter Novels—under an indulgence not extended to several of its compeers. "The Reverberator," which figured at birth (1888) in half a dozen numbers of "Macmillan's Magazine" may be described, I suppose, beyond any fiction here reproduced, as a *jeu d' esprit:* I can think at least of none other on the brow of which I may presume to place that laurel. And yet as I cast about me for the nameable grounds of the hospitality I thus give it I find myself think of it in other rich lights as well; quite in the light of an exemplary anecdote, and at the same time quite in that of a little rounded drama. This is to press hard, it might seem, on so slight a composition; but I brave the extravagance under the interest of recognising again how the weight of expatiation is ever met in such cases—that of the slender production equally with that of the stout—by a surface really much larger than the mere offered face of the work.

The face of the work may be small in itself, and yet the surface, the whole thing, the associational margin and connexion, may spread, beneath the fond remembering eye, like nothing more noble than an insidious grease-spot. It is of the essence of the anecdote to get itself told as it can—which truth represented clearly the best chance of life for the matter involved in "The Reverberator"; but also it is of the essence of the drama to conform to logic, and the pages I here treat of may appear at moments not quite predominantly sure either of their luck or of their law. This, however, I think, but to a cursory glance, for I perhaps do them a wrong in emphasising their anecdotic cast. Might I not, certainly, have invoked for them in some degree the anecdotic grace I would n't have undertaken them at all; but I now see how they were still to have been provided for if this had failed them.

The anecdote consists, ever, of something that has oddly happened to some one, and the first of its duties is to point directly to the person whom it so distinguishes. He may be you or I or any one else, but a condition of our interest—perhaps the principal one—is that the anecdote shall know him, and shall accordingly speak of him, as its subject. Who is it then that by this rule the specimen before us adopts and sticks to? Something happens, and to a certain person, or, better, to a certain group of persons, in "The Reverberator," but of whom, when it comes to the point, is the fable narrated? The anecdote has always a question to answer—of whom necessarily is it told? Is it told here of the Proberts or of the Dossons? To whom in the instance before us does the principal thing, the thing worth the telling, happen? To the fatal Mr. Flack, to Francie Dosson and her father and sister, lumping them, on the ground of their "racial consciousness," all together?—or to the cluster of scandalised Parisians in general, if not to the girl's distracted young lover in particular? It is easy, alas, to defy a clear statement on this head to be made ("No, I can't say whom or what or *which* I'm about: I seem so sometimes to be about one set and sometimes about another!" the little story is free to plead) whereby anecdotic grace does break down. Fortunately there remains another string, a second, to my bow: I should have been nowhere, in the event of a challenge, had I not concomitantly felt my subject, for all its slightness, as a small straight *action,* and so placed it in that blest drama-light which, really making for intelligibility as nothing else does, orders and regulates, even when but faintly turned on; squares things and keeps them in happy relation to each other. What "happens," by that felicity, happens thus to every one concerned, exactly as in much more prodigious recitals: it's a case—just as we have seen it before, in more portentous connexions and with the support of mightier comparisons —of the planned rotation of aspects and of that "scenic" determination of them about which I fear I may already have been a bore.

After which perhaps too vertiginous explanatory flight I feel that I drop indeed to the very concrete and comparatively trivial origin of my story—short, that is, of some competent critical attribution of triviality all round. I am afraid, at any rate, that with this reminiscence I but watch my grease-spot (for I cling to the homely metaphor) engagingly extend its bounds. Who shall say thus—and I have put the vain question but too often before!—where the associational nimbus of the all but lost, of the miraculously recovered, chapter of experience shall absolutely fade and stop? That would be possible only were experience a chessboard of sharp black-and-white squares. Taking one of these for a convenient plot, I have but to see my particle of suggestion lurk in its breast, and then but to repeat in this connexion the act of picking it up, for the whole of the *rest* of the connexion straightway to loom into life, its parts all clinging together and pleading with a collective friendly voice that I can't pretend to resist: "Oh but we too, you know; what were *we* but of the experience?" Which comes to scarce more than saying indeed, no doubt, that nothing more complicates and overloads the act of retrospect than to let one's imagination itself work backward as part of the business. Some art of preventing this by keeping that interference out would be here of a useful application; and would include the question of providing conveniently for the officious faculty in the absence of its natural caretakers, the judgment, the memory, the conscience, occupied, as it were, elsewhere. These truants, the other faculties of the mind without exception, I surmise, would then be free to remount the stream of time (as an earnest and enquiring band) with the flower of the flock, the hope of the family, left at home or "boarded out," say, for the time of the excursion. I have been unable, I confess, to make such an arrangement; the consequence of which failure is that everything I "find," as I look back, lives for me again in the light of *all* the parts, such as they are, of my intelligence. Or to express the phenomenon otherwise, and perhaps with still more complacency for it, the effort to reconstitute the medium and the season that favoured the first stir of life, the first perceived gleam of the vital spark, in the trifle before us, fairly makes everything in the picture revive, fairly even extends the influence to matters remote and strange. The musing artist's imagination—thus *not* excluded and confined—supplies the link that is missing and makes the whole occasion (the occasion of the glorious birth to him of still another infant motive) comprehensively and richly *one*. And this if that addition to his flock—his effusive parental welcome to which seems immediately to cause so splendid and furnished and fitted a world to arch over it—happens to be even of so modest a promise as the tiny principle of "The Reverberator."

It was in a grand old city of the south of Europe (though neither in Rome nor yet in Florence) long years ago, and during a winter spent there in the seeing of many people on the pleasantest terms in the world, as they now seem to me to have been, as well as in the hearing of infinite talk, talk mainly, inexhaustibly, about persons and the "personal equation" and the personal mystery. This somehow *had* to be in an odd, easy, friendly, a miscellaneous, many-coloured little cosmopolis, where the casual exoteric society was a thing of heterogeneous vivid patches, but with a fine old native basis, the basis that held stoutly enough together while the patches dangled and fluttered, stitched on as with thread of silver, pinned on as with pearls, lasting their time above all and brightening the scene. To allude to the scene, alas! seems half an undertaking to reproduce it, any humoursome indulgence in which would lead us much too far. Nor am I strictly —as if I cultivated an ideal of strictness!—concerned with any fact but that of the appearance among us, that winter, of a charming free young person, superlatively introduced and infinitely admired, who, taken to twenty social bosoms, figured "success" in a form, that of the acclaimed and confident pretty girl of our prosaic and temperate climes, for which the old-world salon, with its windows of iridescent view and its different conception of the range of charm, had never much provided. The old-world salon, in our community, still, when all was said, more or less imposed the type and prescribed the tone; yet to the charming stranger even these penetralia had not been closed, and, over them, to be brief, she had shed her influence, just as among them, not less, she had gathered her harvest. She had come, in fine, she had seen and had conquered; after which she had withdrawn with her spoil. Her spoil, to put it plainly, had been a treasure of impressions; her harvest, as I have said, a wealth of revelations. I made an absence of several weeks, I went to Florence and to Rome, but I came back in the spring—and all to encounter the liveliest chatter of surprise that had perhaps ever spent itself under the elegant massive ceilings for which the old-world salons were famous. The ingenious stranger—it was awfully coming to light—had **written** about them, about these still consciously critical retreats, many of them temples harbouring the very altar of the exclusive; she had made free with them, pen in hand, with the best conscience in the world, no doubt, but to a high effect of confidence betrayed, and to the amazement and consternation of every one involved, though most of all, naturally, to the dismay of her primary backers.

The young lady, frankly, a graceful amateur journalist, had made use of her gathered material; she had addressed to a newspaper in her native city (which no power on earth would induce me to designate, so that as to this and to the larger issue, not less, of the glamour of its big State-name, I defy all guesses) a letter as long, as confidential, as "chatty," as full of headlong history and limping legend, of aberration and confusion, as she might have indited to the most trusted of friends. The friend trusted had been, as happened, simply the biggest "reading public" in the world, and the performance, typographically bristling, had winged its way back to its dishonoured nest like some monstrous black bird or beetle, an embodiment of popping eyes, a whirl of brandished feathers and claws. Strange, it struck me, to tell the truth, the fact itself of "anybody's knowing," and still more of anybody's caring—the fact itself, that is, of such prompt repercussion and recognition: one would so little, in advance, have supposed the reverberation of the bomb, its heeded reverberation, conceivable. No such consequence, clearly, had been allowed for by its innocent maker, for whose imagination, one felt sure, the explosion had not been designed to be world-shaking. The recording, slobbering sheet, as an object thinkable or visible in a medium so non-conducting, made of actual recognition, made even of the barest allusion, the falsest of false notes. The scandal reigned, however, and the commotion lasted, a nine days' wonder; the ingenuous stranger's name became anathema, and all to the high profit of an incorrigible collector of "cases." Him in his depth of perversity, I profess, the flurry of resentment could only, after a little, affect as scarce more charged with wisdom than the poor young lady's miscalculated overflow itself; so completely beside the question of the finer *comparative* interest remained that of the force of the libel and that of the degree of the injury. The finer interest was in the facts that made the incident a case, and the true note of that, I promptly made sure, was just in the extraordinary amount of native innocence that positively *had* to be read into the perpetrated act. The couple of columns in the vulgar newspaper constituted no document whatever on the manners and morals of the company of persons "betrayed," but on the other hand, in its indirect way, flooded "American society" with light, became on *that* side in the highest degree documentary. So it was, I soon saw, that though the perpetrated act was in itself and immediately no "situation," it nevertheless pointed to one, and was for that value to be stored up.

It remained for a long time thus a mere sketched finger-post: the perpetrated act had, unmistakeably, *meant* something—one couldn't make out at first exactly what; till at last, after several years of oblivion, its connexions, its illustrative worth, came quite naturally into view. It fell in short into the wider perspective, the very largest fund of impressions and appearances, perhaps, that the particular observer's and designer's mind was to have felt itself for so long queerly weighted with. I have already had occasion to say that the "international" light lay thick, from period to period, on the general scene of my observation—a truth the reasons and bearings of which will require in due course to be intelligibly stated; everything that possibly could, at any rate, managed at that time (as it had done before and was undiscourageably to continue to do) to *be* international for me: which was an immense resource and a happy circumstance from many points of view. Therefore I may say at once that if no particular element or feature of the view had struck me from far back as receiving so much of the illumination as the comparative *state of innocence* of the spirit of my countryfolk, by that same token everything had a price, was of immediate application and found itself closely interwoven, that could tend to emphasise or vivify the innocence. I had indeed early to recognise that I was in a manner shut up to the contemplation of it—really to the point, it has often seemed to me these pages must testify, of appearing to wander, as under some uncanny spell, amid the level sands and across the patchless desert of a single and of a not especially rich or fruitful aspect. Here, for that matter, comes in one of the oddest and most interesting of facts—as I measure it; which again will take much stating, but to which I may provisionally give *this* importance, that, sketchily speaking, if I had n't had, on behalf of the American character, the negative aspects to deal with, I should practically, and given the limits of my range, have had no aspects at all. I shall on a near pretext, as I say, develop the sense of this; but let it now stand for the obvious truth that the negative sides were always *at* me, for illustration, for interpretation, and that though I looked yearningly, from time to time, over their collective head, though, after an experimental baffled sniff, I was apt to find myself languish for sharper air than any they exhaled, they constantly gave me enough, and more than enough, to "tackle," so that I might even well ask myself what more miscellaneous justice I should have been able to render.

Given, after this fashion, my condition of knowledge, the most general appearance of the American (of those days) in Europe, that of being almost incredibly *unaware of life*—as the European order expressed life—had to represent for me the *whole* exhibitional range; the particular initiation on my own part that would have helped me to other apprehensions being absolutely bolted and barred to me. What this alternative would have stood for we shall immediately see; but meanwhile—and nothing could have been at once more inevitable, more logical and more ridiculous—I was reduced to studying my New Yorkers and my Bostonians, since there were enough of these alone and to spare, under the queer rubric of their more or less stranded helplessness. If asked why I describe in such terms the appearances that most appealed to me, I can only wonder how the bewildered state of the persons principally figuring in the Americano-European prospect could have been otherwise expressed. They come back to me, in the lurid light of contrast, as irresistibly destitute of those elements of preparedness that my pages show even the most limited European adventure to call into play. This at least was, by my retrospect, the inveterate case for the men—it differed only for certain of the women, the younger, the youngest, those of whom least might at the best have been expected, and in the interest of whose "success" their share of the characteristic blankness underwent what one might call a sea-change. Conscious of so few things in the world, these unprecedented creatures—since that is what it came to for them—were least of all conscious of deficiencies and dangers; so that, the grace of youth and innocence and freshness aiding, their negatives were converted and became in certain relations lively positives and values. I might give a considerable list of those of my fictions, longer and shorter, in which this curious conversion is noted. Suffice it, at all events, in respect to the show at large, that, even as testifying but to a suffered and suffering state, and working beauty and comedy and pathos but into that compass, my procession of figures—which kept passing, and indeed kept pausing, by no act of my own—left me with all I could manage on my hands.

This will have seemed doubtless a roundabout approach to my saying that I seized the right connexion for our roaring young lioness of the old-world salons from the moment I qualified her as, in spite of the stimulating commerce enjoyed with them, signally "unaware of life." What had she lacked for interest? what had her case lacked for application? what in the world but just that perceived reference to something larger, something more widely significant? What was so large, what so widely significant in its general sphere, as that, "otherwise" so well endowed and appointed, as that, altogether so well constituted and introduced, she *could* have kept up to the end (the end of our concern with her) the state of un-awareness? Immense at any rate the service she so rendered the brooding critic capable of taking a hint from her, for she became on the spot an inimitable link with the question of what it might distinguishably be in their own flourishing Order that could *keep* them, the passionless pilgrims, so un-aware? This was the point—one had caught them in the act of it; of a disposition, which had perhaps even most a comic side, to treat "Europe," collectively, as a vast painted and gilded holiday toy, serving its purpose on the spot and for the time, but to be relinquished, sacrificed, broken and cast away, at the dawn of any other convenience. It seemed to figure thus not only as a gorgeous dressed doll, the most expensive plaything, no doubt, in the world, but as a *living* doll, precisely, who would speak and act and perform, all for a "charge"—which was the reason both of the amusement and of the cost. Only there was no more *responsibility* to a living doll than to a dead —so that, in fine, what seemed most absent from the frolic intercourse was the note of anything like reciprocity: unless in-deed the so prompt and frequent newspaperisation of any quaint confidence extracted by pressure on the poor doll's stomach, of any droll sight of powers set in motion by twitch of whatever string, might serve for a rendering of that ideal. It had reached one's ear again and again from beyond the sea, this inveteracy, as one might almost call it, of the artless ven-tilation, and mainly in the public prints, of European matter originally gathered in under the supposed law of privilege en-joyed on the one hand and security enjoyed on the other. A hundred good instances confirmed this tradition that nothing in the new world was held accountable to anything in the old, that the hemispheres would have been as dissociated as different planets had n't one of them, by a happy miracle, come in for the comparatively antique right of free fishing in the other.

It was the so oft-attested American sense of the matter that was meanwhile the oddity—the sense on the part of remote adventurous islanders that no custom of give-and-take between their bustling archipelago and the far, the massed continent was thinkable. Strangely enough, none the less, the continent was anecdotically interesting to the islands—though as soon as these were reached all difference between the fruit of the private and the fruit of the public garden naturally dropped. More than all was it striking that the "naturalness" was all of American making—in spite, as had ever seemed to me, of the American tradition to the contrary; the tradition that Europe, much rather, had originally made social commerce unequal. Europe had had quite other matters on her hands; Europe had, into the bargain, on what might n't be newspaperised or otherwise ventilated, quite her own religion and her own practice. This superstition held true of the fruits of curiosity *wherever* socially gathered, whether in bustling archipelagos or in neighbouring kingdoms. It did n't, one felt, immensely signify, all the while; small harm was done, and it was surely rare that any was intended; for supreme, more and more, is the blest truth—sole safety, as it mostly seems, of our distracting age— that a given thing has but to be newspaperised *enough* (which it may, at our present rate of perfection, in a few hours) to return, as a quick consequence, to the common, the abysmal air and become without form and void. This life of scant seconds, as it were, by the sky-scraping clock, is as good for our sense and measure of the vulgar thing, for keeping apprehension down and keeping immunity up, as no life at all; since in the midst of such preposterous pretensions to recorded or reflected existence what particular vulgarity, what individual blatancy, can prevail? Still over and above all of which, too, we are made aware of a large new direct convenience or resource—the beautiful facility thus rendered the individual mind for what it shall denominate henceforth ignoring in the lump: than which nothing is more likely to work better, I suggest, toward a finer economy of consciousness. For the new beauty is that the lump, the vast concretion of the negligible, is, thanks to prodigious expensive machinery working all *ad hoc,* carefully wrought and prepared for our so dealing with it; to the great saving of our labour of selection, our own not always too beguiled or too sweetened picking over of the heap.

Our ingenious young friend of the shocked saloons—to finish *her* history—had just simply acted in the tradition; she had figured herself one of the islanders, irresponsible in their very degree, and with a mind as closed to the "coming back" of her disseminated prattle as if it would have had in fact to be wafted from another planet. Thus, as I say, the friendliest initiations offered her among ancient seats had still failed to make her what I have called "aware." Here it was that she became documentary, and that in the flash of some new and accessory light, the continued procession of figures equally fallible, yet as little criminal, her bedimmed precedent shone out for me once more; so that when I got my right and true reference, as I say, for the instance commemorated in "The Reverberator," and which dangled loosely from the peg supplied by the earlier case, this reference was much more directly to the pathetic than to anything else. The Dosson family, here before us, are sunk in their innocence, sunk in their irremediable unawareness almost beyond fishing out. This constituted for handling them, I quite felt, a serious difficulty; they could be too abandoned and pathetic, as the phrase is, to live, and yet be perfectly true; but on the other hand they could be perfectly true and yet too abandoned for vivification, too consentingly feeble to be worth saving. Even this, still, would n't materially limit in them the force of the characteristic—it was exactly in such formless terms that they would speak best for the majority of their congeners; and, in fine, moreover, there was *this* that I absolutely had to save for the love of my subject-matter at large—the special appeal attached to the mild figure of Francina. I need scarcely point out that "round" Francie Dosson the tale is systematically constructed; with which fact was involved for me the clear sense that if I did n't see the Francie Dossons (by whom I mean the general quaint sisterhood, perfectly distinguishable then, but displaced, disfeatured, "discounted" to-day, for all I know) as always and at any cost—at whatever cost of repetition, that is—worth saving, I might as well shut up my international department. For practically—as I have said already more than enough to convey—they were what the American branch of that equation constantly threw me back upon; by reason indeed of a brace of conditions only one of which strictly inhered in the show itself.

In the heavy light of "Europe" thirty or forty years ago, there were more of the Francie Dossons and the Daisy Millers and the Bessie Aldens and the Pandora Days than of all the other attested American objects put together—more of them, of course I mean, from the moment the weird harvester was at all preoccupied with charm, or at all committed to "having to have" it. But quite apart from that truth was always the stiff fact, against which I might have dashed myself in vain, that I hadn't the *data* for a right approach to the minor quantities, such as they might have been made out to be. The minor quantities appeared, consistently, but in a single light—that of promiscuous obscure attendance on the Daisies and Bessies and Francies; a generalized crepuscular state at best, even though yielding little by little a view of dim forms and vague differences. These adumbrations, sufficient tests once applied, claimed identities as fathers, mothers, even sometimes as satellites more directly "engaged"; but there was always, for the author of this record, a prompt and urgent remark to be made about them —which placed him, when all was said, quite at his ease. The men, the non-European, in these queer clusters, the fathers, brothers, playmates, male appendages of whatever presumption, were visible and thinkable only as the American "business-man"; and before the American business-man, as I have been prompt to declare, I was absolutely and irredeemably helpless, with no fibre of my intelligence responding to his mystery. No approach I could make to him on his "business side" really got near it. That is where I was fatally incompetent, and this in turn—the case goes into a nutshell—is so obviously why, for any decent documentation, I was simply shut up to what was left me. It takes but a glance to see how the matter was in such a fashion simplified. With the men wiped out, at a stroke, so far as any grasp of the principle of their activity was concerned (what in the name of goodness did I, or could I, know, to call know, about the very alphabet of their activity?), it wasn't the *elder* woman I could take, on any reckoning, as compensatory: her inveterate blankness of surface had a manner all its own of defying the imagination to hover or to hope. There was really, as a rule, nothing whatever to be done with the elder woman; not only were reason and fancy alike forewarned not to waste their time, but any attempt upon her, one somehow felt, would have been indecorous and almost monstrous. She wasn't so much as in question; since if one could work it out for the men that the depreciated state with which *they* vaguely and, as it were, somnolently struggled, was perhaps but casual and temporary, might be regarded in fact as the mere state of the medal with its right face accidentally turned down, this redemption never glimmered for the wife and mother, in whom nothing was in eclipse, but everything rather (everything there was at all) straight in evidence, and to whom therefore any round and complete embodiment had simply been denied.

"A Passionate Pilgrim," written in the year 1870, the earliest date to which anything in the whole present series refers itself, strikes me to-day, and by the same token indescribably touches me, with the two compositions that follow it, as sops instinctively thrown to the international Cerberus formidably posted where I doubtless then did n't quite make him out, yet from whose capacity to loom larger and larger with the years there must already have sprung some chilling portent. Cerberus would have been, thus, to one's younger artistic conscience, the keeper of the international "books"; the hovering disembodied critical spirit with a disengaged eye upon sneaking attempts to substitute the American romantic for the American real. To that comparatively artless category the fiction I have just named, together with "Madame de Mauves" and "The Madonna of the Future," belong. As American as possible, and even to the pitch of fondly coaxing it, I then desired my ground-stuff to remain; so that such situations as are thus offered must have represented my prime view of the telling effect with which the business-man would be dodged. He *is* dodged, here, doubtless, to a charm—he is made to wait as in the furthest and coldest of an infinite perspective of more or less quaint antechambers; where my ingenuous theory of the matter must have been that, artfully trifled with from room to room and from pretext to pretext, he might be kept indefinitely at bay. Thus if a sufficient amount of golden dust were kicked up in the foreground—and I began to kick it, under all these other possible pretexts, as hard as I knew how, he would probably never be able, to my confusion, to break through at all. I had in the spring of 1869, and again in that of 1870, spent several weeks in England, renewing and extending, with infinite zest, an acquaintance with the country that had previously been but an uneffaced little chapter of boyish, or—putting it again far enough back for the dimmest dawn of sensibility—of infinite experience; and had, perceptively and æsthetically speaking, taken the adventure of my twenty-sixth year "hard," as "A Passionate Pilgrim" quite sufficiently attests.

A part of that adventure had been the never-to-be-forgotten thrill of a first sight of Italy, from late in the summer of 1869 on; so that a return to America at the beginning of the following year was to drag with it, as a lengthening chain, the torment of losses and regrets. The repatriated victim of that unrest was, beyond doubt, acutely conscious of his case: the fifteen months just spent in Europe had absolutely determined his situation. The nostalgic poison had been distilled for him, the future presented to him but as a single intense question: was he to spend it in brooding exile, or might he somehow come into his "own"?—as I liked betimes to put it for a romantic analogy with the state of dispossessed princes and wandering heirs. The question was to answer itself promptly enough—yet after a delay sufficient to give me the measure of a whole previous relation to it. I had from as far back as I could remember carried in my side, buried and unextracted, the head of one of those well-directed shafts from the European quiver to which, of old, tender American flesh was more helplessly and bleedingly exposed, I think, than to-day: the nostalgic cup had been applied to my lips even before I was conscious of it—I had been hurried off to London and to Paris immediately after my birth, and then and there, I was ever afterwards strangely to feel, that poison had entered my veins. This was so much the case that when again, in my thirteenth year, re-exposure was decreed, and was made effective and prolonged, my inward sense of it was, in the oddest way, not of my finding myself in the vague and the uncharted, but much rather restored to air already breathed and to a harmony already disclosed. The unnatural precocity with which I had in fine "taken" to Europe was to be revealed to me later on and during another quite languishing American interval; an interval during which I supposed my young life to have been made bitter, under whatever appearances of smug accommodation, by too prompt a mouthful—recklessly administered to one's helplessness by responsible hands—of the fruit of the tree of knowledge. Why otherwise so queer a taste, always, in so juvenile, so *generally* gaping, a mouth? Well, the queer taste doubtless had been there, but the point of my anecdote, with my brace of infatuated "short stories" for its occasion, is in the infinitely greater queerness it was to take on between the summer of '70 and that of '72, when it set me again in motion.

As I read over "A Passionate Pilgrim" and "The Madonna of the Future" they become in the highest degree documentary for myself—from all measure of such interest as they may possibly have at this time of day for others I stand off; though I disengage from them but one thing, their betrayal of their consolatory use. The deep beguilement of the lost vision recovered, in comparative indigence, by a certain inexpert intensity of art—the service rendered by them at need, with whatever awkwardness and difficulty—sticks out of them for me to the exclusion of everything else and consecrates them, I freely admit, to memory. "Madame de Mauves" and "Louisa Pallant" are another matter; the latter, in especial, belongs to recent years. The former is of the small group of my productions yielding to present research no dimmest responsive ghost of a traceable origin. These remarks have constituted to excess perhaps the record of what may have put this, that and the other treated idea into my head; but I am quite unable to say what, in the summer of 1873, may have put "Madame de Mauves." Save for a single pleasant image, and for the fact that, dispatched to New York, the tale appeared, early in the following year, in "The Galaxy," a periodical to which I find, with this, twenty other remembrances gratefully attached, not a glimmer of attendant reference survives. I recall the tolerably wide court of an old inn at Bad-Homburg in the Taunus hills—a dejected and forlorn little place (its *seconde jeunesse* not yet in sight) during the years immediately following the Franco-Prussian war, which had overturned, with that of Baden-Baden, its altar, the well-appointed worship of the great goddess Chance—a homely enclosure on the ground-level of which I occupied a dampish, dusky, unsunned room, cool, however, to the relief of the fevered muse, during some very hot weather. The place was so dark that I could see my way to and from my inkstand, I remember, but by keeping the door to the court open—thanks to which also the muse, witness of many mild domestic incidents, was distracted and beguiled. In this retreat I was visited by the gentle Euphemia; I sat in crepuscular comfort pouring forth again, and, no doubt, artfully editing, the confidences with which she honoured me. She again, after her fashion, was what I might have called experimentally international; she muffled her charming head in the lightest, finest, vaguest tissue of romance and put twenty questions by. "Lousia Pallant," with still subtler art, I find, completely covers her tracks—her repudiation of every ray of legend being the more marked by the later date (1888) of her appearance. Charitably affected to her and thus disposed, if the term be not arrogant, to hand her down, I yet win from her no shadow of an intelligible account of herself. I had taken possession, at Florence, during the previous year, of a couple of sunny rooms on the Arno just at the point where the Borg' Ognissanti begins to bore duskily westward; and in those cheerful chambers (where the pitch of brightness differed so from that of the others just commemorated) I seem to have found my subject seated in extreme assurance. I did my best for it one February while the light and the colour and the sound of old Italy played in again through my open windows and about my patient table after the bold loud fashion that I had had, from so much before, to teach myself to think directly auspicious when it might be, and indirectly when it might n't.

XI

PREFACE TO "LADY BARBARINA"

(VOLUME XIV IN THE NEW YORK EDITION. CONTAINING: "LADY BARBARINA," "THE SIEGE OF LONDON," "AN INTERNATIONAL EPISODE," "THE PENSION BEAUREPAS," "A BUNDLE OF LETTERS," "THE POINT OF VIEW")

I HAVE gathered into this volume several short fictions of the type I have already found it convenient to refer to as "international"—though I freely recognise, before the array of my productions, of whatever length and whatever brevity, the general applicability of that term. On the interest of *contrasted* things any painter of life and manners inevitably much depends, and contrast, fortunately for him, is easy to seek and to recognise; the only difficulty is in presenting it again with effect, in extracting from it its sense and its lesson. The reader of these volumes will certainly see it offered in no form so frequent or so salient as that of the opposition of aspects from country to country. Their author, I am quite aware, would seem struck with no possibility of contrast in the human lot so great as that encountered as we turn back and forth between the distinctively American and the distinctively European outlook. He might even perhaps on such a showing be representd as scarce aware, before the human scene, of any other sharp antithesis at all. He is far from denying that this one has always been vivid for him; yet there are cases in which, however obvious and however contributive, its office for the particular demonstration, has been quite secondary, and in which the work is by no means merely addressed to the illustration of it. These things have had in the latter case their proper subject: as, for instance, the subject of "The Wings of the Dove," or that of "The Golden Bowl," ha.

not been the exhibited behaviour of certain Americans as Americans, of certain English persons as English, of certain Romans as Romans. Americans, Englishmen, Romans are, in the whole matter, agents or victims; but this is in virtue of an association nowadays so developed, so easily to be taken for granted, as to have created a new scale of relations altogether, a state of things from which *emphasised* internationalism has either quite dropped or is well on its way to drop. The dramatic side of human situations subsists of course on contrast; and when we come to the two novels I have just named we shall see, for example, just how they positively provide themselves with that source of interest. We shall see nevertheless at the same time that the subject could in each case have been perfectly expressed had *all* the persons concerned been only American or only English or only Roman or whatever.

If it be asked then, in this light, why they deviate from that natural harmony, why the author resorts to the greater extravagance when the less would serve, the answer is simply that the course taken has been, on reflexion, the course of the greater amusement. That is an explanation adequate, I admit, only when itself a little explained—but I shall have due occasion to explain it. Let me for the moment merely note that the very condition I here glance at—that of the achieved social fusion, say, without the sense and experience of which neither "The Wings of the Dove," nor "The Golden Bowl," nor "The Portrait of a Lady," nor even, after all, I think, "The Ambassadors," would have been written—represents a series of facts of the highest interest and one that, at this time of day, the late-coming observer and painter, the novelist sometimes depressed by all the drawbacks of a literary form overworked and relaxed, can only rejoice to meet in his path and to measure more and more as a portent and an opportunity. In proportion as he intelligently meets it, and more especially in proportion as he may happen to have "assisted" from far back at so many of the odd and fresh phenomena involved, must he see a vast new province, infinitely peopled and infinitely elastic—by which I mean with incalculable power to grow—annexed to the kingdom of the dramatist. On this point, however, much more is to be said than I can touch on by the way—so that I return to my minor contention; which is that in a whole group of tales I here collect the principle of illustration has on the other hand quite definitely been that the idea could *not* have expressed itself without the narrower application of international terms. The contrast in "Lady Barbarina" depends altogether on the immitigable Anglicism of this young woman and that equally marked projection of New York elements and objects which, surrounding and framing her figure, throws it into eminent relief. She has her personal qualities, but the very interest, the very curiosity of the matter is that her imbroglio is able to attest itself with scarce so much as a reference to them. It plays itself out quite consistently on the plane of her general, her instinctive, her exasperatedly conscious ones. The others, the more intimate, the subtler, the finer—so far as there may have been such—virtually become, while the story is enacted, not relevant, though their relevancy might have come up on some other basis.

But that this is true, always in its degree, of each of the other contributions to the class before us, we shall sufficiently make out, I think, as we take them in their order. I am only struck, I may indeed parenthesise, with the inveteracy of the general ground (not to say of the extension I give it) over which my present remarks play. It does thus in truth come home to me that, combining and comparing in whatever proportions and by whatever lights, my "America" and its products would doubtless, as a theme, have betrayed gaps and infirmities enough without such a kicking-up of the dramatic dust (mainly in the foreground) as I could set my "Europe" in motion for; just as my Europe would probably have limped across our stage to no great effect of processional state without an ingenuous young America (constantly seen as ingenuous and young) to hold up

its legendary train.. At the same time I pretend not at all to regret my having had from the very first to see my workable
world all and only as an unnatural mixture. No mixture, for
that matter, is quite unnatural unless quite sterile, and the
particular range of associations that betimes, to my eyes,
blocked out everything else, blocked out aspects and combinations more simply conditioned, was at least not open to the reproach of not giving me results. These were but what they
could be, of course; but such as they were, at all events, here am
I at this time of day quite earnestly grouping, distinguishing,
discussing them. The great truth in the whole connexion,
however, is, I think, that one never really chooses one's general
range of vision—the experience from which ideas and themes
and suggestions spring: this proves ever what it has *had* to be,
this is one with the very turn one's life has taken; so that whatever it "gives," whatever it makes us feel and think of, we regard very much as imposed and inevitable. The subject thus
pressed upon the artist is the necessity of his case and the fruit
of his consciousness; which truth makes and has ever made of
any quarrel with his subject, any stupid attempt to go behind
that, the true stultification of criticism. The author of these remarks has in any case felt it, from far back, quite his least
stupid course to meet halfway, as it were, the turn taken and
the perceptions engendered by the tenor of his days. Here it is
that he has never pretended to "go behind"—which would have
been for him a deplorable waste of time. The thing of profit
is to *have* your experience—to recognise and understand it, and
for this almost any will do; there being surely no absolute ideal
about it beyond getting from it all it has to give. The artist—
for it is of this strange brood we speak—has but to have his
honest sense of life to find it fed at every pore even as the birds
of the air are fed; with more and more to give, in turn, as a
consequence, and, quite by the same law that governs the responsive affection of a kindly-used animal, in proportion as
more and more is confidently asked.

All of which, however, doubtless wanders a little far from my mild argument—that of my so grateful and above all so well-advised primary acceptance of a *determined* array of appearances. What I was clearly to be treated to by fate—with the early-taken ply I have already elsewhere glanced at—was (should I have the intelligence to embrace it) some considerable occasion to appreciate the mixture of manners. So, as I say, there would be a decent economy in cultivating the intelligence; through the sincerity of which process I have plucked, I hold, every little flower of a "subject" pressed between the leaves of these volumes. I am tempted indeed to make for my original lucidity the claim of something more than bare prudence—almost that of a happy instinctive foresight. This is what I mean by having been "well-advised." It was as if I had, vulgarly speaking, received quite at first the "straight tip"—to back the right horse or buy the right shares. The mixture of manners was to become in other words not a less but a very much more appreciable and interesting subject of study. The mixture of manners was in fine to loom large and constantly larger all round; it was to be a matter, plainly, about which the future would have much to say. Nothing appeals to me more, I confess, as a "critic of life" in any sense worthy of the name, than the finer—if indeed thereby the less easily formulated—group of the conquests of civilisation, the multiplied symptoms among educated people, from wherever drawn, of a common intelligence and a social fusion tending to abridge old rigours of separation. This too, I must admit, in spite of the many-coloured sanctity of such rigours in general, which have hitherto made countries smaller but kept the globe larger, and by which immediate strangeness, immediate beauty, immediate curiosity were so much fostered. Half our instincts work for the maintained differences; without them, for instance, what would have been the point of the history of poor Lady Barbarina? I have out to put that question, I must add, to feel it beautifully large; for there looms before me at its touch the vision of a

LADY BARBARINA

Lady Barbarina reconciled, domesticated, developed, of possibly greater vividness than the quite other vision expressed in these pages. It is a question, however, of the tendency, perceptive as well as reflective too, of the braver imagination—which faculty, in our future, strikes me as likely to be appealed to much less by the fact, by the pity and the misery and the greater or less grotesqueness, of the courageous, or even of the timid, missing their lives beyond certain stiff barriers, than by the picture of their more and more steadily making out their opportunities and their possible communications. Behind all the small comedies and tragedies of the international, in a word, has exquisitely lurked for me the idea of some eventual sublime consensus of the educated; the exquisite conceivabilities of which, intellectual, moral, emotional, sensual, social, political—all, I mean, in the face of felt difficulty and danger—constitute stuff for such "situations" as may easily make many of those of a more familiar type turn pale. *There,* if one will—in the dauntless fusions to come—is the personal drama of the future.

We are far from it certainly—as I have delayed much too long to remark—in the chronicle of Lady Barb. I have placed this composition (1888) at the top of my list, in the present cluster, despite the earlier date of some of its companions; consistently giving it precedence by reason of its greatest length. The idea at the root of it scarcely brooks indication, so inevitable had it surely become, in all the conditions, that a young Englishwoman in some such predicament should figure as the happy pictorial thought. The whole thing rests, I need scarce point out, on the most primitive logic. The international relation had begun to present itself "socially," after the liveliest fashion, a quarter of a century ago and earlier, as a relation of intermarrying; but nothing was meanwhile so striking as that these manifestations took always the same turn. The European of "position" married the young American woman, or the young American woman married the European of position—one scarce knew how best to express the regularity of it; but the social field was scanned in vain for a different pairing. No American citizen appeared to offer his hand to the "European" girl, or if he did so offered it in vain. The bridal migrations were eastward without exception—as rigidly as if settled by statute. Custom clearly had acquired the force of law; a fact remarkable, significant, interesting and even amusing. And yet, withal, it seemed scarce to demand explanations. So far as they appeared indeed they were confident on the American side. The representatives of that interest had no call in life to go "outside" for their wives—having obviously close at hand the largest and choicest assortment of such conveniences; as was sufficiently proved by the European "run" on the market. What American run on any foreign market had been noted?—save indeed always on the part of the women! It all redounded to the honour and glory of the young woman grown in American conditions —to cast discredit on whose general peerlessness by attested preference for other types could but strike the domestic aspirant as an act of disloyalty or treachery. It was just the observed rarity of the case therefore that prompted one to put it to the imaginative test. Any case so unlikely to happen—taking it for at all conceivable—could only be worth attention when it *should*, once in a blue moon, occur. There was nothing meanwhile, in truth, to "go by"; we had seen the American girl "of position" absorbed again and again into the European social system, but we had only seen young foreign candidates for places as cooks and housemaids absorbed into the American. The more one viewed the possible instance, accordingly, the more it appealed to speculative study; so that, failing all valid testimony, one had studiously, as it were, to forge the very documents.

I have only to add that I found mine, once I had produced them, thoroughly convincing: the most one could do, in the conditions, was to make one's picture appear to hang together, and I should have broken down, no doubt, had my own, after a superficial question or two, not struck me as decently hanging.

The essential, at the threshold, I seem to recall, was to get my young man right—I somehow quite took for granted the getting of my young woman. Was this because, for the portrait of Lady Barb, I felt appealed to so little in the name of *shades?* Shades would be decidedly neither of her general world nor of her particular consciousness: the image I had in view was a maiden nature that, after a fashion all its own, should show as fine and complete, show as neither coarse nor poor, show above all as a resultant of many causes, quite without them. I felt in short sure of Lady Barb, and I think there is no question about her, or about the depth of root she might strike in American soil, that I shouldn't have been ready on the spot to answer. Such is the luck of the conception that imposes itself *en bloc*— or such at least the artist's luck in face of it; such certainly, to begin with and "subjectively" speaking, is the great advantage of a character all of a piece: immediacy of representation, the best omens for felicity, then so honourably await it. It was Jackson Lemon and *his* shades, comparatively, and his comparative sense for shades, that, in the tale, most interested me. The one thing fine-drawn in his wife was that she had been able to care for him as he was: to almost every one and every thing else equally American, to almost every one and every thing else so sensibly stamped, toned and warranted, she was to find herself quite otherwise affected. With her husband the law was reversed—he had, much rather, imputed authority and dignity, imputed weight and charm, to the antecedents of which she was so fine and so direct a consequence; his estimate, his appreciation of her being founded thus on a vision of innumerable close correspondences. It is that vision in him that is racked, and at so many fine points, when he finds their experiment come so near failure; all of which—at least as I seem to see it again so late in the day—lights his inward drama as with the never-quenched lamp of a sacred place. His wife's, on the other hand, goes on in comparatively close darkness.

It is indeed late in the day that I thus project the ray of *my* critical lantern, however; for it comes over me even as I write that the general air in which most of these particular flowers of fancy bloom is an air we have pretty well ceased to breathe. "Lady Barbarina" is, as I have said, scarce a quarter of a century old; but so many of the perceived conditions in which it took birth have changed that the account of them embodied in that tale and its associates will already pass for ancient history. "Civilisation" and education move fast, after all, and too many things have happened; too many *sorts* of things, above all, seem more and more likely to happen. This multiplication of kinds of occurrences, I make no doubt, will promote the inspiration of observers and poets to come; but it may meanwhile well make for an effect of superannuation in any record of the leaner years. Jackson Lemon's has become a more frequent adventure and Lady Barbarina is to-day as much at her ease in New York, in Washington, at Newport, as in London or in Rome. If this is her case, moreover, it is still more that of little Mrs. Headway, of "The Siege of London" (1883), who suffers, I feel, by the sad circumstance that her type of complication, or, more exactly speaking perhaps, that of the gentlemen concerned with her, is no longer eminent, or at least salient. Both she and her friends have had too many companions and successors; so that to reinvest them with historic importance, with individual dignity, I have to think of them rather as brave precursors, as adventurous skirmishers and *éclaireurs*. This does n't diminish, I recognise, any interest that may reside in the form either of "The Siege" aforesaid or of its congeners "An International Episode," "A Bundle of Letters" and "The Pension Beaurepas." Or rather indeed perhaps I should distinguish among these things and, if presuming to claim for several some hint of the distinction we may see exemplified in any first-class art-museum, the distinction of the archaic subject treated by a "primitive" master of high finish, yet notice duly that others are no more "quaint" than need be. What has really happened, I think, is that the *great* international cases, those that bristle with fifty sorts of social reference and overflow, and, by the same token, with a hundred illustrations of social incoherence, are now equally taken for granted on all sides of the sea, have simply become incidents and examples of the mixture of manners, as I call it, and the thicker fusion: which may mean nothing more, in truth, but that social incoherence (with the sense for its opposite practically extinct among the nations) has at last got itself accepted, right and left, as normal.

So much, as I put it, for the great cases; but a certain freshness, I make out, still hangs strangely enough about the smaller and the more numerous; those to which we owe it that such anecdotes—in my general array—as "Pandora," as "Fordham Castle," as "Flickerbridge," as "Miss Gunton of Poughkeepsie," are by no means false even to present appearances. "The Pension Beaurepas" is not alone, thanks to some of its associations, in glowing for me with the tender grace of a day that is dead; and yet, though the accidents and accessories, in such a picture, may have been marked for change, why shall not the essence of the matter, the situation of Mr. and Mrs. Ruck and their daughter at old Geneva—for there is of course a new, a newer Geneva—freely recur? I am careful to put it as a question, and all for a particular reason—the reason that, to be frank, I find myself, before the vast diluvian occidental presence in Europe, with its remorseless rising tide and its positive expression of almost nothing but quantity and number, deprived, on definite and ample grounds, of the precious faculty of confidence. This confidence was of old all instinctive, in face of the "common run" of appearances, the even then multitudinous, miscellaneous minor international phenomena, those of which the "short story," as contemporaneously practised, could effect a fairly prompt and easy notation; but it is now unmistakeable that to come forth, from whatever privacy, to almost any one of the great European highways, and more particularly perhaps to approach the ports of traffic for the lately-developed and so flourishing "southern route" from New York and Boston, is te encounter one of those big general questions that sturdily brush away the multiplication of small answers. "Who are they, what are they, whence and whither and why?" the "critic of life," international or other, still, or more and more, asks himself, as he of course always asked, but with the actual difference that the reply that used to come so conveniently straight, "Why, they're just the American vague variety of the dear old Anglo-Saxon race," not only hangs fire and leaves him to wait and wonder, but really affects him as having for this act of deference (as to which he can't choose, I admit) little more than a conscious mocking, baffling, in fact a just all but sinister, grimace. "Don't you wish you knew, or even *could* know?" the inscrutable grin seems to convey; and with resources of cynicism behind it not in the least to be disturbed by any such cheap retort as "Don't you wish that, on your side, *you* could say—or even. for your own convenience, so much as guess?"

For there is no communicating to the diluvian presence, on such a scale, any suspicion that convenience shall anywhere fail it: all its consciousness, on that general head, is that of itself representing and actively *being* the biggest convenience of the world. Little need to insist on the guarantee of subjective ease involved in such an attitude—the immense noted growth of which casts its chill, as I intimate, on the enquirer proceeding from settled premisses. He was aware formerly, when it came to an analysis, of all his presumptions; he had but to glance for an immemorial assurance at a dozen of the myriad "registers" disposed in the vestibules of bankers, the reading-rooms of hotels and "exchanges," open on the most conspicuous table of visited palace and castle, to see them bristle with names of a more or less conceivable tradition. Queer enough often, whether in isolation or in association, were these gages of identity: but their queerness, not independent of some more or less traceable weird law, was exactly, after all, their most familiar note. They had their way of not breaking, through it all, the old sweet Anglo-Saxon spell; they had their way of not failing, when all was said, to suggest more communities and comprehensions than conundrums and "stunts." He would be brave, however, who should say that any such ghost of a quiet conformity presides in the fulness of time over the interminable passenger-lists that proclaim the prosperity of the great conveying companies. If little books have their fates, little names—and long ones still more—have their eloquence; the emphasis of nominal reference in the general roll-call falls so strongly upon alien syllables and sounds, representative signs that fit into our "English" legend (as we were mainly conscious up to a few years since of having inherited that boon) scarcely more than if borrowed from the stony slabs of Nineveh. I may not here attempt to weigh the question of what these exotic symbols positively represent—a prodigious question, I cannot but think; I content myself with noting the difference made for fond fancy by the so rapidly established change, by the so considerable drop of old associations. The point is of one's having the heart to assume that the Ninevites, as I may momentarily call them for convenience, are to be constantly taken as feeling in the same way about fifty associational matters as we used, in all satisfaction, to observe our earlier generations feel. One can but speak for one's self, and my imagination, on the great highways, I find, doesn't rise to such people, who are obviously beyond my divination. They strike one, above all, as giving no account of themselves in any terms already consecrated by human use; to this inarticulate state they probably form, collectively, the most unprecedented of monuments; abysmal the mystery of what they think, what they feel, what they want, what they suppose themselves to be saying. There would appear to be to-day no slim scrap even of a Daisy Miller to bridge the chasm; no light-footed Francie Dosson or Pandora Day to dance before one across the wavering plank.

I plead a blank of memory as to the origin of "The Siege of London"; I get no nearer to the birth of the idea than by recalling a certain agitation of the spirit, a lively irritation of the temper, under which, one evening early in the autumn of 1877, that is more than thirty years ago, I walked away from the close of a performance at the Théâtre Français. The play had been "Le Demi-Monde" of the younger Dumas, a masterpiece which I had not heard for the first time, but a particular feature of which on this occasion more than ever yet filled up the measure of my impatience. I could less than ever swallow it, Olivier de Jalin's denunciation of Madame d'Ange; the play, from the beginning, marches toward it—it is the main hinge of the action; but the very perfection with which the part was rendered in those years by Delaunay (just as Croizette was pure perfection as Suzanne) seemed to have made me present at something inhuman and odious. It was the old story—that from the positive, the prodigious *morality* of such a painter of the sophisticated life as Dumas, not from anything else or less edifying, one must pray to be delivered. There are doubtless many possible views of such a dilemma as Olivier's, the conflict of propriety for him between the man he likes and esteems and the woman he has loved but has n't esteemed and does n't, and as to whom he sees his friend blind, and, as he thinks, befooled; in consequence of which I am not re-judging his case. But I recover with a pensive pleasure that is almost all a pang the intensity with which I could then feel it; to the extent of wondering whether the general situation of the three persons concerned, or something like it, might n't be shown as taking quite another turn. Was there not conceivable an Olivier of our race, a different Olivier altogether, moved to ask himself how at such a juncture a "real gentleman," distressed and perplexed, would yet most naturally act? The question would be interesting, it was easy to judge, if only by the light it might throw on some of the other, the antecedent and concomitant, phases of a real gentleman's connexion "at all at all" with such a business and such a world. It remained with me, at all events, and was to prove in time the germ of "The Siege of London"; of the conception of which the state of mind so reflected strikes me as making, I confess, very ancient history.

Far away and unspeakably regretted the days, alas, or, more exactly, the nights, on which one could walk away from the Français under the spell of such fond convictions and such deep and agitating problems. The emphasis of the international proposition has indeed had time, as I say, to place itself elsewhere—if, for that matter, there be any emphasis or any proposition left at all—since the age when that particular pleasure seemed the keenest in life. A few months ago, one evening, I found myself withdrawing from the very temple and the supposedly sacred rites before these latter were a third over: beneath that haunted dome itself they seemed to have become at last so accessible, cynically making their bargain with them, to the profanations long kept at bay. Only, with that evolution of taste possible on the part of the old worshipper in question, what world-convulsions might n't, in general, well have taken place? Let me continue to speak of the rest of the matter here before us as therefore of almost pre-historic reference. I was to make, in due course, at any rate, my limited application of that glimmering image of a M. de Jalin with whom we might have more fellow-feeling, and I sent "The Siege of London" accordingly to my admirable friend the late Leslie Stephen, then editor of "The Cornhill Magazine," where it appeared during the two first months of 1883. That is all I remember about it save always the particular London light in which at that period I invoked the muse and drove the pen and with which the compositions resulting strike my fancy to-day as so closely interfused that in reading over those of them I here preserve every aspect and element of my scene of application lives again for me. This scene consisted of small chambers in a small street that opened, at a very near corner, into Piccadilly and a view of the Green Park; I had dropped into them almost instantaneously, under the accepted heavy pressure of the autumnal London of 1876, and was to sit scribbling in them for nearly ten years. The big human rumble of Piccadilly (all human and equine then and long after) was close at hand; I liked to think that Thackeray's Curzon Street, in which Becky Sharp, or rather Mrs. Rawdon Crawley, had lived, was not much further off: I thought of it preponderantly, in my comings and goings, as Becky's and her creator's; just as I was to find fifty other London neighbourhoods speak to me almost only with the voice, the thousand voices, of Dickens.

A "great house," forming the southwest corner of Piccadilly and with its long and practically featureless side, continued by the high wall of its ample court, opposite my open-eyed windows, gloomed, in dusky brick, as the extent of my view, but with a vast convenient neutrality which I found, soon enough, protective and not inquisitive, so that whatever there was of my sedentary life and regular habits took a sort of local wealth of colour from the special greyish-brown tone of the surface always before me. This surface hung there like the most voluminous of curtains—it masked the very stage of the great theatre of the town. To sit for certain hours at one's desk before it was somehow to occupy in the most suitable way in the world the proportionately ample interests of the mightiest of dramas. When I went out it was as if the curtain rose; so that, to repeat, I think of my tolerably copious artistry of that time as all the fruit of the inter-acts, with the curtain more or less quietly down and with the tuning of fiddles and only the vague rumble of shifted scenery playing round it and through it. There were absences of course: "A Bundle of Letters," here reproduced took birth (1879) during certain autumn weeks spent in Paris, where a friend of those years, a young London journalist, the late Theodore Child (of Merton College Oxford, who was to die, prematurely and lamentedly, during a gallant professional tour of exploration in Persia) was fondly carrying on, under difficulties, an Anglo-American periodical called "The Parisian." He invited me to contribute to its pages, and again, a small sharply-resonant street off the Rue de la Paix, where all existence somehow went on as a repercussion from well-brushed asphalt, lives for me as the scene of my response. A snowstorm of a violence rare in Paris raged, I recollect, for many hours, for the greater part of a couple of days; muffling me noiselessly into the small, shiny, shabby salon of an *hôtel garni* with a droll combinational, almost cosmic sign, and promoting (it comes back to me) a deep concentration, an unusual straightness of labour. "A Bundle of Letters" was written in a single long session and, the temperature apart, at a "heat." Its companion-piece, "The Point of View," marks not less for memory, I find, an excursion associated with diligence. I have no heart to "go into" these mere ingenious and more or less effective pleasantries to any tune beyond this of glancing at the *other*, the extinct, actualities they hold up the glimmering taper to. They are still faintly scented, doubtless, with something of that authenticity, and a living work of art, however limited, pretends always, as for part of its grace, to some good faith of community, however indirect, with its period and place.

To read over "The Point of View" has opened up for me, I confess, no contentious vista whatever, nothing but the faded iridescence of a far-away Washington spring. This, in 1881, had been my first glimpse of that interesting city, where I then spent a few weeks, a visit repeated the following year; and I remember beginning on the first occasion a short imaginary correspondence after the pattern of the then already published "Bundle of Letters." After an absence from America of some five years I inevitably, on the spot again, had impressions; and not less inevitably and promptly, I remember, recognised the truth that if one really was subject to such, and to a good many, and they were at all worth entertaining or imparting, one was likely to bristle with a quite proportionately smaller number of neat and complacent conclusions. Impressions could mutually conflict—

which was exactly the interest of them; whereas in ninety-nine connexions out of a hundred, conclusions could but raise the wind for large groups of persons incapable, to all appearance, of intelligently opening their eyes, though much occupied, to make up for it, with opening, and all vociferously, their mouths. "The Point of View," in fine, I fear, was but to commemorate, punctually enough, its author's perverse and incurable disposition to interest himself less in his own (always so quickly stale) experience, under certain sorts of pressure, than in that of conceivable fellow mortals, which might be mysteriously and refreshingly different. The thing indeed may also serve, in its degree, as a punctual small monument to a recognition that was never to fail; that of the nature of the burden bequeathed by such rash multiplications of the candid consciousness. They are splendid for experience, the multiplications, each in its way an intensifier; but expression, liking things above all to be made comfortable and easy for it, views them askance. The case remains, none the less—alas for this faculty!—that no representation of life worth speaking of can go forward without them. All of which will perhaps be judged to have but a strained relevance, however, to the fact that, though the design of the short imaginary correspondence I speak of was interrupted during those first weeks in Washington, a second visit, the following spring, served it better; I had kept the thread (through a return to London and a return again thence) and, if I remember rightly, I brought my small scheme to a climax on the spot. The finished thing appeared in "The Century Magazine" of December 1882. I recently had the chance to "look up," for old sake's sake, that momentary seat of the good-humoured satiric muse —the seats of the muses, even when the merest flutter of one of their robes has been involved, losing no scrap of sanctity for me, I profess, by the accident of my having myself had the honour to offer the visitant the chair. The chair I had anciently been able to push forward in Washington had not, I found, survived the ravage of nearly thirty years; its place knew it no more, infirm and precarious dependence as it had struck me even at the time as being. So, quite exquisitely, as whenever that lapse occurs, the lost presence, the obliterated scene, translated itself for me at last into terms of almost more than earthly beauty and poetry. Fifty intimate figures and objects flushed with life in the other time had passed away since then; a great chapter of history had made itself, tremendous things had happened; the ghosts of old cherished names, of old tragedies, of old comedies, even of old mere mystifications, had marshalled their array. Only the little rounded composition remained; which glowed, ever so strangely, like a swinging, playing lantern, with a light that brought out the past. The past had been most concretely that vanished and slightly sordid tenement of the current housing of the muse. I had had "rooms" in it, and I could remember how the rooms, how the whole place, a nest of rickety tables and chairs, lame and disqualified utensils of every sort, and of smiling, shuffling, procrastinating persons of colour, had exhaled for me, to pungency, the domestic spirit of the "old South." I had nursed the unmistakeable scent; I had read history by its aid; I had learned more than I could say of what had anciently been the matter under the reign of the great problem of persons of colour—so badly the matter, by my vision, that a deluge of blood and fire and tears had been needed to correct it. These complacencies of perception swarmed for me again—while yet no brick of the little old temple of the revelation stood on another.

I could scarcely have said where the bricks *had* stood; the other, the superseded Washington of the exquisite springtime, of the earlier initiation, of the hovering plaintive ghosts, reduced itself to a great vague blur of warmth and colour and fragrance. It kept flushing through the present—very much as if I had had my small secret for making it. I could turn on my finger the magic ring—it was strange how slight a thing, a mere handful of pages of light persistent prose, could act as that talisman. So, at all events, I like to date, and essentially to synchronise, these sincere little studies in general. Nothing perhaps can vouch better for their having applied to conditions that superficially at least have changed than the fact that to fond memory—I speak of my own—there hangs about the last item on this list, the picture of "The Pension Beaurepas," the unearthly poetry, as I call it, of the Paquis, and that I should yet have to plunge into gulfs of explanation as to where and what the Paquis may have been. An old-world nook of one's youth was so named, a scrap of the lakeside fringe of ancient Geneva, now practically quite reformed and improved away. The Pension Beaurepas, across the years, looks to me prodigiously archaic and incredibly quaint; I ask myself why, at the time, I so wasted the precious treasure of a sense that absolutely primitive pre-revolutionary "Europe" had never really been swept out of its cupboards, shaken out of its curtains, thumped out of its mattresses. The echoes of the eighteenth century, to go no further back, must have been thick on its rather greasy stone staircase, up and down which, unconscious of the character of the fine old wrought-iron *rampe,* as of most other things in the world besides, Mr. and Mrs. and Miss Ruck, to speak only of them, used mournfully to straggle. But I mustn't really so *much* as speak only, as even speak, of them. They would carry me too far back—which possibly outlived verisimilitude in them is what I wish to acknowledge.

XII

PREFACE TO "THE LESSON OF THE MASTER"

(VOLUME XV IN THE NEW YORK EDITION. CONTAINING: "THE LESSON OF THE MASTER," "THE DEATH OF THE LION," "THE NEXT TIME," "THE FIGURE IN THE CARPET," "THE COXON FUND")

MY clearest remembrance of any provoking cause connected with the matter of the present volume applies, not to the composition at the head of my list—which owes that precedence to its greatest length and earliest date—but to the next in order, an effort embalmed, to fond memory, in a delightful association. I make the most of this passage of literary history—I like so, as I find, to recall it. It lives there for me in old Kensington days; which, though I look back at them over no such great gulf of years—"The Death of the Lion" first appeared but in 1894—have already faded for me to the complexion of ever so long ago. It was of a Sunday afternoon early in the spring of that year: a young friend, a Kensington neighbour and an ardent man of letters, called on me to introduce a young friend of his own and to bespeak my interest for a periodical about to take birth, in his hands, on the most original "lines" and with the happiest omens. What omen could be happier for instance than that this infant *recueil*, joyously christened even before reaching the cradle, should take the name of "The Yellow Book"?—which so certainly would command for it the liveliest attention. What, further, should one rejoice more to hear than that this venture was, for all its constitutional gaiety, to brave the quarterly form, a thing hitherto of austere, of awful tradition, and was indeed in still other ways to sound the note of bright young defiance? The project, modestly and a little vaguely but all communicatively set forth, amused me, charmed me, on the spot—or at least the touchingly convinced and inflamed projector did. It was the happy fortune of the late Henry Harland to charge everything he touched, whether in life or in literature, with that influence—an effect by which he was always himself the first to profit. If he came to me, about "The Yellow Book," amused, he pursued the enterprise under the same hilarious star; its difficulties no less than its felicities excited, in the event, his mirth; and he was never more amused (nor, I may certainly add, more amusing) than when, after no very prolonged career, it encountered suddenly and all distressfully its term. The thing had then been to him, for the few years, a humorous uneasy care, a business attended both with other troubles and other pleasures; yet when, before the too prompt harshness of his final frustration, I reflect that he had adventurously lived, wrought and enjoyed, the small square lemon-coloured quarterly, "failure" and all, figures to me perhaps his most beguiling dream and most rewarding hours.

The bravest of the portents that Sunday afternoon—the intrinsic, of course I mean; the only ones to-day worth speaking of—I have yet to mention; for I recall my rather embarrassed inability to measure as yet the contributory value of Mr. Aubrey Beardsley, by whom my friend was accompanied and who, as his prime illustrator, his perhaps even quite independent picture-maker, was to be in charge of the "art department." This young man, slender, pale, delicate, unmistakeably intelligent, somehow invested the whole proposition with a detached, a slightly ironic and melancholy grace. I had met him before, on a single occasion, and had seen an example or two of his so curious and so disconcerting talent—my appreciation of which seems to me, however, as I look back, to have stopped quite short. The young *recueil* was to have pictures, yes, and they were to be as often as possible from Beardsley's hand; but they were to wear this unprecedented distinction, and were to scatter it all about them, that they should have nothing to do with the text—which put the whole matter on an ideal basis. To those who remember the short string of numbers of "The Yellow Book" the spasmodic independence of these contributions will still be present. They were, as illustrations, related surely to nothing else in the same pages—save once or twice, as I imperfectly recall, to some literary effort of Beardsley's own that matched them in perversity; and I might well be at peace as to any disposition on the part of the strange young artist ever to emulate *my* comparatively so incurious text. There would be more to say about him, but he must not draw me off from a greater relevance—my point being simply that he had associated himself with Harland that brave day to dangle before me the sweetest aid to inspiration ever snatched by a poor scribbler from editorial lips. I should sooner have come to this turn of the affair, which at once bathed the whole prospect in the rosiest glow.

I was invited, and all urgently, to contribute to the first number, and was regaled with the golden truth that my composition might absolutely assume, might shamelessly parade in, its own organic form. It was disclosed to me, wonderfully, that—so golden the air pervading the enterprise—any projected contribution might conform, not only unchallenged but by this circumstance itself the more esteemed, to its true intelligible nature. For any idea I might wish to express I might have space, in other words, elegantly to express it— an offered licence that, on the spot, opened up the millennium to the "short story." One had so often known this product to struggle, in one's hands, under the rude prescription of brevity at any cost, with the opposition so offered to its really becoming a story, that my friend's emphasised indifference to the arbitrary limit of length struck me, I remember, as the fruit of the finest artistic intelligence. We had been at one—that we already knew—on the truth that the forms of wrought things, in this order, *were,* all exquisitely and effectively, the things; so that, for the delight of mankind, form might compete with form and might correspond to fitness; might, that is, in the given case, have an inevitability, a marked felicity. Among forms, moreover, we had had, on the dimensional ground—for length and breadth—our ideal, the beautiful and blest *nouvelle;* the generous, the enlightened hour for which appeared thus at last to shine. It was under the star of the *nouvelle* that, in other languages, a hundred interesting and charming results, such studies on the minor scale as the best of Turgenieff's, of Balzac's, of Maupassant's, of Bourget's, and just lately, in our own tongue, of Kipling's, had been, all economically, arrived at—thanks to their authors', as "contributors," having been able to count, right and left, on a wise and liberal support. It had taken the blank misery of our Anglo-Saxon sense of such matters to organise, as might be said, the general indifference to this fine type of composition. In that dull view a "short story" was a "short story," and that was the end of it. Shades and differences, varieties and styles, the value above all of the idea happily *developed,* languished, to extinction, under the hard-and-fast rule of the "from six to eight thousand words"—when, for one's benefit, the rigour was a little relaxed. For myself, I delighted in the shapely *nouvelle*—as, for that matter, I had from time to time and here and there been almost encouraged to show.

However, these are facts quite of the smaller significance and at which I glance only because I seem still to recognise in those of my three bantlings held by Harland at the baptismal font—"The Death of the Lion" (1894), "The Coxon Fund" (1894), "The Next Time" (1895), *plus* a paper not here to be reproduced—something of the less troubled confidence with which they entered on their first state of being. These pieces have this in common that they deal all with the literary life, gathering their motive, in each case, from some noted adventure, some felt embarrassment, some extreme predicament, of the artist enamoured of perfection, ridden by his idea or paying for his sincerity. They testify indeed, as they thus stand together, to no general intention—they minister only, I think, to an emphasised effect. The particular case, in respect to each situation depicted, appealed to me but on its merits; though I was to note with interest, as my sense more and more opened itself, that situations of the order I speak of might again and again be conceived. They rose before me, in fine, as numerous, and thus, here, even with everything not included, they have added themselves up. I must further mention that if they enjoy in common their reference to the troubled artistic consciousness, they make together, by the same stroke, this other rather blank profession, that few of them recall to me, however dimly, any scant pre-natal phase.

In putting them sundry such critical questions so much after the fact I find it interesting to make out—critically interesting of course, which is all our interest here pretends to be—that whereas any anecdote about life pure and simple, as it were, proceeds almost as a matter of course from some good jog of fond fancy's elbow, some pencilled note on somebody else's case, so the material for any picture of personal states so specifically complicated as those of my hapless friends in the present volume will have been drawn preponderantly from the depths of the designer's own mind. This, amusingly enough, is what, on the evidence before us, I seem critically, as I say, to gather—that the states represented, the embarrassments and predicaments studied, the tragedies and comedies recorded, can be intelligibly fathered but on his own intimate experience. I have already mentioned the particular rebuke once addressed me on all this ground, the question of where on earth, where roundabout us at this hour, I had "found" my Neil Paradays, my Ralph Limberts, my Hugh Verekers and other such supersubtle fry. I was reminded then, as I have said, that these represented eminent cases fell to the ground, as by their foolish weight, unless I could give chapter and verse for the eminence. I was reduced to confessing I couldn't, and yet must repeat again here how little I was so abashed. On going over these things I see, to our critical edification, exactly why— which was because I was able to plead that my postulates, my animating presences, were all, to their great enrichment, their intensification of value, ironic; the strength of applied irony being surely in the sincerities, the lucidities, the utilities that stand behind it. When it's not a campaign, of a sort, on behalf of the something better (better than the obnoxious, the provoking object) that blessedly, as is assumed, *might* be, it's not worth speaking of. But this is exactly what we mean by operative irony. It implies and projects the possible other case, the case rich and edifying where the actuality is pretentious and vain. So it plays its lamp; so, essentially, it carries that smokeless flame, which makes clear, with all the rest, the good cause that guides it. My application of which remarks is that the studies here collected have their justification in the ironic spirit, the spirit expressed by my being able to reply promptly enough to my friend: "If the life about us for the last thirty years refuses warrant for these examples, then so much the worse for that life. The *constatation* would be so deplorable that instead of making it we must dodge it: there are decencies that in the name of the general self-respect we must take for granted, there's a kind of rudimentary intellectual honour to which we must, in the interest of civilisation, at least pretend." But I must really reproduce the whole passion of my retort.

"What does your contention of non-existent conscious *exposures,* in the midst of all the stupidity and vulgarity and hypocrisy, imply but that we have been, nationally, so to speak, graced with no instance of recorded sensibility fine enough to react against these things?—an admission too distressing. What one would accordingly fain do is to baffle any such calamity, to *create* the record, in default of any other enjoyment of it; to imagine, in a word, the honourable, the producible case. What better example than this of the high and helpful public and, as it were, civic use of the imagination?—a faculty for the possible fine employments of which in the interest of morality my esteem grows every hour I live. How can one consent to make a picture of the preponderant futilities and vulgarities and miseries of life without the impulse to exhibit as well from time to time, in its place, some fine example of the reaction, the opposition or the escape? One does, thank heaven, encounter here and there symptoms of immunity from the general infection; one recognises with rapture, on occasion, signs of a protest against the rule of the cheap and easy; and one sees thus that the tradition of a high æsthetic temper need n't, after all, helplessly and ignobly perish. These reassurances are one's warrant, accordingly, for so many recognitions of the apparent doom and the exasperated temper—whether with the spirit and the career fatally bruised and finally broken in the fray, or privileged but to gain from it a finer and more militant edge I have had, I admit, to project *signal* specimens—have had, naturally, to make and to keep my cases interesting; the only way to achieve which was to suppose and represent them eminent. In other words I was inevitably committed, always, to the superior case; so that if this is what you reprehensively mean, that I have been thus beguiled into citing celebrities without analogues and painting portraits without models, I plead guilty to the critical charge. Only what I myself mean is that I carry my guilt lightly and have really in face of each perpetrated licence scarce patience to defend myself." So I made my point and so I continued.

"I can't tell you, no, who it is I 'aimed at' in the story of Henry St. George; and it wouldn't indeed do for me to name his exemplar publicly even were I able. But I none the less maintain his situation to have been in *essence* an observed reality- -though I should be utterly ashamed, I equally declare, if I hadn't done quite my best for it. It was the fault of this notable truth, and not my own, that it too obscurely lurked—dim and disengaged; but where is the work of the intelligent painter of life if not precisely in some such aid given to true meanings to be born? He must bear up as he can if it be in consequence laid to him that the flat grows salient and the tangled clear, the common—worst of all!—even amusingly rare, by passing through his hands. Just so when you ask who in the world I had in mind for a victim, and what in the world for a treasure, so sacrificed to the advertisement not even of their own merits but of all sorts of independent, of really indifferent, exhibitory egotism, as the practically harried and hunted Neil Paraday and his borrowed, brandished and then fatally mislaid manuscript, I'm equally confident of having again and again closely noted in the social air all the elements of such a drama. I've put these elements together—that was my business, and in doing this wished of course to give them their maximum sense, which depended, for irony, for comedy, for tragedy, in other words for beauty, on the 'importance' of the poor foredoomed monarch of the jungle. And then, I'm not ashamed to allow, it was *amusing* to make these people 'great,' so far as one could do so without making them intrinsically false. (Yes—for the mere accidental and relative falsity I don't care.) It was amusing because it was more difficult—from the moment, of course I mean, that one worked out at all their greatness; from the moment one didn't simply give it to be taken on trust. Working out economically almost anything is the very life of the art of representation; just as the request to take on trust, tinged with the least extravagance, is the very death of the same. (There may be such a state of mind brought about on the reader's part, I think, as a positive desire to take on trust; but that is only the final fruit of insidious proceedings, operative to a sublime end, on the author's side; and is at any rate a different matter.) As for the all-ingen-

ious "Figure in the Carpet," let me perhaps a little pusillanimously conclude, nothing would induce me to come into
close quarters with you on the correspondences of this anecdote. Here exactly is a good example for you of the virtue
of your taking on trust—when I have artfully begotten in
you a disposition. All I can at this point say is that if ever
I was aware of ground and matter for a significant fable, I
was aware of them in that connexion."

My plea for "correspondences" will perhaps, however, after
all, but bring my reader back to my having, at the outset
of these remarks, owned to full unconsciousness of seed
dropped here by that quick hand of occasion that had elsewhere generally operated; which comes to saying, no doubt,
that in the world of letters things don't at this time of day
very strikingly happen. Suggestive and illuminating incident
is indeed scarce frequent enough to be referred to as admin-
istering the shake that starts up fresh the stopped watch of attention. I shouldn't therefore probably have accumulated these
illustrations without the sense of something interchangeable,
or perhaps even almost indistinguishable, between my own
general adventure and the more or less lively illustration into
which I was to find this experiment so repeatedly flower. Let
it pass that if I am so oddly unable to say here, at any point,
"what gave me my idea," I must just a trifle freely have
helped myself to it from hidden stores. But, burdened thus
with the imputation of that irregularity, I shall give a poor
account of my homogeneous group without the charity of a
glance, however brief, at its successive components. However
I might have been introduced in fact to Henry St. George,
of "The Lesson of the Master," or however I might have been
deprived of him, my complete possession of him, my active
sympathy with him as a known and understood and admired
and pitied, in fine as a fully measured, quantity, hangs about
the pages still as a vague scent hangs about thick orchard
trees. The great sign of a grasped warrant—for identification,

arrest or whatever—is, after all, in the confidence that dissipates vagueness; and the logic of such developed situations as those of the pair commemorated at the head of my list imposed itself all triumphantly. Had n't one again and again caught "society" in the very fact of not caring in the least what might become of the subject, however essentially fine and fragile, of a patronage reflecting such credit on all concerned, so long as the social game might be played a little more intensely, and if possible more irrelevantly, by this unfortunate's aid? Given the Lion, his "death" was but too conceivably the issue of the cruel exposure thus involved for him; and if it be claimed by what I can but feel rather a pedantic view that so precious an animal exactly could n't, in our conditions, have been "given," I must reply that I yet had met him—though in a preserve not perhaps known in all its extent to geographers.

Of such a fantasy as "The Next Time" the principle would surely soon turn up among the consulted notes of any sincere man of letters—taking literature, that is, on the side of the money to be earned by it. There are beautiful talents the exercise of which yet is n't lucrative, and there are pressing needs the satisfaction of which may well appear difficult under stress of that failure of felicity. Just so there are other talents that leave any fine appreciation mystified and gaping, and the active play of which may yet be observed to become on occasion a source of vast pecuniary profit. Nothing then is at moments more attaching, in the light of "comparative" science, than the study of just where and when, just how and why recognition denies itself to the appeal at all artfully, and responds largely to the appeal coarsely enough, commingled. The critical spirit—with leisure indeed to spare—may well, in its restlessness, seek to fix a bit exactly the point at which a beautiful talent, as I have called it, ceases, when imperilled by an empty pocket, to be a "worldly" advantage. The case in which impunity, for the *malheureux* ridden by that questionable boon, insists on breaking down would seem thus to become susceptible of

much fine measurement. I don't know, I confess, that it
proveably is; but the critical spirit at all afraid of so slight
a misadventure as a waste of curiosity is of course deplorably false to its nature. The difficulty here, in truth, is that,
from the moment a straight dependence on the broad-backed
public is a part of the issue, the explicative quantity to be
sought is precisely the mood of that monster—which, consistently and consummately unable to give the smallest account
of itself, naturally renders no grain of help to enquiry. Such
a study as that of Ray Limbert's so prolonged, so intensified,
but so vain continuance in hope (hope of successfully grow-
ing in his temperate garden some specimen of the rank exotic whose leaves are rustling cheques) is in essence a "story
about the public," only wearing a little the reduced face by
reason of the too huge scale, for direct portrayal, of the monstrous countenance itself. Herein resides, as I have hinted, the
anxious and easy interest of almost any sincere man of letters in the mere vicinage, even if that be all, of such strained
situations as Ray Limbert's. They speak of the public, such
situations, to whomever it may concern. They at all events had
from far back insidiously beset the imagination of the author
of "The Next Time," who can scarce remember the day when
he wasn't all sympathetically, all tenderly occupied with some
presumed literary watcher—and quite of a sublime constitution
—for that postponed redress. Therefore in however developed
a state the image in question was at last to hover before him,
some form of it had at least never been far to seek.

I to *this* extent recover the acute impression that may have
given birth to "The Figure in the Carpet," that no truce, in
English-speaking air, had ever seemed to me really struck, or
even approximately strikeable, with our so marked collective
mistrust of anything like close or analytic appreciation—appreciation, to *be* appreciation, implying of course some such rudimentary zeal; and this though that fine process be the Beautiful
Gate itself of enjoyment. To have become consistently aware

of this odd numbness of the general sensibility, which seemed ever to condemn it, in presence of a work of art, to a view scarce of half the intentions embodied, and moreover but to the scantest measure of these, was to have been directed from an early day to some of the possible implications of the matter, and so to have been led on by seductive steps, albeit perhaps by devious ways, to such a congruous and, as I would fain call it, fascinating case as that of Hugh Vereker and his undiscovered, not to say undiscoverable, secret. That strikes me, when all is said, as an ample indication of the starting-point of this particular portrayal. There may be links missing between the chronic consciousness I have glanced at—that of Hugh Vereker's own analytic projector, speaking through the mouth of the anonymous scribe—and the poor man's attributive dependence, for the sense of being understood and enjoyed, on some responsive reach of critical perception that he is destined never to waylay with success; but even so they scarce signify, and I may not here attempt to catch them. This too in spite of the amusement almost always yielded by such recoveries and reminiscences, or to be gathered from the manipulation of any string of evolutionary pearls. What I most remember of my proper process is the lively impulse, at the root of it, to reinstate analytic appreciation, by some ironic or fantastic stroke, so far as possible, in its virtually forfeited rights and dignities. Importunate to this end had I long found the charming idea of some artist whose most characteristic intention, or cluster of intentions, should have taken all vainly for granted the public, or at the worst the not unthinkable private, exercise of penetration. I couldn't, I confess, be indifferent to those rare and beautiful, or at all events odd and attaching, elements that might be imagined to grow in the shade of so much spent intensity and so much baffled calculation. The mere quality and play of an ironic consciousness in the designer left wholly alone, amid a chattering unperceiving world, with the thing he has most wanted to do, with the design more or less realised—some effectual glimpse of that might by itself, for instance, reward one's experiment. I came to Hugh Vereker, in fine, by this travelled road of a generalisation; the habit of having noted for many years how strangely and helplessly, among us all, what we call criticism—its curiosity never emerging from the limp state—is apt to stand off from the intended sense of things, from such finely-attested matters, on the artist's part, as a spirit and a form, a bias and a logic, of his own. From my definite preliminary it was no far cry to the conception of an intent worker who should find himself to the very end in presence but of the limp curiosity. Vereker's drama indeed—or I should perhaps rather say that of the aspiring young analyst whose report we read and to whom, I ruefully grant, I have ventured to impute a developed wit— is that at a given moment the limpness begins vaguely to throb and heave, to become conscious of a comparative tension. As an effect of this mild convulsion acuteness, at several points, struggles to enter the field, and the question that accordingly comes up, the issue of the affair, can be but whether the very secret of perception hasn't been lost. That is the situation, and "The Figure in the Carpet" exhibits a small group of well-meaning persons engaged in a test. The reader is, on the evidence, left to conclude.

The subject of "The Coxon Fund," published in "The Yellow Book" in 1894, had long been with me, but was, beyond doubt, to have found its interest clinched by my perusal, shortly before the above date, of Mr. J. Dyke Campbell's admirable monograph on S. T. Coleridge. The wondrous figure of that genius had long haunted me, and circumstances into which I need n't here enter had within a few years contributed much to making it vivid. Yet it's none the less true that the Frank Saltram of "The Coxon Fund" pretends to be of his great suggester no more than a dim reflexion and above all a free rearrangement. More interesting still than the man—for the dramatist at any rate—is the S. T. Coleridge *type*, so what

I was to do was merely to recognise the type, to borrow it, to
re-embody and freshly place it; an ideal under the law of which
I could but cultivate a free hand. I proceeded to do so; I recon-
structed the scene and the figures—I had my own idea, which
required, to express itself, a new set of relations—though, when
all this is said, it had assuredly taken the recorded, transmitted
person, the image embalmed in literary history, to fertilise my
fancy. What I should, for that matter, like most to go into here,
space serving, is the so interesting question—for the most part,
it strikes me, too confusedly treated—of the story-teller's "real
person" or actual contemporary transplanted and exhibited.
But this pursuit would take us far, such radical revision do the
common laxities of the case, as generally handled, seem to call
for. No such process is *effectively* possible, we must hold, as
the imputed act of transplanting; an act essentially not mechanical, but thinkable rather—so far as thinkable at all—in
chemical, almost in mystical terms. We can surely account for
nothing in the novelist's work that has n't passed through the
crucible of his imagination, has n't, in that perpetually simmer-
ing cauldron his intellectual *pot-au-feu,* been reduced to savoury
fusion. We here figure the morsel, of course, not as boiled to
nothing, but as exposed, in return for the taste it gives out, to
a new and richer saturation. In this state it is in due course
picked out and served, and a meagre esteem will await, a poor
importance attend it, if it does n't speak most of its late genial
medium, the good, the wonderful company it has, as I hint,
æsthetically kept. It has entered, in fine, into new relations,
it emerges for new ones. Its final savour has been consituted,
but its prime identity destroyed—which is what was to be demonstrated. Thus it has become a different and, thanks to a rare
alchemy, a better thing. Therefore let us have here as little
as possible about its "being" Mr. This or Mrs. That. If it ad-
justs itself with the least truth to its new life it can't possibly
be either. If it gracelessly refers itself to either, if it persists as
the impression not artistically dealt with, it shames the honour

230

offered it and can only be spoken of as having ceased to be a thing of fact and yet not become a thing of truth. I am tempted to add that this recommemorative strain might easily woo me to another light step or two roundabout "The Coxon Fund." For I find myself look at it most interestedly to-day, after all, in the light of a significance quite other than that just noted. A marked example of the possible scope, at once, and the possible neatness of the *nouvelle,* it takes its place for me in a series of which the main merit and sign is the effort to do the complicated thing with a strong brevity and lucidity—to arrive, on behalf of the multiplicity, at a certain science of control. Infinitely attractive—though I risk here again doubtless an effect of reiteration—the question of how to exert this control in accepted conditions and how yet to sacrifice no real value; problem ever dearest to any economic soul desirous to keep renewing, and with a frugal splendour, its ideal of economy. Sacred altogether to memory, in short, such labours and such lights. Thus "The Coxon Fund" is such a complicated thing that if it still seems to carry itself—by which I mean if its clearness still rules here, or still serves—some pursued question of how the trick was played would probably not be thankless.

XIII

PREFACE TO "THE AUTHOR OF BELTRAFFIO"

(VOLUME XVI IN THE NEW YORK EDITION. CONTAINING:
"THE AUTHOR OF BELTRAFFIO," "THE MIDDLE YEARS," "GRE-
VILLE FANE," "BROKEN WINGS," "THE TREE OF KNOWLEDGE,"
"THE ABASEMENT OF THE NORTHMORES," "THE GREAT GOOD
PLACE," "FOUR MEETINGS," "PASTE," " 'EUROPE'," "MISS
GUNTON OF POUGHKEEPSIE")

WHAT I had lately and most particularly to say of "The
Coxon Fund" is no less true of "The Middle Years," first
published in "Scribner's Magazine" (1893)—that recollection
mainly and most promptly associates with it the number of
times I had to do it over to make sure of it. To get it right was
to squeeze my subject into the five or six thousand words I
had been invited to make it consist of—it consists, in fact,
should the curious care to know, of some 5550—and I scarce
perhaps recall another case, with the exception I shall presently
name, in which my struggle to keep compression rich, if not,
better still, to keep accretions compressed, betrayed for me such
community with the anxious effort of some warden of the
insane engaged at a critical moment in making fast a victim's
straitjacket. The form of "The Middle Years" is not that
of the *nouvelle,* but that of the concise anecdote; whereas
the subject treated would perhaps seem one comparatively
demanding "developments"—if indeed, amid these mysteries,
distinctions were so absolute. (There is of course neither
close nor fixed measure of the reach of a development, which
in some connexions seems almost superfluous and then in others
to represent the whole sense of the matter; and we should

doubtless speak more thoroughly by book had we some secret for exactly tracing deflexions and returns.) However this may be, it was as an anecdote, an anecdote only, that I was determined my little situation here should figure; to which end my effort was of course to follow it as much as possible from its outer edge in, rather than from its centre outward. That fond formula, I had alas already discovered, may set as many traps in the garden as its opposite may set in the wood; so that after boilings and reboilings of the contents of my small cauldron, after added pounds of salutary sugar, as numerous as those prescribed in the choicest recipe for the thickest jam, I well remember finding the whole process and act (which, to the exclusion of everything else, dragged itself out for a month) one of the most expensive of its sort in which I had ever engaged.

But I recall, by good luck, no less vividly how much finer a sweetness than any mere spooned-out saccharine dwelt in the fascination of the questions involved. Treating a theme that "gave" much in a form that, at the best, would give little, might indeed represent a peck of troubles; yet who, none the less, beforehand, was to pronounce with authority such and such an idea anecdotic and such and such another developmental? One had, for the vanity of *a priori* wisdom here, only to be so constituted that to see any form of beauty, for a particular application, proscribed or even questioned, was forthwith to covet that form more than any other and to desire the benefit of it exactly there. One had only to be reminded that for the effect of quick roundness the small smooth situation, though as intense as one will, is prudently indicated, and that for a fine complicated entangled air nothing will serve that doesn't naturally swell and bristle—one had only, I say, to be so warned off or warned on, to see forthwith no beauty for the simple thing that should n't, and even to perversity, enrich it, and none for the other, the comparatively intricate, that should n't press it out as a mosaic. After which fashion the careful craftsman would have prepared himself the special inviting treat of scarce being able to say, at his highest infatuation, before any series, which might be the light thing weighted and which the dense thing clarified. The very attempt so to discriminate leaves him in fact at moments even a little ashamed; whereby let him shirk here frankly certain of the issues presented by the remainder of our company—there being, independently of these mystic matters, other remarks to make. Blankness overtakes me, I confess, in connexion with the brief but concentrated "Greville Fane"—*that* emerges, how concentrated I tried to make it—which must have appeared in a London weekly journal at the beginning of the "nineties"; but as to which I further retain only a dim warm pleasantness as of old Kensington summer hours. I re-read, ever so kindly, to the promotion of a mild aftertaste—that of a certain feverish pressure, in a cool north room resorted to in heavy London Augusts, with stray, rare echoes of the town, beyond near roofs and chimneys, making harmless detonations, and with the perception, over my page, as I felt poor Greville grow, that her scant record, to be anything at all, would have to be a minor miracle of foreshortening. For here is exactly an illustrative case: the subject, in this little composition, is "developmental" enough, while the form has to make the anecdotic concession; and yet who shall say that for the right effect of a small harmony the fusion has failed? We desire doubtless a more detailed notation of the behaviour of the son and daughter, and yet had I believed the right effect missed "Greville Fane" wouldn't have figured here.

Nothing, by the same stroke, could well have been condemned to struggle more for that harmony than "The Abasement of the Northmores" and "The Tree of Knowledge": the idea in these examples (1900) being developmental with a vengeance and the need of an apparent ease and a general congruity having to enforce none the less—as on behalf of some victim of the income-tax who would minimise his "return"—an almost heroic dissimulation of capital. These things, especially the former, are novels intensely compressed, and with that character in them yet keeping at bay, under stress of their failing else to be good short stories, any air of mutilation. They had had to be good short stories in order to earn, however precariously, their possible wage and "appear"— so certain was it that there would be no appearance, and consequently no wage, for them as frank and brave *nouvelles*. They could but conceal the fact that they *were* "nouvelles"; they could but masquerade as little anecdotes. I include them here by reason of that successful, that achieved and consummate— as it strikes me—duplicity: which, however, I may add, was in the event to avail them little—since they were to find nowhere, the unfortunates, hospitality and the reward of their effort. It is to "The Tree of Knowledge" I referred just above, I may further mention, as the production that had cost me, for keeping it "down," even a greater number of full revolutions of the merciless screw than "The Middle Years." On behalf also of this member of the group, as well as for "The Author of Beltraffio," I recover exceptionally the sense of the grain of suggestion, the tiny air-blown particle. In presence of a small interesting example of a young artist long dead, and whom I had yet briefly seen and was to remember with kindness, a friend had made, thanks to a still greater personal knowledge of him and of his quasi-conspicuous father, likewise an artist, one of those brief remarks that the dramatist feels as fertilising. "And then," the lady I quote had said in allusion to certain troubled first steps of the young man's career, to complications of consciousness that had made his early death perhaps less strange and less lamentable, even though superficially more tragic; "and then he had found his father out, artistically: having grown up in so happy a personal relation with him only to feel, at last, quite awfully, that he did n't and could n't believe in him." That fell on one's ear of course only to prompt the inward cry: "How can there possibly *not* be all sorts of good things in it?" Just so for "The Author of Beltraffio"—long before this and some time before the first appearance of the tale in "The English Illustrated Magazine" (1884): it had been said to me of an eminent author, these several years dead and on some of the embarrassments of whose life and character a common friend was enlarging: "Add to them all, moreover, that his wife objects intensely to what he writes. She can't bear it (as you can for that matter rather easily conceive) and that naturally creates a tension—!" *There* had come the air-blown grain which, lodged in a handful of kindly earth, was to produce the story of Mark Ambient.

Elliptic, I allow, and much of a skipping of stages, so bare an account of such performances; yet with the constitutive process for each idea quite sufficiently noted by my having had, always, only to say to myself sharply enough: "Dramatise it, dramatise it!" That answered, in the connexion, always, all my questions—that provided for all my "fun." The two tales I have named but represent therefore their respective grains of seed dramatically handled. In the case of "Broken Wings" (1900), however, I but see to-day the produced result—I fail to disinter again the buried germ. Little matters it, no doubt, that I recall as operative here the brush of no winged word; for when had I been, as a fellow scribbler, closed to the general admonition of such adventures as poor Mrs. Harvey's, the elegant representative of literature at Mundham?—to such predicaments as Stuart Straith's, gallant victim of the same hospitality and with the same confirmed ache beneath his white waistcoat? The appeal of mature purveyors obliged, in the very interest of their presumed, their marketable, freshness, to dissimulate the grim realities of shrunken "custom," the felt chill of a lower professional temperature—any old note-book would show *that* laid away as a tragic "value" not much less tenderly than some small plucked flower of association left between the leaves for pressing. What had happened here, visibly, was that the value had had to wait long to become active. "Dramatise, dramatise, dramatise!" had been just there more of an easy admonition than of a ready feat; the case for dramatisation was somehow not whole. Under some forgotten touch, however, at its right hour, it was to round itself. What the single situation lacked the *pair* of situations would supply—there was drama enough, with economy, from the moment sad companions, looking each other, with their identities of pluck and despair, a little hard in the face, should confess each to the other, relievingly, what they kept from every one else. With the right encounter and the right surprise, that is with the right persons, postulated, the relief, if in the right degree exquisite, might be the drama—and the right persons, in fine, to make it exquisite, were Stuart Straith and Mrs. Harvey. There remains "The Great Good Place" (1900)—to the spirit of which, however, it strikes me, any gloss or comment would be a tactless challenge. It embodies a calculated effect, and to plunge into it, I find, even for a beguiled glance—a course I indeed recommend—is to have left all else outside. There then my indications must wait.

The origin of "Paste" is rather more expressible, since it was to consist but of the ingenious thought of transposing the terms of one of Guy de Maupassant's admirable *contes*. In "La Parure" a poor young woman, under "social" stress, the need of making an appearance on an important occasion, borrows from an old school friend, now much richer than herself, a pearl necklace which she has the appalling misfortune to lose by some mischance never afterwards cleared up. Her life and her pride, as well as her husband's with them, become subject, from the hour of the awful accident, to the redemption of their debt; which, effort by effort, sacrifice by sacrifice, franc by franc, with specious pretexts, excuses, a rage of desperate explanation of their failure to restore the missing object, they finally obliterate—all to find that their whole consciousness and life have been convulsed and deformed in vain, that the pearls were but highly artful "imitation" and that their passionate penance has ruined them for nothing. It seemed harmless sport simply to turn that situation round—to shift, in other words, the ground of the horrid mistake, making this a matter not of a false treasure supposed to be true and precious, but of a real treasure supposed to be false and hollow: though a new little "drama," a new setting for *my* pearls—and as different as possible from the other—had of course withal to be found.

"Europe," which is of 1899, when it appeared in "Scribner's Magazine," conspicuously fails, on the other hand, to disown its parentage; so distinct has its "genesis" remained to me. I had preserved for long years an impression of an early time, a visit, in a sedate American city—for there *were* such cities then —to an ancient lady whose talk, whose allusions and relics and spoils and mementoes and credentials, so to call them, bore upon a triumphant sojourn in Europe, long years before, in the hey-day of the high scholarly reputation of her husband, a dim displaced superseded celebrity at the time of my own observation. They had been "much made of," he and she, at various foreign centres of polite learning, and above all in the England of early Victorian days; and my hostess had lived ever since on the name and fame of it; a treasure of legend and anecdote laid up against the comparatively lean half-century, or whatever, that was to follow. For myself even, after this, a good slice of such a period had elapsed; yet with my continuing to believe that fond memory would still somehow be justified of this scrap too, along with so many others: the unextinguished sense of the temperature of the January morning on which the little Sunday breakfast-party, at half-past nine across the snow, had met to the music of a chilly ghostly kindly tinkle; that of the roomful of cherished echoes and of framed and glazed, presented and autographed and thumb-marked mementoes—the wealth of which was somehow explained (this was part of the legend) by the ancient, the at last almost prehistoric, glory of like matutinal hours, type and model of the emulous shrunken actual.

The justification I awaited, however, only came much later, on my catching some tender mention of certain admirable ladies, sisters and spinsters under the maternal roof, for whom the century was ebbing without remedy brought to their eminent misfortune (such a ground of sympathy always in the "good old" American days when the touching case was still possible) of not having "been to Europe." Exceptionally prepared by culture for going, they yet couldn't leave their immemorial mother, the headspring, precisely, of that grace in them, who on the occasion of each proposed start announced her approaching end—only to postpone it again after the plan was dished and the flight relinquished. So the century ebbed, and so Europe altered—for the worse—and so perhaps even a little did the sisters who sat in bondage; only so didn't at all the immemorial, the inextinguishable, the eternal mother. Striking to the last degree, I thought, that obscure, or at least that muffled, tragedy, which had the further interest of giving me on the spot a setting for my own so long uninserted gem and of enabling me to bring out with maximum confidence my inveterate "Dramatise!" "Make this *one* with such projection as you are free to permit yourself of the brooding parent in the other case," I duly remarked, "and the whole thing falls together; the paradise the good sisters are apparently never to attain becoming by this conversion just the social cake on which they have always been fed and that has so notoriously opened their appetite." Or something of that sort. I recognise that I so but express here the "plot" of my tale as it stands; except for so far as my formula, "something of that sort," was to make the case bristle with as many vivid values, with as thick and yet as clear a little complexity of interest, as possible. The merit of the thing is in the feat, once more, of the transfusion; the receptacle (of form) being so exiguous, the brevity imposed so great. I undertook the brevity, so often undertaken on a like scale before, and again arrived at it by the innumerable repeated chemical reductions and condensations that tend to make of the very short story, as I risk again noting, one of the costliest, even if, like the hard, shining sonnet, one of the most indestructible, forms of composition in general use. I accepted the rigour of its having, all sternly, in this case, to treat so many of its most appealing values as waste; and I now seek my comfort perforce in the mere exhibited result, the union of whatever fulness with whatever clearness.

XIV

PREFACE TO "THE ALTAR OF THE DEAD"

(VOLUME XVII IN THE NEW YORK EDITION. CONTAINING: "THE ALTAR OF THE DEAD," "THE BEAST IN THE JUNGLE," "THE BIRTHPLACE," "THE PRIVATE LIFE," "OWEN WINGRAVE," "THE FRIENDS OF THE FRIENDS," "SIR EDMUND ORME," "THE REAL RIGHT THING")

"The Altar of the Dead" forms part of a volume bearing the title of "Terminations," which appeared in 1895. Figuring last in that collection of short pieces, it here stands at the head of my list, not as prevailing over its companions by length, but as being ample enough and of an earlier date than several. I have to add that with this fact of its temporal order, and the fact that, as I remember, it had vainly been "hawked about," knocking, in the world of magazines, at half a dozen editorial doors impenetrably closed to it, I shall have exhausted my fund of allusion to the influences attending its birth. I consult memory further to no effect; so that if I should seem to have lost every trace of "how I came to think" of such a motive, did n't I, by a longer reach of reflexion, help myself back to the state of not having *had* to think of it? The idea embodied in this composition must in other words never have been so absent from my view as to call for an organised search. It was "there"—it had always, or from ever so far back, been there, not interfering with other conceits, yet at the same time not interfered with; and it naturally found expression at the first hour something more urgently undertaken happened not to stop the way. The way here, I recognise, would ever have been easy to stop, for the general patience, the inherent waiting faculty, of the principle of interest involved, was conscious of no strain, and above all of no loss, in amusedly biding its time. Other conceits might indeed come and go, born of light impressions and passing hours, for what sort of free intelligence would it be that, addressed to the human scene, should propose to itself, all vulgarly, never to be waylaid or arrested, never effectively inspired, by some imaged appeal of the lost Dead? The subject of my story is obviously, and quite as usual, the exhibition of a case; the case being that of an accepted, a cultivated habit (the cultivation is really the point) of regularly taking thought for them. Frankly, I can but gather, the desire, at last of the acutest, to give an example and represent an instance of some such practised communion, was a foredoomed consequence of life, year after year, amid the densest and most materialised aggregation of men upon earth, the society most wedded by all its conditions to the immediate and the finite. More exactly speaking, it was impossible for any critic or "creator" at all worth his wage not, as a matter of course, again and again to ask himself what may not become of individual sensibility, of the faculty and the fibre itself, when everything makes against the indulgence of it save as a conscious, and indeed highly emphasised, dead loss.

The impression went back for its full intensity, no doubt, neither to a definite moment nor to a particular shock; but the author of the tale before us was long to cherish the memory of a pair of illuminating incidents that, happily for him —by which I mean happily for the generalisation he here makes—placed themselves, at no great distance apart, so late in a sustained experience of London as to find him profitably prepared for them, and yet early enough to let confirmatory matter gather in abundance round. Not to this day, in fine, has he forgotten the hard, handsome, gentlemanly face, as it was expressionally affected in a particular conjunction, of a personage occasionally met in other years at one of the friendliest, the most liberal of "entertaining" houses and then lost to sight till after a long interval. The end of all mortal things had, during this period, and in the fulness of time, overtaken our delightful hosts and the scene of their long hospitality, a scene of constant welcome to my personage, as I have called him (a police-magistrate then seated, by reason of his office, well in the eye of London, but as conspicious for his private urbanity as for his high magisterial and penal mask). He too has now passed away, but what could exactly better attest the power of prized survival in personal signs than my even yet felt chill as I saw the old penal glare rekindled in him by the form of my aid to his memory. "We used sometimes to meet, in the old days, at the dear So-and-So's, you may recall." "The So-and-So's?" said the awful gentleman, who appeared to recognise the name, across the table, only to be shocked at the allusion. "Why, they're Dead, sir—dead these many years." "Indeed they are, sir, alas," I could but reply with spirit; "and it's precisely why I like so to speak of them!—Il ne manquerait plus que cela, that because they're dead I should n't!" is what I came within an ace of adding; or rather *might* have come hadn't I felt my indecency too utterly put in its place. I was left with it in fact on my hands—where however I was quite everlastingly, as you see, to cherish it. My anecdote is mild and its companion perhaps milder; but impressions come as they can and stay as they will.

A distinguished old friend, a very eminent lady and highly marked character, though technically, as it were, a private person, unencompassed by literary luggage or other monumental matter, had dropped from the rank at a great age and, as I was to note after a sufficient interval, to my surprise, with a singularly uncommemorated and unchronicled effect: given, I mean, her social and historical value. One blushed, as the days passed, for the want of manners in it—there being twenty reasons in the case why manners should have been remembered. A friend of the interesting woman, there-

upon, seeing his opportunity, asked leave of an acquaintance of his own, the conductor of a "high class" periodical, to intervene on behalf of her memory in the pages under the latter's control. The amiable editor so far yielded to a first good impulse as to welcome the proposal; but the proposer was disconcerted to receive on the morrow a colder retractation. "I really don't see why I should publish **an article** about Mrs. X *because*—and because *only,* so far as I can make out—she's dead." Again I felt the inhibition, as the psychologists say, that I had felt in the other case; the vanity, *in the conditions,* of any yearning plea that this was the most beautiful of reasons. Clearly the conditions were against its being for an effective moment felt as such; and the article in question never appeared—nor, to the best of my knowledge, anything else of the sort; which fact was to take its place among other grim values. These pointed, as they all too largely accumulated, to the general black truth that London was a terrible place to die in; doubtless not so much moreover by conscious cruelty or perversity as under the awful doom of general dishumanisation. It takes space to feel, it takes time to know, and great organisms as well as small have to pause, more or less, to possess themselves and to be aware. Monstrous masses are, by this truth, so impervious to vibration that the sharpest forces of feeling, locally applied, no more penetrate than a pin or a paper-cutter penetrates an elephant's hide. Thus the very tradition of sensibility would perish if left only to their care. It has here and there to be rescued, to be saved by independent, intelligent zeal; which type of effort however, to avail, has to fly in the face of the conditions.

These are easily, one is obliged to add, too many for it; nothing being more visible for instance than that the life of inordinately numerous companies is hostile to friendship and intimacy—unless indeed it be the impropriety of such names applied to the actual terms of intercourse. The sense of the

state of the dead is but part of the sense of the state of the
living; and, congruously with that, life is cheated to almost
the same degree of the finest homage (precisely this our possible friendships and intimacies) that we fain would render
it. We clutch indeed at some shadow of these things, we stay
our yearning with snatches and stop-gaps; but our struggle
yields to the other arrayed things that defeat the *cultivation,*
in such an air, of the finer flowers—creatures of cultivation as the finer flowers essentially are. We perforce fall
back, for the application of that process, on the coarser—
which form together the rank and showy bloom of "success,"
of multiplied contact and multiplied motion; the bloom of a
myriad many-coloured "relations"—amid which the precious
plant that is rare at the best becomes rare indeed. "The
Altar of the Dead" then commemorates a case of what I have
called the individual independent effort to keep it none the
less tended and watered, to cultivate it, as I say, with an
exasperated piety. I am not however here reconstituting my
more or less vivid fable, but simply glancing at the natural
growth of its prime idea, that of an invoked, a restorative
reaction against certain general brutalities. Brutal, more and
more, to wondering eyes, the great fact that the poor dead,
all about one, were nowhere so dead as there; where to be
caught in any rueful glance at them was to be branded at
once as "morbid." "Mourir, à Londres, c'est être bien mort!"
—I have not forgotten the ironic emphasis of a distinguished
foreign friend, for some years officially resident in England,
as we happened once to watch together a funeral-train, on its
way to Kensal Green or wherever, bound merrily by. That
truth, to any man of memories, was too repeatedly and intol-
erably driven home, and the situation of my depicted George
Stransom is that of the poor gentleman who simply at last
could n't "stand" it.

To desire, amid these collocations, to place, so far as possible, like with like, was to invite "The Beast in the Jungle"

to stand here next in order. As to the accidental determinant of which composition, once more—of comparatively recent date and destined, like its predecessor, first to see the light in a volume of miscellanies ("The Better Sort," 1903)—I remount the stream of time, all enquiringly, but to come back empty-handed. The subject of this elaborated fantasy—which, I must add, I hold a successful thing only as its motive may seem to the reader to stand out sharp—can't quite have belonged to the immemorial company of such solicitations; though in spite of this I meet it, in ten lines of an old note-book, but as a recorded conceit and an accomplished fact. Another poor sensitive gentleman, fit indeed to mate with Stransom of "The Altar"—my attested predilection for poor sensitive gentlemen almost embarrasses me as I march! —was to have been, after a strange fashion and from the threshold of his career, condemned to keep counting with the unreasoned prevision of some extraordinary fate; the conviction, lodged in his brain, part and parcel of his imagination from far back, that experience would be marked for him, and whether for good or for ill, by some rare distinction, some incalculable violence or unprecedented stroke. So I seemed to see him start in life—under the so mixed star of the extreme of apprehension and the extreme of confidence; all to the logical, the quite inevitable effect of the complication aforesaid: his having to wait and wait for the right recognition; none of the mere usual and normal human adventures, whether delights or disconcertments, appearing to conform to the great type of his fortune. So it is that he's depicted. No gathering appearance, no descried or interpreted promise or portent, affects his superstitious soul either as a damnation deep enough (if damnation be in question) for his appointed *quality* of consciousness, or as a translation into bliss sublime enough (on *that* hypothesis) to fill, in vulgar parlance, the bill. Therefore as each item of experience comes, with its possibilities, into view, he can but dismiss it under this sterilising habit of the failure to find it good enough and thence to appropriate it.

His one desire remains of course to meet his fate, or at least to divine it, to see it as intelligible, to learn it, in a word; but none of its harbingers, pretended or supposed, speak his ear in the true voice; they wait their moment at his door only to pass on unheeded, and the years ebb while he holds his breath and stays his hand and—from the dread not less of imputed pride than of imputed pusillanimity—stifles his distinguished secret. He perforce lets everything go—leaving all the while his general presumption disguised and his general abstention unexplained; since he's ridden by the idea of what things may lead to, since they mostly always lead to human communities, wider or intenser, of experience, and since, above all, in his uncertainty, he must n't compromise others. Like the blinded seeker in the old-fashioned game he "burns," on occasion, as with the sense of the hidden thing near—only to deviate again however into the chill; the chill that indeed settles on him as the striking of his hour is deferred. His career thus resolves itself into a great negative adventure, my report of which presents, for its centre, the fine case that has caused him most tormentedly to "burn," and then most unprofitably to stray. He is afraid to recognise what he incidentally misses, since what his high belief amounts to is not that he shall have felt and vibrated less than any one else, but that he shall have felt and vibrated more; which no acknowledgement of the minor loss must conflict with. Such a course of existence naturally involves a climax—the final flash of the light under which he reads his lifelong riddle and sees his conviction proved. He has indeed been marked and indeed suffered his fortune—which is precisely to have been the man in the world to whom nothing whatever was to happen. My picture leaves him overwhelmed—at last he has understood; though in thus disengaging my treated theme for the reader's benefit I seem to acknowledge that this more detached witness may not successfully have done so. I certainly grant that any felt merit in the thing must all depend on the clearness and charm with which the subject just noted expresses itself.

If "The Birthplace" deals with another poor gentleman —of interest as being yet again too fine for his rough fate —here at least I can claim to have gone by book, here once more I lay my hand, for my warrant, on the clue of actuality. It was one of the cases in which I was to say at the first brush of the hint: "How can there possibly *not* be innumerable things in it?" "It" was the mentioned adventure of a good intelligent man rather recently appointed to the care of a great place of pilgrimage, a shrine sacred to the piety and curiosity of the whole English-speaking race, and haunted by other persons as well; who, coming to his office with infinite zest, had after a while desperately thrown it up—as a climax to his struggle, some time prolonged, with "the awful nonsense he found himself expected and paid, and thence quite obliged, to talk." It was in these simple terms his predicament was named to me—not that I would have had a word more, not indeed that I had n't at once to turn my back for very joy of the suppressed details: so unmistakeably, on the spot, was a splendid case all there, so complete, in fine, as it stood, was the appeal to fond fancy; an appeal the more direct, I may add, by reason, as happened, of an acquaintance, lately much confirmed, on my own part, with the particular temple of our poor gentleman's priesthood. It struck me, at any rate, that here, if ever, was the perfect theme of a *nouvelle*—and to some such composition I addressed myself with a confidence unchilled by the certainty that it would nowhere, at the best (a prevision not falsified) find "acceptance." For the rest I must but leave "The Birthplace" to plead its own cause; only adding that here afresh and in the highest degree were the conditions reproduced for that mystic, that "chemical" change wrought in the impression of life by its dedication to an æsthetic use, that I lately spoke of in connexion with "The Coxon Fund." Beautiful on all this ground exactly, to the projector's mind, the process by which the small cluster of actualities latent in the fact reported to him was to be reconstituted and, so far as they might need, altered; the felt fermentation, ever interesting, but flagrantly so in the example before us, that enables the sense originally communicated to make fresh and possibly quite different terms for the new employment there awaiting it. It has been liberated (to repeat, I believe, my figure) after the fashion of some sound young draught-horse who may, in the great meadow, have to be re-captured and re-broken for the saddle.

I proceed almost eagerly, in any case, to "The Private Life"—and at the cost of reaching for a moment over "The Jolly Corner": I find myself so fondly return to ground on which the history even of small experiments may be more or less written. This mild documentation fairly thickens for me, I confess, the air of the first-mentioned of these tales; the scraps of records flit through that medium, to memory, as with the incalculable brush of wings of the imprisoned bat at eventide. This piece of ingenuity rests for me on such a handful of acute impressions as I may not here tell over at once; so that, to be brief, I select two of the sharpest. Neither of these was, in old London days, I make out, to be resisted even under its single pressure; so that the hour struck with a vengeance for "Dramatise it, dramatise it!" (dramatise, that is, the combination) from the first glimpse of a good way to work together two cases that happened to have been given me. They were those—as distinct as possible save for belonging alike to the "world," the London world of a time when Discrimination still a little lifted its head—of a highly distinguished man, constantly to be encountered, whose fortune and whose peculiarity it was to bear out personally as little as possible (at least to *my* wondering sense) the high denotements, the rich implications and rare associations, of the genius to which he owed his position and his renown. One may go, naturally, in such a connexion, but by one's own applied measure; and I have never ceased to ask myself, in this particular loud, sound, normal, hearty presence, all so assertive and so whole, all bristling with prompt responses and expected opinions and usual views, radiating all a broad daylight equality of emphasis and impartiality of address (for most relations)— I never ceased, I say, to ask myself what lodgement, on such premises, the rich proud genius one adored could ever have contrived, what domestic commerce the subtlety that was its prime ornament and the world's wonder have enjoyed, under what shelter the obscurity that was its luckless drawback and the world's despair have flourished. The whole aspect and *allure* of the fresh sane man, illustrious and undistinguished— no "sensitive poor gentleman" he!—was mystifying; they made the question of who then had written the immortal things such a puzzle.

So at least one could but take the case—though one's need for relief depended, no doubt, on what one (so to speak) suffered. The writer of these lines, at any rate, suffered so much—I mean of course but by the unanswered question— that light *had* at last to break under pressure of the whimsical theory of two distinct and alternate presences, the assertion of either of which on any occasion directly involved the entire extinction of the other. This explained to the imagination the mystery: our delightful inconceivable celebrity was *double*, constructed in two quite distinct and "water-tight" compartments—one of these figured by the gentleman who sat at a table all alone, silent and unseen, and wrote admirably deep and brave and intricate things; while the gentleman who regularly came forth to sit at a quite different table and substantially and promiscuously and multitudinously dine stood for its companion. They had nothing to do, the so dissimilar twins, with each other; the diner could exist but by the cessation of the writer, whose emergence, on his side, depended on his—

and our!—ignoring the diner. Thus it was amusing to think of the real great man as a presence known, in the late London days, all and only to himself—unseen of other human eye and converted into his perfectly positive, but quite secondary, *alter ego* by any approach to a social contact. To the same tune was the social personage known all and only to society, was he conceivable but as "cut dead," on the return home and the threshold of the closed study, by the waiting spirit who would flash at that signal into form and possession. Once I had so seen the case I could n't see it otherwise; and so to see it moreover was inevitably to feel in it a situation and a motive. The ever-importunate murmur, "Dramatise it, dramatise it!" haunted, as I say, one's perception; yet without giving the idea much support till, by the happiest turn, the whole possibility was made to glow.

For didn't there immensely flourish in those very days and exactly in that society the apparition the most qualified to balance with the odd character I have referred to and to supply to "drama," if "drama" there was to be, the precious element of contrast and antithesis?—that most accomplished of artists and most dazzling of men of the world whose effect on the mind repeatedly invited to appraise him was to beget in it an image of representation and figuration so exclusive of any possible inner self that, so far from there being here a question of an *alter ego,* a double personality, there seemed scarce a question of a real and single one, scarce foothold or margin for any private and domestic *ego* at all. Immense in this case too, for any analytic witness, the solicitation of wonder—which struggled all the while, not less amusingly than in the other example, toward the explanatory secret; a clear view of the perpetual, essential performer, consummate, infallible, impeccable, and with his high shining elegance, his intensity of presence, on these lines, involving to the imagination an absolutely blank reverse or starved residuum, no *other* power of presence whatever. One said it under one's breath, one really yearned to know: was he, such an embodiment of skill and taste and tone and composition, of every public gloss and grace, thinkable even as occasionally single?—since to be truly single is to be able, under stress, to be separate, to be *solus*, to know at need the interlunar swoon of *some* independent consciousness. Yes, *had* our dazzling friend any such alternative, could he so unattestedly exist, and was the withdrawn, the sequestered, the unobserved and unhonoured condition so much as imputable to him? Was n't his potentiality of existence public, in fine, to the last squeeze of the golden orange, and when he passed from our admiring sight into the chamber of mystery what, the next minute, was on the other side of the door? It was irresistible to believe at last that there was at such junctures inveterately nothing; and the more so, once I had begun to dramatise, as this supplied the most natural opposition in the world to my fond companion-view—the other side of the door *only* cognisant of the true Robert Browning. One's harmless formula for the poetic employment of this pair of conceits could n't go much further than "Play them against each other"—the ingenuity of which small game "The Private Life" reflects as it can.

I fear I can defend such doings but under the plea of my amusement in them—an amusement I of course hoped others might succeed in sharing. But so comes in exactly the principle under the wide strong wing of which several such matters are here harvested; things of a type that might move me, had I space, to a pleading eloquence. Such compositions as "The Jolly Corner," printed here not for the first time, but printed elsewhere only as I write and after my quite ceasing to expect it; "The Friends of the Friends," to which I here change the colourless title of "The Way It Came" (1896), "Owen Wingrave" (1893), "Sir Edmund Orme" (1891), "The Real Right Thing" (1900), would obviously never have existed but for that love of "a story as a story" which had from far back beset and beguiled their author. To this passion, the vital flame at the heart of any sincere attempt to lay a scene and launch a drama, he flatters himself he has never been false; and he will indeed have done his duty but little by it if he has failed to let it, whether robustly or quite insidiously, fire his fancy and rule his scheme. He has consistently felt it (the appeal to wonder and terror and curiosity and pity and to the delight of fine recognitions, as well as to the joy, perhaps sharper still, of the mystified state) the very source of wise counsel and the very law of charming effect. He has revelled in the creation of alarm and suspense and surprise and relief, in all the arts that practise, with a scruple for nothing but any lapse of application, on the credulous soul of the candid or, immeasurably better, on the seasoned spirit of the cunning, reader. He has built, rejoicingly, on that blest faculty of wonder just named, in the latent eagerness of which the novelist so finds, throughout, his best warrant that he can but pin his faith and attach his car to it, rest in fine his monstrous weight and his queer case on it, as on a strange passion planted in the heart of man for his benefit, a mysterious provision made for him in the scheme of nature. He has seen this particular sensibility, the need and the love of wondering and the quick response to any pretext for it, as the beginning and the end of his affair—thanks to the innumerable ways in which that chord may vibrate. His prime care has been to master those most congruous with his own faculty, to make it vibrate as finely as possible—or in other words to the production of the interest appealing most (by its kind) to himself. This last is of course the particular clear light by which the genius of representation ever best proceeds—with its beauty of adjustment to any strain of attention whatever. Essentially, meanwhile, excited wonder must have a subject, must face in a direction, must be, increasingly, *about* something. Here comes in then the artist's bias and his range—determined, these things, by his own fond inclination. About what, good man, does he himself most wonder?—for upon that, whatever it may be, he will naturally most abound. Under that star will he gather in what he shall most seek to represent; so that if you follow thus his range of representation you will know how, you will see where, again, good man, he for himself most aptly vibrates.

All of which makes a desired point for the little group of compositions here placed together; the point that, since the question has ever been for me but of wondering and, with all achievable adroitness, of causing to wonder, so the whole fairy-tale side of life has used, for its tug at my sensibility, a cord all its own. When we want to wonder there's no such good ground for it as the wonderful—premising indeed always, by an induction as prompt, that this element can but be at best, to fit its different cases, a thing of appreciation. What is wonderful in one set of conditions may quite fail of its spell in another set; and, for that matter, the peril of the unmeasured strange, in fiction, being the silly, just as its strength, when it saves itself, is the charming, the wind of interest blows where it lists, the surrender of attention persists where it can. The ideal, obviously, on these lines, is the straight fairy-tale, the case that has purged in the crucible all its *bêtises* while keeping all its grace. It may seem odd, in a search for the amusing, to try to steer wide of the silly by hugging close the "supernatural"; but one man's amusement is at the best (we have surely long had to recognise) another's desolation; and I am prepared with the confession that the "ghost-story," as we for convenience call it, has ever been for me the most possible form of the fairy-tale. It enjoys, to my eyes, this honour by being so much the neatest—neat with that neatness without which *representation,* and therewith beauty, drops. One's working of the spell is of course—decently and effectively—but by the represented thing, and the grace of the more or less closely represented state is the measure of any success; a truth by the general smug neglect of which it's difficult not to be struck. To begin to wonder, over a case, I

must begin to believe—to begin to give out (that is to attend)
I must begin to take in, and to enjoy *that* profit I must begin
to see and hear and feel. This would n't seem, I allow, the general requirement—as appears from the fact that so many persons profess delight in the picture of marvels and prodigies
which by any, even the easiest, critical measure *is* no picture;
in the recital of wonderful horrific or beatific things that are
neither represented nor, so far as one makes out, seen as repre-
sentable: a weakness not invalidating, round about us, the
most resounding appeals to curiosity. The main condition of
interest—that of some appreciable rendering of sought effects—
is absent from them; so that when, as often happens, one is
asked how one "likes" such and such a "story" one can but
point responsively to the lack of material for a judgement.

The apprehension at work, we thus see, would be of certain projected conditions, and its first need therefore is that
these appearances be constituted in some other and more col-
ourable fashion than by the author's answering for them on
his more or less gentlemanly honour. This is n't enough; *give*
me your elements, *treat* me your subject, one has to say—
I must wait till then to tell you how I like them. I might
"rave" about them all were they given and treated; but there
is no basis of opinion in such matters without a basis of
vision, and no ground for that, in turn, without some communicated closeness of truth. There are portentous situations,
there are prodigies and marvels and miracles as to which this
communication, whether by necessity or by chance, works comparatively straight—works, by our measure, to some convincing
consequence; there are others as to which the report, the picture, the plea, answers no tithe of the questions we would put.
Those questions *may* perhaps then, by the very nature of the
case, be unanswerable—though often again, no doubt, the felt
vice is but in the quality of the provision made for them:
on any showing, my own instinct, even in the service of great
adventures, is all for the best *terms* of things; all for ground

on which touches and tricks may be multiplied, the greatest number of questions answered, the greatest appearance of truth conveyed. With the preference I have noted for the "neat" evocation—the image, of any sort, with fewest attendant vaguenesses and cheapnesses, fewest loose ends dangling and fewest features missing, the image kept in fine the most susceptible of intensity—with this predilection, I say, the safest arena for the play of moving accidents and mighty mutations and strange encounters, or whatever odd matters, is the field, as I may call it, rather of their second than of their first exhibition. By which, to avoid obscurity, I mean nothing more cryptic than I feel myself show them best by showing almost exclusively the way they are felt, by recognising as their main interest some impression strongly made by them and intensely received. We but too probably break down, I have ever reasoned, when we attempt the prodigy, the appeal to mystification, in itself; with its "objective" side too emphasised the report (it is ten to one) will practically run thin. We want it clear, goodness knows, but we also want it thick, and we get the thickness in the human consciousness that entertains and records, that amplifies and interprets it. That indeed, when the question is (to repeat) of the "supernatural," constitutes the only thickness we do get; here prodigies, when they come straight, come with an effect imperilled; they keep all their character, on the other hand, by looming through some other history—the indispensable history of somebody's *normal* relation to something. It's in such connexions as these that they most interest, for what we are then mainly concerned with is their imputed and borrowed dignity. Intrinsic values they have none—as we feel for instance in such a matter as the would-be portentous climax of Edgar Poe's "Arthur Gordon Pym," where the indispensable history is absent, where the phenomena evoked, the moving accidents, coming straight, as I say, are immediate and flat, and the attempt is all at the horrific in itself. The result is that, to my sense, the climax fails—fails because it stops short, and stops short for want of connexions. There *are* no connexions; not only, I mean, in the sense of further statement, but of our own further relation to the elements, which hang in the void: whereby we see the effect lost, the imaginative effort wasted.

I dare say, to conclude, that whenever, in quest, as I have noted, of the amusing, I have invoked the horrific, I have invoked it, in such air as that of "The Turn of the Screw," that of "The Jolly Corner," that of "The Friends of the Friends," that of "Sir Edmund Orme," that of "The Real Right Thing," in earnest aversion to waste and from the sense that in art economy is always beauty. The apparitions of Peter Quint and Miss Jessel, in the first of the tales just named, the elusive presence nightly "stalked" through the New York house by the poor gentleman in the second, are matters as to which in themselves, really, the critical challenge (essentially nothing ever but the spirit of fine attention) may take a hundred forms—and a hundred felt or possibly proved infirmities is too great a number. Our friends' respective minds about them, on the other hand, are a different matter—challengeable, and repeatedly, if you like, but never challengeable without some consequent further stiffening of the whole texture. Which proposition involves, I think, a moral. The moving accident, the rare conjunction, whatever it be, doesn't make the story—in the sense that the story is our excitement, our amusement, our thrill and our suspense; the human emotion and the human attestation, the clustering human conditions we expect presented, only make it. The extraordinary is most extraordinary in that it happens to you and me, and it's of value (of value for others) but so far as visibly brought home to us. At any rate, odd though it may sound to pretend that one feels on safer ground in tracing such an adventure as that of the hero of "The Jolly Corner" than in pursuing a bright career among pirates or detectives, I allow that composition to pass as the measure or limit, on my own part, of any achievable comfort in the "adventure-story"; and this not because I may "render"—well, what my poor gentleman attempted and suffered in the New York house—better than I may render detectives or pirates or other splendid desperadoes, though even here too there would be something to say; but because the spirit engaged with the forces of violence interests me most when I can think of it as engaged most deeply, most finely and most "subtly" (precious term!). For then it is that, as with the longest and firmest prongs of consciousness, I grasp and hold the throbbing subject; *there* it is above all that I find the steady light of the picture.

After which attempted demonstration I drop with scant grace perhaps to the admission here of a general vagueness on the article of my different little origins. I have spoken of these in three or four connexions, but ask myself to no purpose, I fear, what put such a matter as "Owen Wingrave" or as "The Friends of the Friends," such a fantasy as "Sir Edmund Orme," into my head. The habitual teller of tales finds these things in old note-books—which however but shifts the burden a step; since how, and under what inspiration, did they first wake up in these rude cradles? One's notes, as all writers remember, sometimes explicitly mention, sometimes indirectly reveal, and sometimes wholly dissimulate, such clues and such obligations. The search for these last indeed, through faded or pencilled pages, is perhaps one of the sweetest of our more pensive pleasures. Then we chance on some idea we *have* afterwards treated; then, greeting it with tenderness, we wonder at the first form of a motive that was to lead us so far and to show, no doubt, to eyes not our own, for so other; then we heave the deep sigh of relief over all that is never, thank goodness, to be done again. Would we have embarked on *that* stream had we known?—and what might n't we have made of this one *had n't* we known! How, in a proportion of cases, could we have dreamed "there might be something"?—and why, in another proportion, did n't we *try* what there might be, since there are sorts of trials (ah indeed more than one sort!) for which the day will soon have passed? Most of all, of a certainty, is brought back, before these promiscuities, the old burden of the much life and the little art, and of the portentous dose of the one it takes to make any show of the other. It is n't however that one "minds" not recovering lost hints; the special pride of any tinted flower of fable, however small, is to be able to opine with the celebrated Topsy that it can only have "growed." Does n't the fabulist himself indeed recall even as one of his best joys the particular pang (both quickening and, in a manner, profaning possession) of parting with some conceit of which he can give no account but that his sense—of beauty or truth or whatever—has been for ever so long saturated with it? Not, I hasten to add, that measurements of time may n't here be agreeably fallacious, and that the "ever so long" of saturation shan't often have consisted but of ten minutes of perception. It comes back to me of "Owen Wingrave," for example, simply that one summer afternoon many years ago, on a penny chair and under a great tree in Kensington Gardens, I must at the end of a few such visionary moments have been able to equip him even with details not involved or not mentioned in the story. Would that adequate intensity all have sprung from the fact that while I sat there in the immense mild summer rustle and the ever so softened London hum a young man should have taken his place on another chair within my limit of contemplation, a tall quiet slim studious young man, of admirable type, and have settled to a book with immediate gravity? Did the young man then, on the spot, just *become* Owen Wingrave, establishing by the mere magic of type the situation, creating at a stroke all the implications and filling out all the picture? That he would have been capable of it is all I can say—unless it be, otherwise put, that I should have been capable of letting him; though there hovers the happy alternative that Owen Wingrave, nebulous and fluid, may only, at the touch, have found *himself* in this gentleman; found, that is, a figure and a habit, a form, a face, a fate, the interesting aspect presented and the dreadful doom recorded; together with the required and multiplied connexions, not least that presence of some self-conscious dangerous girl of lockets and amulets offered by the full-blown idea to my very first glance. These questions are as answerless as they are, luckily, the reverse of pressing—since my poor point is only that at the beginning of my session in the penny chair the seedless fable had n't a claim to make or an excuse to give, and that, the very next thing, the pennyworth still partly unconsumed, it was fairly bristling with pretexts. "Dramatise it, dramatise it!" would seem to have rung with sudden intensity in my ears. But dramatise what? The young man in the chair? Him perhaps indeed—however disproportionately to his mere inoffensive stillness; though no imaginative response *can* be disproportionate, after all, I think, to any right, any really penetrating, appeal. Only, where and whence and why and how sneaked in, during so few seconds, so much penetration, so very much rightness? However, these mysteries are really irrecoverable; besides being doubtless of interest, in general, at the best, but to the infatuated author.

Moved to say that of "Sir Edmund Orme" I remember absolutely nothing, I yet pull myself up ruefully to retrace the presumption that this morsel must first have appeared, with a large picture, in a weekly newspaper and, as then struck me, in the very smallest of all possible print—at sight of which I felt sure that, in spite of the picture (a thing, in its way, to be thankful for) no one would ever read it. I was never to hear in fact that any one had done so—and I therefore surround it here with every advantage and give it without compunction a new chance. For as I meditate I do a little live it over, do a little remember in connexion with it the felt challenge of some experiment or two in one of the finest shades, the finest (*that* was the point) of the gruesome. The gruesome gross and obvious might be charmless enough; but why should n't one, with ingenuity, almost infinitely refine upon it?—as one was prone at any time to refine almost on anything? The study of certain of the situations that keep, as we say, the heart in the mouth might renew itself under this star; and in the recital in question, as in "The Friends of the Friends," "The Jolly Corner" and "The Real Right Thing," the pursuit of such verily leads us into rarefied air. Two sources of effect must have seemed to me happy for "Sir Edmund Orme"; one of these the bright thought of a state of *unconscious* obsession or, in romantic parlance, hauntedness, on the part of a given person; the consciousness of it on the part of some other, in anguish lest a wrong turn or forced betrayal shall determine a break in the blest ignorance, becoming thus the subject of portrayal, with plenty of suspense for the occurrence or non-occurrence of the feared mischance. Not to be liable herself to a dark visitation, but to see such a danger play about her child as incessantly as forked lightning may play unheeded about the blind, this is the penalty suffered by the mother, in "Sir Edmund Orme," for some hardness or baseness of her own youth. There I must doubtless have found my escape from the obvious; there I avoided a low directness and achieved one of those redoubled twists or sportive—by which I don't at all mean wanton—gambols dear to the fastidious, the creative fancy and that make for the higher interest. The higher interest—and this is the second of the two flowers of evidence that I pluck from the faded cluster —must further have dwelt, to my appraisement, in my placing my scene at Brighton, the old, the mid-Victorian, the Thackerayan Brighton; where the twinkling sea and the breezy air, the great friendly, fluttered, animated, many-coloured "front," would emphasise the note I wanted; that of the strange and sinister embroidered on the very type of the normal and easy.

This was to be again, after years, the idea entertained for

"The Jolly Corner," about the composition of which there would be more to say than my space allows; almost more in fact than categorical clearness might see its way to. A very limited thing being on this occasion in question, I was moved to adopt as my motive an analysis of some one of the conceivably rarest and intensest grounds for an "unnatural" anxiety, a *malaise* so incongruous and discordant, in the given prosaic prosperous conditions, as almost to be compromising. Spencer Brydon's adventure however is one of those finished fantasies that, achieving success or not, speak best even to the critical sense for themselves—which I leave it to do, while I apply the remark as well to "The Friends of the Friends" (and all the more that this last piece allows probably for no other comment).

I have placed "Julia Bride," for material reasons, at the end of this Volume, quite out of her congruous company, though not very much out of her temporal order; and mainly with this drawback alone that any play of criticism she may seem formed to provoke rather misses its link with the reflexions I have here been making. That link is with others to come, and I must leave it to suggest itself on the occasion of these others; when I shall be inevitably saying, for instance, that if there are voluminous, gross and obvious ways of seeking that effect of the distinctively rich presentation for which it has been my possibly rather thankless fate to strive, so doubtless the application of patches and the multiplication of parts make up a system with a train of votaries; but that the achieved iridescence from within works, I feel sure, more kinds of magic; and our interest, our decency and our dignity can of course only be to work as many kinds as possible. Such value as may dwell in "Julia Bride," for example, seems to me, on re-perusal, to consist to a high degree in the strength of the flushing through on the part of the subject-matter, and in the mantle of iridescence naturally and logically so produced. Julia is "foreshortened," I admit, to within

an inch of her life; but I judge her life still saved and yet
at the same time the equal desideratum, its depicted full
fusion with other lives that remain undepicted, not lost.
The other lives, the rest of the quantity of life, press in,
squeeze forward, to the best of their ability; but, restricted
as the whole thing is to implications and involutions only,
they prevail at best by indirectness; and the bid for amusement, the effect presumably sought, is by making us conceive and respond to them, making us feel, taste, smell and
enjoy them, without our really knowing why or how. Full-
fed statement here, to repeat my expression—the imaged
résumé of as many of the vivifying elements as may be co-
herently packed into an image at once—is the predominant
artifice; thanks to which we catch by the very small reflector, which is of absolutely minimum size for its task, a quite
"unlikely" amount, I surmise, of the movement of life. But,
again and again, it would take me long to retail the refinements of ingenuity I felt poor re-invoked Julia all anxiously,
all intelligently invite me to place, for this belated, for this
positively final appearance, at her disposal. "Here we are
again!" she seemed, with a chalked grimace, to call out to me,
even as the clown at the circus launches the familiar greeting;
and it was quite as if, while she understood all I asked of her,
I confessed to her the oddity of my predicament. This was but
a way, no doubt, of confessing it to myself—except indeed that
she might be able to bear it. Her plea was—well, anything she
would; but mine, in return, was that I really did n't take her
for particularly important in herself, and would in fact have
had no heart for her without the note, attaching to her as not
in the least to poor little dim and archaic Daisy Miller, say;
the note, so to call it, of multitudinous reference. I had had,
for any confidence, to make it out to myself that my little frisk-
ing haunter, under private stress, of the New York public
scene, was related with a certain intensity to the world about
her; so that her case might lose itself promptly enough in a

complexus of larger and stranger cases—even in the very air, by what seemed to promise, of the largest possibilities of comedy. What if she were the silver key, tiny in itself, that would unlock a treasure?—the treasure of a whole view of manners and morals, a whole range of American social aspects?

To put that question was to see one's subject swell at its mere touch; but to do this, by the same stroke, was to ask one's self, alas, how such a majestic mass could be made to turn round in a *nouvelle*. For, all tainted with the up-town debility though it still might be—and this too, after all, comparative—did n't it yet strain the minor key, to re-employ my expression, almost to breaking? How had the prime idea come to me, in the first place, but as possibly and perhaps even minutely illustrating, in respect of consequences and remoter bearings, that freedom repeatedly to contract for the fond preliminaries of marriage which has been immemorially cherished by the American female young? The freedoms of American life are, together with some of its queer restrictions and timidities, the suggestive matter for painter, poet or satirist; and who should say that one of the greatest of all such birthrights, the large juvenile licence as to getting "engaged," disengaged and re-engaged, had received half the attention the charmed dramatist or moralist would appear consistently to owe it? Presumably of the greatest its bearing on the social tone at large, on the manners, habits and ideals of communities clinging to it—of generations wedded, that is, to the young *speculative* exchange of intimate vows—as to the palladium of their liberties. What had struck me nevertheless was that, in common with a hundred other native traditions and practices, it had suffered from the attitude of poets and statisticians banded alike to display it as quite devoid of attendant signs or appreciable effects. From far back a more perverse student, doubtless, of the human scene in general had ventured to suspect in it some at least of the properties of presentable truth:

so hard it appeared to believe that the number of a young lady's
accepted lovers would n't in some degree determine the mixture
of the elements in the young lady's consciousness and have
much to "say," in one way and another, to the young lady's
general case. *What* it might have to say (of most interest to
poet and moralist) was certainly meanwhile no matter for *a
priori* judgement—it might have to say but the most charming, the most thrilling things in the world; this, however, was
exactly the field for dramatic analysis, no such fine quantities
being ever determinable till they have with due intelligence
been "gone into." "Dramatise, dramatise!" one had, in fine,
before the so signal appearance, said to one's self: then, and
not sooner, would one see.

By the same token and the same process would one arrive
at a similar profit on the score of that other almost equally
prized social provision—which has indeed received more critical attention—the unrestricted freedom of re-marriage in the
lifetime of the parties, the unhampered ease of rupture and
repudiation for each. On this ground, as I say, the fond interpreter of life has had, wherever we observe him, the acute
appeal apparently enough in his ears; and it was to reach
me in the present connexion but as a source of sound re-
enforcement to my possibly too exiguous other example.
"Superadd some view of the so enjoyed and so typical freedoms of the mother to the element, however presented, of the
daughter's inimitable career of licence; work in, as who should
say, a tablespoonful of the due display of responsible consc'ous-
ness, of roused and reflective taste, of delicacy spreading a
tentative wing; season and stir according to judgement and
then set the whole to simmer, to stew, or whatever, serving hot
and with extreme neatness"; such, briefly stated, had been
my careful formula or recipe—by which I of course had to
abide in spite of suspecting the process to promise, from an
early stage, a much stronger broth, smoking in a much bigger
bowl, than I had engaged to prepare. The fumes exhaled by

the mixture were the gage, somehow, of twenty more ingredients than I had consciously put in; and this means in short that, even with the actual liquid drained off, I make out a residuum of admirable rich "stock," which—in common deference to professional and technical thirft—must again certainly serve. Such are both the penalties and the profits of that obsession by the sense of an ampler comedy in human things—latent and a little lost, but all responsive to the interested squeeze, to the roused passion of pursuit—than even quite expert and anxious preliminaries of artistic relation to any theme may always be trusted to give the measure of. So what does this truth amount to, after all, but a sort of consecration of what I have called, for "Julia Bride," my predicament?—the consciousness, in that connexion, but of finding myself, after so many years astride the silver-shod, sober-paced, short-stepping, but oh so hugely nosing, so tenderly and yearningly and ruefully sniffing, grey mule of the "few thousand words," ridiculously back where I had started. I clutch at the claim in question indeed, since I feel that without it the shadow I may have cast might n't bear comparison even with that of limping Don Quixote assisted through his castle-gate and showing but thankless bruises for laurels —might in fact resign itself rather to recalling Moses Primrose welcomed home from the Fair.

XV

PREFACE TO "DAISY MILLER"

(VOLUME XVIII IN THE NEW YORK EDITION. CONTAINING: "DAISY MILLER," "PANDORA," "THE PATAGONIA," "THE MAR- RIAGES," "THE REAL THING," "BROOKSMITH," "THE BELDONALD HOLBEIN," "THE STORY IN IT," "FLICKERBRIDGE," "MRS. MEDWIN")

IT was in Rome during the autumn of 1877; a friend then living there but settled now in a South less weighted with appeals and memories happened to mention—which she might perfectly not have done—some simple and uninformed American lady of the previous winter, whose young daughter, a child of nature and of freedom, accompanying her from hotel to hotel, had "picked up" by the wayside, with the best con- science in the world, a good-looking Roman, of vague iden- tity, astonished at his luck, yet (so far as might be, by the pair) all innocently, all serenely exhibited and introduced: this at least till the occurrence of some small social check, some interrupting incident, of no great gravity or dignity, and which I forget. I had never heard, save on this showing, of the amiable but not otherwise eminent ladies, who were n't in fact named, I think, and whose case had merely served to point a familiar moral; and it must have been just their want of salience that left a margin for the small pencil-mark inveterately signifying, in such connexions, "Dramatise, dram- atise!" The result of my recognising a few months later the sense of my pencil-mark was the short chronicle of "Daisy Miller," which I indited in London the following spring and then addressed, with no conditions attached, as I remember, to the editor of a magazine that had its seat of publication at Philadelphia and had lately appeared to appreciate my contributions. That gentleman however (an historian of some repute) promptly returned me my missive, and with an absence of comment that struck me at the time as rather grim—as, given the circumstances, requiring indeed some explanation: till a friend to whom I appealed for light, giving him the thing to read, declared it could only have passed with the Philadelphian critic for "an outrage on American girlhood." This was verily a light, and of bewildering intensity; though I was presently to read into the matter a further helpful inference. To the fault of being outrageous this little composition added that of being essentially and pre-eminently a *nouvelle;* a signal example in fact of that type, foredoomed at the best, in more cases than not, to editorial disfavour. If accordingly I was afterwards to be cradled, almost blissfully, in the conception that "Daisy" at least, among my productions, might approach "success," such success for example, on her eventual appearance, as the state of being promptly pirated in Boston—a sweet tribute I hadn't yet received and was never again to know—the irony of things yet claimed its rights, I couldn't but long continue to feel, in the circumstance that quite a special reprobation had waited on the first appearance in the world of the ultimately most prosperous child of my invention. So doubly discredited, at all events, this bantling met indulgence, with no great delay, in the eyes of my admirable friend the late Leslie Stephen and was published in two numbers of "The Cornhill Magazine" (1878).

It qualified itself in that publication and afterwards as "a Study"; for reasons which I confess I fail to recapture unless they may have taken account simply of a certain flatness in my poor little heroine's literal denomination. Flatness indeed, one must have felt, was the very sum of her story; so that perhaps after all the attached epithet was meant but as a deprecation, addressed to the reader, of any great critical hope of stirring scenes. It provided for mere concentration, and on an object scant and superficially vulgar—from which, however, a sufficiently brooding tenderness might eventually extract a shy incongruous charm. I suppress at all events here the appended qualification—in view of the simple truth, which ought from the first to have been apparent to me, that my little exhibition is made to no degree whatever in critical but, quite inordinately and extravagantly, in poetical terms. It comes back to me that I was at a certain hour long afterwards to have reflected, in this connexion, on the characteristic free play of the whirligig of time. It was in Italy again—in Venice and in the prized society of an interesting friend, now dead, with whom I happened to wait, on the Grand Canal, at the animated water-steps of one of the hotels. The considerable little terrace there was so disposed as to make a salient stage for certain demonstrations on the part of two young girls, children *they,* if ever, of nature and of freedom, whose use of those resources, in the general public eye, and under our own as we sat in the gondola, drew from the lips of a second companion, sociably afloat with us, the remark that there before us, with no sign absent, were a couple of attesting Daisy Millers. Then it was that, in my charming hostess's prompt protest, the whirligig, as I have called it, at once betrayed itself. "How can you liken *those* creatures to a figure of which the only fault is touchingly to have transmuted so sorry a type and to have, by a poetic artifice, not only led our judgement of it astray, but made *any* judgement quite impossible?" With which this gentle lady and admirable critic turned on the author himself. "You *know* you quite falsified, by the turn you gave it, the thing you had begun with having in mind, the thing you had had, to satiety, the chance of 'observing': your pretty perversion of it, or your unprincipled mystification of our sense of it does it really too much honour—in spite of which, none the less, as anything charming or touching always to that extent justifies itself, we after a fashion forgive and understand you. But why *waste* your romance? There are cases, too many, in which you 've done it again; in which, provoked by a spirit of observation at first no doubt sufficiently sincere, and with the measured and felt truth fairly twitching your sleeve, you have yielded to your incurable prejudice in favour of grace—to whatever it is in you that makes so inordinately for form and prettiness and pathos; not to say sometimes for misplaced drolling. Is it that you 've after all too much imagination? Those awful young women capering at the hotel-door, *they* are the real little Daisy Millers that were; whereas yours in the tale is such a one, more 's the pity, as—for pitch of the ingenuous, for quality of the artless—could n't possibly have been at all." My answer to all which bristled of course with more professions than I can or need report here; the chief of them inevitably to the effect that my supposedly typical little figure was of course pure poetry, and had never been anything else; since this is what helpful imagination, in however slight a dose, ever directly makes for. As for the original grossness of readers, I dare say I added, that was another matter—but one which at any rate had then quite ceased to signify.

A good deal of the same element has doubtless sneaked into "Pandora," which I also reprint here for congruity's sake, and even while the circumstances attending the birth of this anecdote, given to the light in a New York newspaper (1884), pretty well lose themselves for me in the mists of time. I do nevertheless connect "Pandora" with one of the scantest of memoranda, twenty words jotted down in New York during a few weeks spent there a year or two before. I had put a question to a friend about a young lady present at a certain pleasure-party, but present in rather perceptibly unsupported and unguaranteed fashion, as without other connexions without more operative "backers," than a

proposer possibly half-hearted and a slightly sceptical sec-
onder; and had been answered to the effect that she was an
interesting representative of a new social and local variety, the
"self-made," or at least self-making, girl, whose sign was that
—given some measurably amusing appeal in her to more or less
ironic curiosity or to a certain complacency of patronage—
she was anywhere made welcome enough if she only came,
like one of the dismembered charges of Little Bo-Peep, leaving
her "tail" behind her. Docked of all natural appendages and
having enjoyed, as was supposed, no natural advantages; with
the "line drawn," that is, at her father and her mother, her
sisters and her brothers, at everything that was hers, and
with the presumption crushing as against these adjuncts, she
was yet held free to prove her case and sail her boat herself; even quite quaintly or quite touchingly free, as might
be—working out thus on her own lines her social salvation.
This was but five-and-twenty years ago; yet what to-day
most strikes me in the connexion, and quite with surprise,
is that at a period so recent there should have been novelty
for me in a situation so little formed by more contemporary lights to startle or waylay. The evolution of varieties
moves fast; the Pandora Days can no longer, I fear, pass
for quaint or fresh or for exclusively native to any one tract
of Anglo-Saxon soil. Little Bo-Peep's charges may, as manners have developed, leave their tails behind them for the
season, but quite knowing what they have done with them and
where they shall find them again—as is proved for the most
part by the promptest disavowal of any apparent ground for
ruefulness. To "dramatise" the hint thus gathered was of
course, rudimentarily, to see the self-made girl apply her very
first independent measure to the renovation of her house,
founding its fortunes, introducing her parents, placing her
brothers, marrying her sisters (this care on her own behalf
being—a high note of superiority—quite secondary), in fine
floating the heavy mass on the flood she had learned to breast.

Something of that sort must have proposed itself to me at that time as the latent "drama" of the case; very little of which, however, I am obliged to recognise, was to struggle to the surface. What is more to the point is the moral I at present find myself drawing from the fact that, then turning over my American impressions, those proceeding from a brief but profusely peopled stay in New York, I should have fished up that none so very precious particle as one of the pearls of the collection. Such a circumstance comes back, for me, to that fact of my insuperably restricted experience and my various missing American clues—or rather at least to my felt lack of the most important of them all—on which the current of these remarks has already led me to dilate. There had been indubitably and multitudinously, for me, in my native city, the world "down-town"—since how otherwise should the sense of "going" down, the sense of hovering at the narrow gates and skirting the so violently overscored outer face of the monstrous labyrinth that stretches from Canal Street to the Battery, have taken on, to me, the intensity of a worrying, a tormenting impression? Yet it was an impression any attempt at the active cultivation of which, one had been almost violently admonished, could but find one in the last degree unprepared and uneducated. It was essentially New York, and New York was, for force and accent, nothing else worth speaking of; but without the special lights it remained impenetrable and inconceivable; so that one but mooned about superficially, circumferentially, taking in, through the pores of whatever wistfulness, no good material at all. I had had to retire, accordingly, with my yearning presumptions all unverified—presumptions, I mean, as to the privilege of the imaginative initiation, as to the hived stuff of drama, at the service there of the literary adventurer really informed enough and bold enough; and with my one drop of comfort the observation already made—that at least I descried, for my own early humiliation and exposure, no semblance of such a competitor slipping in at any door or perched, for raking the scene, on any coign of vantage. *That* invidious attestation of my own appointed and incurable deafness to the major key I frankly surmise I could scarce have borne. For there it was; not only that the major key was "down-town" but that down-town was, all itself, the major key—absolutely, exclusively; with the inevitable consequence that if the minor was "up-town," and (by a parity of reasoning) up-town the minor, so the field was meagre and the inspiration thin for any unfortunate practically banished from the true pasture. Such an unfortunate, even at the time I speak of, had still to confess to the memory of a not inconsiderably earlier season when, seated for several months at the very moderate altitude of Twenty-Fifth Street, he felt himself day by day alone in that scale of the balance; alone, I mean, with the music-masters and French pastry-cooks, the ladies and children —immensely present and immensely numerous these, but testifying with a collective voice to the extraordinary absence (save as pieced together through a thousand gaps and indirectnesses) of a serious male interest. One had heard and seen novels and plays appraised as lacking, detrimentally, a serious female; but the higher walks in that community might at the period I speak of have formed a picture bright and animated, no doubt, but marked with the very opposite defect.

Here it was accordingly that loomed into view more than ever the anomaly, in various ways dissimulated to a first impression, rendering one of the biggest and loudest of cities one of the very least of Capitals; together with the immediate reminder, on the scene, that an adequate muster of Capital characteristics would have remedied half my complaint. To have lived in capitals, even in some of the smaller, was to be sure of that and to know why—and all the more was this a consequence of having happened to live in some of the greater. Neither scale of the balance, in these, had ever struck one as so monstrously heaped-up at the expense of the other; there had been manners and customs enough, so to speak, there had been features and functions, elements, appearances, social material, enough to go round. The question was to have appeared, however, and the question was to remain, this interrogated mystery of what American town-life had left to entertain the observer withal—when nineteen twentieths of it, or in other words the huge organised mystery of the consummately, the supremely applied money-passion, were inexorably closed to him. My own practical answer figures here perforce in the terms, and in them only, of such propositions as are constituted by the four or five longest tales comprised in this series. What it came to was that up-town would do for me simply what up-town could—and seemed in a manner apologetically conscious that this might n't be described as much. The kind of appeal to interest embodied in these portrayals and in several of their like companions was the measure of the whole minor exhibition, which affected me as virtually saying: "Yes I 'm either *that*—that range and order of things, or I 'm nothing at all; therefore make the most of me!" Whether "Daisy Miller," "Pandora," "The Patagonia," "Miss Gunton," "Julia Bride" and *tutti quanti* do in fact conform to any such admonition would be an issue by itself and which must n't overcome my shyness; all the more that the point of interest is really but this—that I was on the basis of the loved *nouvelle* form, with the best will in the world and the best conscience, almost helplessly cornered. To ride the *nouvelle* down-town, to prance and curvet and caracole with it there—that would have been the true ecstasy. But a single "spill"—such as I so easily might have had in Wall Street or wherever—would have forbidden me, for very shame, in the eyes of the expert and the knowing, ever to mount again; so that in short it was n't to be risked on any terms.

There were meanwhile the alternatives of course—that I might renounce the *nouvelle*, or else might abjure that "American life" the characteristic towniness of which was lighted for me, even though so imperfectly, by New York and Boston— by those centres only. Such extremities, however, I simply could n't afford—artistically, sentimentally, financially, or by any other sacrifice—to face; and if the fact nevertheless remains that an adjustment, under both the heads in question, had eventually to take place, every inch of my doubtless meagre ground was yet first contested, every turn and twist of my scant material economically used. Add to this that if the other constituents of the volume, the intermediate ones, serve to specify what I was then thrown back on, I need n't perhaps even at the worst have found within my limits a thinness of interest to resent: seeing that still after years the common appeal remained sharp enough to flower again into such a composition as "Julia Bride" (which independently of its appearance here has seen the light but in "Harper's Magazine," 1908). As I wind up with this companion-study to "Daisy Miller" the considerable assortment of my shorter tales I seem to see it symbolise my sense of my having waited with something of a subtle patience, my having still hoped as against hope that the so ebbing and obliging seasons would somehow strike for me some small flash of what I have called the major light —would suffer, I mean, to glimmer out, through however odd a crevice or however vouchsafed a contact, just enough of a wandering air from the down-town penetralia as might embolden, as might inform, as might, straining a point, even conceivably inspire (always where the *nouvelle,* and the *nouvelle* only, should be concerned); all to the advantage of my extension of view and my variation of theme. A whole passage of intellectual history, if the term be not too pompous, occupies in fact, to my present sense, the waiting, the so fondly speculative interval: in which I seem to see myself rather a high and dry, yet irrepressibly hopeful artistic Micawber, cocking an ostensibly confident hat and practising an almost passionate system of "bluff"; insisting, in fine, that something (out of the just-named penetralia) *would* turn up if only the right imaginative hanging-about on the chance, if only the true intelligent attention, were piously persisted in.

I forget exactly what Micawber, who had hung about so on the chance, I forget exactly what *he*, at the climax of his exquisite consciousness, found himself in fact reverting to; but I feel that my analogy loses nothing from the circumstance that so recently as on the publication of "Fordham Castle" (1904), for which I refer my reader to Volume XVI, the miracle, after all, alas, had n't happened, the stray emitted gleam had n't fallen across my page, the particular supreme "something" those who live by their wits finally and *most* yearningly look for had n't, in fine, turned up. What better proof of this than that, with the call of the "four or five thousand words" of "Fordham Castle" for instance to meet, or even with the easier allowance of space for its successor to rise to, I was but to feel myself fumble again in the old limp pocket of the minor exhibition, was but to know myself reduced to finger once more, not a little ruefully, a chord perhaps now at last too warped and rusty for complicated music at short order? I trace myself, for that matter, in "Fordham Castle" positively "squirming" with the ingenuity of my effort to create for my scrap of an up-town subject—*such* a scrap as I at the same time felt myself admonished to keep it down to! —a certain larger connexion; I may also add that of the exceedingly close complexus of intentions represented by the packed density of those few pages it would take some ampler glance here to give an account. My point is that my pair of little up-town identities, the respectively typical objects of parental and conjugal interest, the more or less mitigated, more or less embellished or disfigured, intensified or modernised Daisy Millers, Pandora Days, Julia Brides, Miss Guntons or whatever, of the anxious pair, the ignored husband and relegated mother, brought together in the Swiss lakeside pension—my point is that these irrepressible agents yet betrayed the conscious need of tricking-out their time-honoured case. To this we owe it that the elder couple bear the brunt of immediate appearance and are charged with the function of adorning at least the foreground of the general scene; they convey, by implication, the moral of the tale, at least its æsthetic one, if there be such a thing: they fairly hint, and from the very centre of the familiar field, at positive deprecation (should an imagined critic care not to neglect such a shade) of too unbroken an eternity of mere international young ladies. It's as if the international young ladies, felt by me as once more, as verily once too much, my appointed thematic doom, had inspired me with the fond thought of attacking them at an angle and from a quarter by which the peril and discredit of their rash inveteracy might be a bit conjured away.

These in fact are the saving sanities of the dramatic poet's always rather mad undertaking—the rigour of his artistic need to cultivate almost at any price variety of appearance and experiment, to dissimulate likenesses, samenesses, stalenesses, by the infinite play of a form pretending to a life of its own. There are not so many quite distinct things in his field, I think, as there are sides by which the main masses may be approached; and he is after all but a nimble besieger or nocturnal sneaking adventurer who perpetually plans, watches, circles for penetrable places. I offer "Fordham Castle," positively for a rare little memento of that truth: once I had to be, for the light wind of it in my sails, "internationally" American, what amount of truth my subject might n't aspire to was urgently enough indicated—which condition straightway placed it in the time-honoured category; but the range of choice as to treatment, by which I mean as to my pressing the clear liquor of amusement and refreshment from the golden apple of composition, *that* blest freedom, with its infinite power of renewal, was still my resource, and I felt myself invoke it not in vain. There was always the difficulty—I have in the course of these so numerous preliminary observations repeatedly referred to it, but the point is so interesting that it can scarce be made too often—that the simplest truth about a human entity, a situation, a relation, an aspect of life, however small, on behalf of which the claim to charmed attention is made, strains ever, under one's hand, more intensely, *most* intensely, to justify that claim; strains ever, as it were, toward the uttermost end or aim of one's meaning or of its own numerous connexions; struggles at each step, and in defiance of one's raised admonitory finger, fully and completely to express itself. Any real art of representation is, I make out, a controlled and guarded acceptance, in fact a perfect economic mastery, of that conflict: the general sense of the expansive, the explosive principle in one's material thoroughly noted, adroitly allowed to flush and colour and animate the disputed value, but with its other appetites and treacheries, its characteristic space-hunger and space-cunning, kept down. The fair flower of this artful compromise is to my sense the secret of "foreshortening"—the particular economic device for which one must have a name and which has in its single blessedness and its determined pitch, I think, a higher price than twenty other clustered loosenesses; and just because full-fed statement, just because the picture of as many of the conditions as possible made and kept proportionate, just because the surface iridescent, even in the short piece, by what is beneath it and what throbs and gleams through, are things all conducive to the only compactness that has a charm, to the only spareness that has a force, to the only simplicity that has a grace—those, in each order, that produce the *rich* effect.

Let me say, however, that such reflexions had never helped to close my eyes, at any moment, to all that had come and gone, over the rest of the field, in the fictive world of adventure more complacently so called—the American world, I particularly mean, that might have put me so completely out of countenance by having drawn its inspiration, that of thousands of celebrated works, neither from up-town nor from down-town nor from my lady's chamber, but from the vast wild garden of "unconventional" life in no matter what part of our country. I grant in fact that this demonstration of how consummately my own meagrely-conceived sources were to be dispensed with by the more initiated minds would but for a single circumstance, grasped at in recovery of self-respect, have thrown me back in absolute dejection on the poverty of my own categories. Why hadn't so quickened a vision of the great neglected native quarry *at large* more troubled my dreams, instead of leaving my imagination on the whole so resigned? Well, with many reasons I could count over, there was one that all exhaustively covered the ground and all completely answered the question: the reflexion, namely, that the common sign of the productions "unconventionally" prompted (and this positively without exception) was nothing less than the birthmark of Dialect, general or special—dialect with the literary rein loose on its agitated back and with its shambling power of traction, not to say, more analytically, of *at*traction, trusted for all such a magic might be worth. Distinctly that was the odd case: the key to the *whole* of the treasure of romance independently garnered was the riot of the vulgar tongue. One might state it more freely still and the truth would be as evident: the plural number, the vulgar tongues, each with its intensest note, but pointed the moral more luridly. Grand generalised continental riot or particular pedantic, particular discriminated and "sectional" and self-conscious riot—to feel the thick breath, to catch the ugly snarl, of all or of either, was to be reminded afresh of the only conditions that guard the grace, the only origins that save the honour, or even the life, of dialect: those precedent to the invasion, to the sophistication, of schools and unconscious of the smartness of echoes and the taint of slang. The thousands of celebrated productions raised their monument but to the bastard vernacular of communities disinherited of the felt difference between the speech of the soil and the speech of the newspaper, and capable thereby, accordingly, of taking slang for simplicity, the composite for the quaint and the vulgar for the natural. These were unutterable depths, and, as they yawned about one, *what* appreciable coherent sound did they seem most to give out? Well, to my ear surely, at the worst, none that determined even a tardy compunction. The monument was there, if one would, but was one to regret one's own failure to have contributed a stone? Perish, and all ignobly, the thought!

Each of the other pieces of which this volume is composed would have its small history; but they have above all in common that they mark my escape from the predicament, as I have called it, just glanced at; my at least partial way out of the dilemma formed by the respective discouragements of down-town, of up-town and of the great dialectic tracts. Various up-town figures flit, I allow, across these pages; but they too, as it were, have for the time dodged the dilemma; I meet them, I exhibit them, in an air of different and, I think, more numerous alternatives. Such is the case with the young American subject in "Flickerbridge" (1902) and with the old American subject, as my signally mature heroine may here be pronounced, in "The Beldonald Holbein" (1901). In these two cases the idea is but a stray spark of the old "international" flame; of course, however, it was quite internationally that I from far back sought my salvation. Let such matters as those I have named represent accordingly so many renewed, and perhaps at moments even rather desperate, clutches of that useful torch. We may put it in this way that the scale of variety had, by the facts of one's situation, been rather oddly predetermined—with Europe so constantly in requisition as the more salient American stage or more effective *repoussoir,* and yet with any particular *action* on this great lighted and decorated scene depending for half its sense on one of my outland importations. Comparatively few those of my productions in which I appear to have felt, and with confidence, that source of credit freely negligible; "The Princess Casamassima,"

'The Tragic Muse," "The Spoils of Poynton," "The Other House," "What Maisie Knew," "The Sacred Fount," practically, among the more or less sustained things, exhausting the list—in which moreover I have set down two compositions not included in the present series. Against these longer and shorter novels stand many of the other category; though when it comes to the array of mere brevities—as in "The Marriages" (1891) and four of its companions here—the balance is more evenly struck: a proof, doubtless, that confidence in what he may call the *indirect* initiation, in the comparatively hampered saturation, may even after long years often fail an earnest worker in these fields. Conclusive that, in turn, as to the innumerable parts of the huge machine, a thing of a myriad parts, about which the intending painter of even a few aspects of the life of a great old complex society must either be right or be ridiculous. He has to be, for authority—and on all such ground authority is everything—but continuously and confidently right; to which end, in many a case, if he happens to be but a civil alien, he had best be simply born again—I mean born differently.

Only then, as he's quite liable to say to himself, what would perhaps become, under the dead collective weight of those knowledges that he may, as the case stands for him, often separately miss, what would become of the free intensity of the perceptions which serve him in their stead, in which he never hesitates to rejoice, and to which, in a hundred connexions, he just impudently trusts? The question is too beguiling, alas, now to be gone into; though the mere putting of it fairly *describes* the racked consciousness of the unfortunate who has incurred the dread heritage of easy comparisons. His wealth, in this possession, is supposed to be his freedom of choice, but there are too many days when he asks himself if the artist mayn't easily know an excess of that freedom. Those of the smaller sort never use all the freedom they have—which is the sign, exactly, by which we know them; but those of the greater have never had too much immediately to use—which is the sovereign mark of their felicity. From which range of speculation let me narrow down none the less a little ruefully; since I confess to no great provision of "history" on behalf of "The Marriages." The embodied notion, for this matter, sufficiently tells its story; one has never to go far afield to speculate on the possible pangs of filial piety in face of the successor, in the given instance, to either lost parent, but perhaps more particularly to the lost mother, often inflicted on it by the parent surviving. As in the classic case of Mrs. Glasse's receipt, it's but a question of "first catching" the example of piety intense enough. Granted that, the drama is all there—all in the consciousness, the fond imagination, the possibly poisoned and inflamed judgement, of the suffering subject; where, exactly, "The Marriages" was to find it.

As to the "The Real Thing" (1890) and "Brooksmith" (1891) my recollection is sharp; the subject of each of these tales was suggested to me by a briefly-reported case. To begin with the second-named of them, the appreciative daughter of a friend some time dead had mentioned to me a visit received by her from a servant of the late distinguished lady, a devoted maid whom I remembered well to have repeatedly seen at the latter's side and who had come to discharge herself so far as she might of a sorry burden. She had lived in her mistress's delightful society and in that of the many so interesting friends of the house; she had been formed by nature, as unluckily happened, to enjoy this privilege to the utmost, and the deprivation of everything was now bitterness in her cup. She had had her choice, and had made her trial, of common situations or of a return to her own people, and had found these ordeals alike too cruel. She had in her years of service tasted of conversation and been spoiled for life; she had, in recall of Stendhal's inveterate motto, caught a glimpse, all untimely, of "la beauté parfaite," and should never find again what she had lost—so that nothing was left her but to languish to her end. *There* was a touched spring, of course, to make "Drama-tise, dramatise!" ring out; only my little derived drama, in the event, seemed to require, to be ample enough, a hero rather than a heroine. I desired for my poor lost spirit the measured maximum of the fatal experience: the thing became, in a word, to my imagination, the obscure tragedy of the "intelligent" butler present at rare table-talk, rather than that of the more effaced tirewoman; with which of course was involved a corre-sponding change from mistress to master.

In like manner my much-loved friend George du Maurier had spoken to me of a call from a strange and striking couple desirous to propose themselves as artist's models for his weekly "social" illustrations to "Punch," and the acceptance of whose services would have entailed the dismissal of an undistin-guished but highly expert pair, also husband and wife, who had come to him from far back on the irregular day and whom, thanks to a happy, and to that extent lucrative, ap-pearance of "type" on the part of each, he had reproduced, to the best effect, in a thousand drawing-room attitudes and combinations. Exceedingly modest members of society they earned their bread by looking and, with the aid of supplied toggery, dressing, greater favourites of fortune to the life; or, otherwise expressed, by skilfully feigning a virtue not in the least native to them. Here meanwhile were their so handsome proposed, so anxious, so almost haggard competi-tors, originally, by every sign, of the best condition and estate, but overtaken by reverses even while conforming impeccably to the standard of superficial "smartness" and pleading with well-bred ease and the right light tone, not to say with fever-ish gaiety, that (as in the interest of art itself) *they* at least should n't have to "make believe." The question thus thrown up by the two friendly critics of the rather lurid little passage was of whether their not having to make believe *would* in fact serve them, and above all serve their interpreter as well as the borrowed graces of the comparatively sordid professionals who had had, for dear life, to *know how* (which was to have learnt how) to do something. The question, I recall, struck me as exquisite, and out of a momentary fond consideration of it "The Real Thing" sprang at a bound.

"Flickerbridge" indeed I verily give up: so thoroughly does this highly-finished little anecdote cover its tracks; looking at me, over the few years and out of its bland neatness, with the fine inscrutability, in fact the positive coquetry, of the refusal to answer free-and-easy questions, the mere cold smile for their impertinence, characteristic of any complete artistic thing. "Dramatise, dramatise!"—there had of course been that preliminary, there could n't not have been; but how represent here clearly enough the small succession of steps by which such a case as the admonition is applied to in my picture of Frank Granger's visit to Miss Wenham came to issue from the whole thick-looming cloud of the noted appearances, the dark and dismal consequences, involved more and more to-day in our celebration, our commemoration, our unguardedly-uttered appreciation, of any charming impression? Living as we do under permanent visitation of the deadly epidemic of publicity, any rash word, any light thought that chances to escape us, may instantly, by that accident, find itself propagated and perverted, multiplied and diffused, after a fashion poisonous, practically, and speedily fatal, to its subject—that is to our idea, our sentiment, our figured interest, our too foolishly blabbed secret. Fine old leisure, in George Eliot's phrase, was long ago extinct, but rarity, precious rarity, its twin-sister, lingered on a while only to begin, in like manner, to perish by inches—to learn, in other words, that to be so much as breathed about is to be handed over to the big drum and the brazen blare, with all the effects of the vulgarised, trampled, desecrated state after the cyclone of sound and fury has spent itself. To have observed that, in turn, is to learn to dread reverberation, mere mechanical ventilation, more than the Black Death; which lesson the hero of my little apologue is represented as, all by himself and with anguish at his heart, spelling out the rudiments of. Of course it was a far cry, over intervals of thought, artistically speaking, from the dire truth I here glance at to my small projected example, looking so all unconscious of any such portentous burden of sense; but through that wilderness I shall not attempt to guide my reader. Let the accomplishment of the march figure for him, on the author's part, the arduous sport, in such a waste, of "dramatising."

Intervals of thought and a desolation of missing links strike me, not less, as marking the approach to any simple expression of my "original hint" for "The Story In It." What I definitely recall of the history of this tolerably recent production is that, even after I had exerted a ferocious and far from fruitless ingenuity to keep it from becoming a *nouvelle*— for it is in fact one of the briefest of my compositions— it still haunted, a graceless beggar, for a couple of years, the cold avenues of publicity; till finally an old acquaintance, about to "start a magazine," begged it in turn of me and published it (1903) at no cost to himself but the cost of his confidence, in that first number which was in the event, if I mistake not, to prove only one of a pair. I like perhaps "morbidly" to think that the Story in it may have been more than the magazine could carry. There at any rate—*for* the "story," that is for the pure pearl of my idea—I had to take, in the name of the particular instance, no less deep and straight a dive into the deep sea of a certain general truth than I had taken in quest of "Flickerbridge." The general truth had been positively phrased for me by a distinguished friend, a novelist not to *our* manner either born or bred, on the occasion of his having made such answer as he could to an interlocutor (he, oh distinctly, indigenous and glib!) bent on learning from him why the adventures he imputed to his heroines were so perversely and persistently but of a type impossible to ladies respecting themselves. My friend's reply had been, not unnaturally, and above all not incongruously, that ladies who respected themselves took particular care never to *have* adventures; not the least little adventure that would be worth (worth any self-respecting novelist's) speaking of. There were certainly, it was to be hoped, ladies who practised that reserve—which, however beneficial to themselves, was yet fatally detrimental to literature, in the sense of promptly making any artistic harmony pitched in the same low key trivial and empty. A picture of life founded on the mere reserves and omissions and suppressions of life, what sort of a performance—for beauty, for interest, for tone—could *that* hope to be? The enquiry was n't answered in any hearing of mine, and of course indeed, on all such ground, discussion, to be really luminous, would have to rest on some such perfect definition of terms as is not of this muddled world. It is, not surprisingly, one of the rudiments of criticism that a human, a personal "adventure" is no *a priori,* no positive and absolute and inelastic thing, but just a matter of relation and appreciation—a name we conveniently give, after the fact, to any passage, to any situation, that has added the sharp taste of uncertainty to a quickened sense of life. Therefore the thing is, all beautifully, a matter of interpretation and of the particular conditions; without a view of which latter some of the most prodigious adventures, as one has often had occasion to say, may vulgarly show for nothing. However that may be, I hasten to add, the mere stir of the air round the question reflected in the brief but earnest interchange I have just reported was to cause a "subject," to my sense, immediately to bloom there. So it suddenly, on its small scale, seemed to stand erect—or at least quite intelligently to lift its head; just *a* subject, clearly, though I could n't immediately tell which or what. To find out I had to get a little closer to it, and "The Story In It" precisely represents that undertaking.

As for "The Beldonald Holbein," about which I have said nothing, *that* story—by which I mean the story *of* it—would take us much too far. "Mrs. Medwin," published in "Punch"

(1902) and in "The Better Sort" (1903), I have also accommodated here for convenience. There is a note or two I would fain add to this; but I check myself with the sense of having, as it is, to all probability, vindicated with a due zeal, not to say a due extravagance, the most general truth of many a story-teller's case: the truth, already more than once elsewhere glanced at, that what longest lives to his backward vision, in the whole business, is not the variable question of the "success," but the inveterate romance of the labour.

XVI

PREFACE TO "THE WINGS OF THE DOVE"

(VOLUME XIX IN THE NEW YORK EDITION)

"THE WINGS OF THE DOVE," published in 1902, represents to my memory a very old—if I should n't perhaps rather say a very young—motive; I can scarce remember the time when the situation on which this long-drawn fiction mainly rests was not vividly present to me. The idea, reduced to its essence, is that of a young person conscious of a great capacity for life, but early stricken and doomed, condemned to die under short respite, while also enamoured of the world; aware moreover of the condemnation and passionately desiring to "put in" before extinction as many of the finer vibrations as possible, and so achieve, however briefly and brokenly, the sense of having lived. Long had I turned it over, standing off from it, yet coming back to it; convinced of what might be done with it, yet seeing the theme as formidable. The image so figured would be, at best, but half the matter; the rest would be all the picture of the struggle involved, the adventure brought about, the gain recorded or the loss incurred, the precious experience somehow compassed. These things, I had from the first felt, would require much working-out; that indeed was the case with most things worth working at all; yet there are subjects and subjects, and this one seemed particularly to bristle. It was formed, I judged, to make the wary adventurer walk round and round it—it had in fact a charm that invited and mystified alike that attention; not being somehow what one thought of as a "frank" subject, after the fashion of some, with its elements well in view and its whole character in its

face. It stood there with secrets and compartments, with possible treacheries and traps; it might have a great deal to give,
but would probably ask for equal services in return, and would
collect this debt to the last shilling. It involved, to begin with,
the placing in the strongest light a person infirm and ill—a case
sure to prove difficult and to require much handling; though
giving perhaps, with other matters, one of those chances for
good taste, possibly even for the play of the very best in the
world, that are not only always to be invoked and cultivated,
but that are absolutely to be jumped at from the moment they
make a sign.

Yes then, the case prescribed for its central figure a sick
young woman, at the whole course of whose disintegration
and the whole ordeal of whose consciousness one would have
quite honestly to assist. The expression of her state and that of
one's intimate relation to it might therefore well need to be
discreet and ingenious; a reflexion that fortunately grew and
grew, however, in proportion as I focussed my image—roundabout which, as it persisted, I repeat, the interesting possibilities
and the attaching wonderments, not to say the insoluble mysteries, thickened apace. Why had one to look so straight in
the face and so closely to cross-question that idea of making
one's protagonist "sick"?—as if to be menaced with death or
danger had n't been from time immemorial, for heroine or
hero, the very shortest of all cuts to the interesting state. Why
should a figure be disqualified for a central position by the
particular circumstance that might most quicken, that might
crown with a fine intensity, its liability to many accidents, its
consciousness of all relations? This circumstance, true enough,
might disqualify it for many activities—even though we should
have imputed to it the unsurpassable activity of passionate,
of inspired resistance. This last fact was the real issue, for
the way grew straight from the moment one recognised that
the poet essentially *can't* be concerned with the act of dying.
Let him deal with the sickest of the sick, it is still by the

act of living that they appeal to him, and appeal the more as the conditions plot against them and prescribe the battle. The process of life gives way fighting, and often may so shine out on the lost ground as in no other connexion. One had had moreover, as a various chronicler, one's secondary physical weaklings and failures, one's accessory invalids—introduced with a complacency that made light of criticism. To Ralph Touchett in "The Portrait of a Lady," for instance, his deplorable state of health was not only no drawback; I had clearly been right in counting it, for any happy effect he should produce, a positive good mark, a direct aid to pleasantness and vividness. The reason of this moreover could never in the world have been his fact of sex; since men, among the mortally afflicted, suffer on the whole more overtly and more grossly than women, and resist with a ruder, an inferior strategy. I had thus to take *that* anomaly for what it was worth, and I give it here but as one of the ambiguities amid which my subject ended by making itself at home and seating itself quite in confidence.

With the clearness I have just noted, accordingly, the last thing in the world it proposed to itself was to be the record predominantly of a collapse. I don't mean to say that my offered victim was not present to my imagination, constantly, as dragged by a greater force than any she herself could exert; she had been given me from far back as contesting every inch of the road, as catching at every object the grasp of which might make for delay, as clutching these things to the last moment of her strength. Such an attitude and such movements, the passion they expressed and the success they in fact represented, what were they in truth but the soul of drama?—which is the portrayal, as we know, of a catastrophe determined in spite of oppositions. My young woman would *herself* be the opposition—to the catastrophe announced by the associated Fates, powers conspiring to a sinister end and, with their command of means, finally achieving it, yet in such straits really to *stifle* the sacred spark that, obviously, a creature so animated, **an adversary so subtle**, could n't but be felt worthy, **under whatever weaknesses**, of the foreground and the limelight. **She** would meanwhile wish, moreover, all along, to live for particular things, she would found her struggle on particular human interests, which would inevitably determine, in respect to her, the attitude of other persons, persons affected in such a manner as to make them part of the action. If her impulse to wrest from her shrinking hour still as much of the fruit of life as possible, if this longing can take effect only by the aid of others, their participation (appealed to, entangled and coerced as they find themselves) becomes their drama too—that of their promoting her illusion, under her importunity, for reasons, for interests and advantages, from motives and points of view, of their own. Some of these promptings, evidently, would be of the highest order—others doubtless might n't; but they would make up together, for her, contributively, her sum of experience, represent to her somehow, in good faith or in bad, what she should have *known*. Somehow, too, at such a rate, one would see the persons subject to them drawn in as by some pool of a Lorelei—see them terrified and tempted and charmed; bribed away, it may even be, from more prescribed and natural orbits, inheriting from their connexion with her strange difficulties and still stranger opportunities, confronted with rare questions and called upon for new discriminations. Thus the scheme of her situation would, in a comprehensive way, see itself constituted; the rest of the interest would be in the number and nature of the particulars. Strong among these, naturally, the need that life should, apart from her infirmity, present itself to our young woman as quite dazzlingly liveable, and that if the great pang for her is in what she must give up we shall appreciate it the more from the sight of all she has.

One would see her then as possessed of all things, all but the single most precious assurance; freedom and money and a mobile mind and personal charm, the power to interest and attach; attributes, each one, enhancing the value of a future. From the moment his imagination began to deal with her at close quarters, in fact, nothing could more engage her designer than to work out the detail of her perfect rightness for her part; nothing above all more solicit him than to recognise fifty reasons for her national and social status. She should be the last fine flower—blooming alone, for the fullest attestation of her freedom—of an "old" New York stem; the happy congruities thus preserved for her being matters, however, that I may not now go into, and this even though the fine association that shall yet elsewhere await me is of a sort, at the best, rather to defy than to encourage exact expression. There goes with it, for the heroine of "The Wings of the Dove," a strong and special implication of liberty, liberty of action, of choice, of appreciation, of contact—proceeding from sources that provide better for large independence, I think, than any other conditions in the world—and this would be in particular what we should feel ourselves deeply concerned with. I had from far back mentally projected a certain sort of young American as more the "heir of all the ages" than any other young person whatever (and precisely on those grounds I have just glanced at but to pass them by for the moment); so that here was a chance to confer on some such figure a supremely touching value. To be the heir of all the ages only to know yourself, as that consciousness should deepen, balked of your inheritance, would be to play the part, it struck me, or at least to arrive at the type, in the light on the whole the most becoming. Otherwise, truly, what a perilous part to play *out*—what a suspicion of "swagger" in positively attempting it! So at least I could reason—so I even think I *had* to—to keep my subject to a decent compactness. For already, from an early stage, it had begun richly to people itself: the difficulty was to see whom the situation I had primarily projected might, by this, that or the other turn, *not* draw in. My business was to watch its turns as the fond parent watches a child perched, for its first riding-lesson, in the saddle; yet its interest, I had all the while to recall, was just in its making, on such a scale, for developments.

What one had discerned, at all events, from an early stage, was that a young person so devoted and exposed, a creature with her security hanging so by a hair, could n't but fall somehow into some abysmal trap—this being, dramatically speaking, what such a situation most naturally implied and imposed. Did n't the truth and a great part of the interest also reside in the appearance that she would constitute for others (given her passionate yearning to live while she might) a complication as great as any they might constitute for herself?—which is what I mean when I speak of such matters as "natural." They would be as natural, these tragic, pathetic, ironic, these indeed for the most part sinister, liabilities, to her living associates, as they could be to herself as prime subject. If her story was to consist, as it could so little help doing, of her being let in, as we say, for this, that and the other irreducible anxiety, how could she not have put a premium on the acquisition, by any close sharer of her life, of a consciousness similarly embarrassed? I have named the Rhine-maiden, but our young friend's existence would create rather, all round her, very much that whirlpool movement of the waters produced by the sinking of a big vessel or the failure of a great business; when we figure to ourselves the strong narrowing eddies, the immense force of suction, the general engulfment that, for any neighbouring object, makes immersion inevitable. I need scarce say, however, that in spite of these communities of doom I saw the main dramatic complication much more prepared *for* my vessel of sensibility than by her—the work of other hands (though with her own imbrued too, after all, in the measure of their never not being, in some direction, generous and extravagant, and thereby provoking).

The great point was, at all events, that if in a predicament she was to be, accordingly, it would be of the essence to create the predicament promptly and build it up solidly, so that it should have for us as much as possible its ominous air of awaiting her. That reflexion I found, betimes, not less inspiring than urgent; one begins so, in such a business, by looking about for one's compositional key, unable as one can only be to move till one has found it. To start without it is to pretend to enter the train and, still more, to remain in one's seat, without a ticket. Well—in the steady light and for the continued charm of these verifications—I had secured my ticket over the tolerably long line laid down for "The Wings of the Dove" from the moment I had noted that there could be no full presentation of Milly Theale as *engaged* with elements amid which she was to draw her breath in such pain, should not the elements have been, with all solicitude, duly prefigured. If one had seen that her stricken state was but half her case, the correlative half being the state of others as affected by her (they too should have a "case," bless them, quite as much as she!) then I was free to choose, as it were, the half with which I should begin. If, as I had fondly noted, the little world determined for her was to "bristle"—I delighted in the term!—with meanings, so, by the same token, could I but make my medal hang free, its obverse and its reverse, its face and its back, would beautifully become optional for the spectator. I somehow wanted them correspondingly embossed, wanted them inscribed and figured with an equal salience; yet it was none the less visibly my "key," as I have said, that though my regenerate young New Yorker, and what might depend on her, should form my centre, my circumference was every whit as treatable. Therefore I must trust myself to know when to proceed from the one and when from the other. Preparatively and, as it were, yearningly—given the whole ground—one began, in the event, with the outer ring, approaching the centre thus by narrowing circumvallations. There, full-blown, accordingly, from one hour to the other, rose one's process—for which there remained all the while so many amusing formulae.

The medal *did* hang free—I felt this perfectly, I remember, from the moment I had comfortably laid the ground provided in my first Book, ground from which Milly is superficially so absent. I scarce remember perhaps a case—I like even with this public grossness to insist on it—in which the curiosity of "beginning far back," as far back as possible, and even of going, to the same tune, far "behind," that is behind the face of the subject, was to assert itself with less scruple. The free hand, in this connexion, was above all agreeable—the hand the freedom of which I owed to the fact that the work had ignominiously failed, in advance, of all power to see itself "serialised." This failure had repeatedly waited, for me, upon shorter fictions; but the considerable production we here discuss was (as "The Golden Bowl" was to be, two or three years later) born, not otherwise than a little bewilderedly, into a world of periodicals and editors, of roaring "successes" in fine, amid which it was well-nigh unnotedly to lose itself. There is fortunately something bracing, ever, in the alpine chill, that of some high icy *arête,* shed by the cold editorial shoulder; sour grapes may at moments fairly intoxicate and the story-teller worth his salt rejoice to feel again how many accommodations he can practise. Those addressed to "conditions of publication" have in a degree their interesting, or at least their provoking, side; but their charm is qualified by the fact that the prescriptions here spring from a soil often wholly alien to the ground of the work itself. They are almost always the fruit of another air altogether and conceived in a light liable to represent *within* the circle of the work itself little else than darkness. Still, when not too blighting, they often operate as a tax on ingenuity—that ingenuity of the expert craftsman which likes to be taxed very much to the same tune to which a well-bred horse likes to be saddled. The best and finest ingenuities, nevertheless, with all respect to that truth, are apt to be, not one's compromises, but one's fullest conformities, and I well remember, in the case before us, the pleasure of feeling my divisions, my proportions and general rhythm, rest all on permanent rather than in any degree on momentary proprieties. It was enough for my alternations, thus, that they were good in themselves; it was in fact so much for them that I really think any further account of the constitution of the book reduces itself to a just notation of the law they followed.

There was the "fun," to begin with, of establishing one's successive centres—of fixing them so exactly that the portions of the subject commanded by them as by happy points of view, and accordingly treated from them, would constitute, so to speak, sufficiently solid *blocks* of wrought material, squared to the sharp edge, as to have weight and mass and carrying power; to make for construction, that is, to conduce to effect and to provide for beauty. Such a block, obviously, is the whole preliminary presentation of Kate Croy, which, from the first, I recall, absolutely declined to enact itself save in terms of amplitude. Terms of amplitude, terms of atmosphere, those terms, and those terms only, in which images assert their fulness and roundness, their power to revolve, so that they have sides and backs, parts in the shade as true as parts in the sun—these were plainly to be my conditions, right and left, and I was so far from overrating the amount of expression the whole thing, as I saw and felt it, would require, that to retrace the way at present is, alas, more than anything else, but to mark the gaps and the lapses, to miss, one by one, the intentions that, with the best will in the world, were not to fructify. I have just said that the process of the general attempt is described from the moment the "blocks" are numbered, and that would be a true enough picture of my plan. Yet one's plan, alas, is one thing and one's result another; so I am perhaps nearer the point in saying that this last strikes me at present as most characterised by the happy features that *were,* under my first and most blest illusion, to have contributed

to it. I meet them all, as I renew acquaintance, I mourn for
them all as I remount the stream, the absent values, the palpable voids, the missing links, the mocking shadows, that reflect,
taken together, the early bloom of one's good faith. Such
cases are of course far from abnormal—so far from it that
some acute mind ought surely to have worked out by this
time the "law" of the degree in which the artist's energy
fairly depends on his fallibility. How much and how often,
and in what connexions and with what almost infinite variety,
must he be a dupe, that of his prime object, to be at all measurably a master, that of his actual substitute for it—or in other
words at all appreciably to exist? He places, after an earnest
survey, the piers of his bridge—he has at least sounded deep
enough, heaven knows, for their brave position; yet the bridge
spans the stream, after the fact, in apparently complete independence of these properties, the principal grace of the original
design. *They* were an illusion, for their necessary hour; but
the span itself, whether of a single arch or of many, seems by
the oddest chance in the world to be a reality; since, actually,
the rueful builder, passing under it, sees figures and hears
sounds above: he makes out, with his heart in his throat, that
it bears and is positively being "used."

The building-up of Kate Croy's consciousness to the capacity
for the load little by little to be laid on it was, by way of example, to have been a matter of as many hundred close-packed
bricks as there are actually poor dozens. The image of her so
compromised and compromising father was all effectively to
have pervaded her life, was in a certain particular way to have
tampered with her spring; by which I mean that the shame and
the irritation and the depression, the general poisonous influence of him, were to have been *shown,* with a truth beyond the
compass even of one's most emphasised "word of honour" for
it, to do these things. But where do we find him, at this time
of day, save in a beggarly scene or two which scarce arrives at
the dignity of functional reference? He but "looks in," poor

beautiful dazzling, damning apparition that he was to have been; he sees his place so taken, his company so little missed, that, cocking again that fine form of hat which has yielded him for so long his one effective cover, he turns away with a whistle of indifference that nobly misrepresents the deepest disappointment of his life. One's poor word of honour has *had* to pass muster for the show. Every one, in short, was to have enjoyed so much better a chance that, like stars of the theatre condescending to oblige, they have had to take small parts, to content themselves with minor identities, in order to come on at all. I have n't the heart now, I confess, to adduce the detail of so many lapsed importances; the explanation of most of which, after all, I take to have been in the crudity of a truth beating full upon me through these reconsiderations, the odd inveteracy with which picture, at almost any turn, is jealous of drama, and drama (though on the whole with a greater patience, I think) suspicious of picture. Between them, no doubt, they do much for the theme; yet each baffles insidiously the other's ideal and eats round the edges of its position; each is too ready to say "I can take the thing for 'done' only when done in *my* way." The residuum of comfort for the witness of these broils is of course meanwhile in the convenient reflexion, invented for him in the twilight of time and the infancy of art by the Angel, not to say by the Demon, of Compromise, that nothing is so easy to "do" as not to be thankful for almost any stray help in its getting done. It was n't, after this fashion, by making good one's dream of Lionel Croy that my structure was to stand on its feet—any more than it was by letting him go that I was to be left irretrievably lamenting. The who and the what, the how and the why, the whence and the whither of Merton Densher, these, no less, were quantities and attributes that should have danced about him with the antique grace of nymphs and fauns circling round a bland Hermes and crowning him with flowers. One's main anxiety, for each one's agents, is that the air of each shall be *given;* but what does the whole thing become, after all, as one goes, but a series of sad places at which the hand of generosity has been cautioned and stayed? The young man's situation, personal, professional, social, was to have been so decanted for us that we should get all the taste; we were to have been penetrated with Mrs. Lowder, by the same token, saturated with her presence, her "personality," and felt all her weight in the scale. We were to have revelled in Mrs. Stringham, my heroine's attendant friend, her fairly choral Bostonian, a subject for innumerable touches, and in an extended and above all an *animated* reflexion of Milly Theale's experience of English society; just as the strength and sense of the situation in Venice, for our gathered friends, was to have come to us in a deeper draught out of a larger cup, and just as the pattern of Densher's final position and fullest consciousness there was to have been marked in fine stitches, all silk and gold, all pink and silver, that have had to remain, alas, but entwined upon the reel.

It isn't, no doubt, however—to recover, after all, our critical balance—that the pattern didn't, for each compartment, get itself somehow wrought, and that we mightn't thus, piece by piece, opportunity offering, trace it over and study it. The thing has doubtless, as a whole, the advantage that each piece is true to its pattern, and that while it pretends to make no simple statement it yet never lets go its scheme of clearness. Applications of this scheme are continuous and exemplary enough, though I scarce leave myself room to glance at them. The clearness is obtained in Book First—or otherwise, as I have said, in the first "piece," each Book having its subordinate and contributive pattern—through the associated consciousness of my two prime young persons, for whom I early recognised that I should have to consent, under stress, to a practical *fusion* of consciousness. It is into the young woman's "ken" that Merton Densher is represented as swimming; but her mind is not here, rigorously, the one reflector. There are occasions when it plays this part, just as there are others when his plays it, and an intelligible plan consists naturally not a little in fixing such occasions and making them, on one side and the other, sufficient to themselves. Do I sometimes in fact forfeit the advantage of that distinctness? Do I ever abandon one centre for another after the former has been postulated? From the moment we proceed by "centres"—and I have never, I confess, embraced the logic of any superior process—they must *be,* each, as a basis, selected and fixed; after which it is that, in the high interest of economy of treatment, they determine and rule. There is no economy of treatment without an adopted, a related point of view, and though I understand, under certain degrees of pressure, a represented community of vision between several parties to the action when it makes for concentration, I understand no breaking-up of the register, no sacrifice of the recording consistency, that doesn't rather scatter and weaken. In this truth resides the secret of the discriminated occasion—that aspect of the subject which we have our noted choice of treating either as picture or scenically, but which is apt, I think, to show its fullest worth in the Scene. Beautiful exceedingly, for that matter, those occasions or parts of an occasion when the boundary line between picture and scene bears a little the weight of the double pressure.

Such would be the case, I can't but surmise, for the long passage that forms here before us the opening of Book Fourth, where all the offered life centres, to intensity, in the disclosure of Milly's single throbbing consciousness, but where, for a due rendering, everything has to be brought to a head. This passage, the view of her introduction to Mrs. Lowder's circle, has its mate, for illustration, later on in the book and at a crisis for which the occasion submits to another rule. My registers or "reflectors," as I so conveniently name them (burnished indeed as they generally are by the intelligence, the curiosity, the passion, the force of the moment, whatever it be, directing them), work, as we have seen, in arranged alternation; so that in the second connexion I here glance at it is Kate Croy who is, "for all she is worth," turned on. She is turned on largely at Venice, where the appearances, rich and obscure and portentous (another word I rejoice in) as they have by that time become and altogether exquisite as they remain, are treated almost wholly through her vision of them and Densher's (as to the lucid interplay of which conspiring and conflicting agents there would be a great deal to say). It is in Kate's consciousness that at the stage in question the drama is brought to a head, and the occasion on which, in the splendid saloon of poor Milly's hired palace, she takes the measure of her friend's festal evening, squares itself to the same synthetic firmness as the compact constructional block inserted by the scene at Lancaster Gate. Milly's situation ceases at a given moment to be "renderable" in terms closer than those supplied by Kate's intelligence, or, in a richer degree, by Densher's, or, for one fond hour, by poor Mrs. Stringham's (since to that sole brief futility is this last participant, crowned by my original plan with the quaintest functions, in fact reduced); just as Kate's relation with Densher and Densher's with Kate have ceased previously, and are then to cease again, to be projected for us, so far as Milly is concerned with them, on any more responsible plate than that of the latter's admirable anxiety. It is as if, for these aspects, the impersonal plate—in other words the poor author's comparatively cold affirmation or thin guarantee—had felt itself a figure of attestation at once too gross and too bloodless, likely to affect us as an abuse of privilege when not as an abuse of knowledge.

Heaven forbid, we say to ourselves during almost the whole Venetian climax, heaven forbid we should "know" anything more of our ravaged sister than what Densher darkly pieces together, or than what Kate Croy pays, heroically, it must be owned, at the hour of her visit alone to Densher's lodging, for her superior handling and her dire profanation of. For we have time, while this passage lasts, to turn round critically; we have time to recognise intentions and proprieties; we have time to catch glimpses of an economy of composition, as I put it, interesting in itself: all in spite of the author's scarce more than half-dissimulated despair at the inveterate displacement of his general centre. "The Wings of the Dove" happens to offer perhaps the most striking example I may cite (though with public penance for it already performed) of my regular failure to keep the appointed halves of my whole equal. Here the makeshift middle—for which the best I can say is that it's always rueful and never impudent—reigns with even more than its customary contrition, though passing itself off perhaps too with more than its usual craft. Nowhere, I seem to recall, had the need of dissimulation been felt so as anguish; nowhere had I condemned a luckless theme to complete its revolution, burdened with the accumulation of its difficulties, the difficulties that grow with a theme's development, in quarters so cramped. Of course, as every novelist knows, it is difficulty that inspires; only, for that perfection of charm, it must have been difficulty inherent and congenital, and not difficulty "caught" by the wrong frequentations. The latter half, that is the false and deformed half, of "The Wings" would verily, I think, form a signal object-lesson for a literary critic bent on improving his occasion to the profit of the budding artist. This whole corner of the picture bristles with "dodges"—such as he should feel himself all committed to recognise and denounce—for disguising the reduced scale of the exhibition, for foreshortening at any cost, for imparting to patches the value of presences, for dressing objects in an *air* as of the dimensions they can't possibly have. Thus he would have his free hand for pointing out what a tangled web we weave when—well, when, through our mislaying or otherwise trifling with our blest pair of compasses, we have to produce the illusion of mass without the illusion of extent. *There* is a job quite to the measure of most of our monitors—and with the interest for them well enhanced by the preliminary cunning quest for the spot where deformity has begun.

I recognise meanwhile, throughout the long earlier reach of the book, not only no deformities but, I think, a positively close and felicitous application of method, the preserved consistencies of which, often illusive, but never really lapsing, it would be of a certain diversion, and might be of some profit, to follow. The author's accepted task at the outset has been to suggest with force the nature of the tie formed between the two young persons first introduced— to give the full impression of its peculiar worried and baffled, yet clinging and confident, ardour. The picture constituted, so far as may be, is that of a pair of natures well-nigh consumed by a sense of their intimate affinity and congruity, the reciprocity of their desire, and thus passionately impatient of barriers and delays, yet with qualities of intelligence and character that they are meanwhile extraordinarily able to draw upon for the enrichment of their relation, the extension of their prospect and the support of their "game." They are far from a common couple, Merton Densher and Kate Croy, as befits the remarkable fashion in which fortune was to waylay and opportunity was to distinguish them— the whole strange truth of their response to which opening involves also, in its order, no vulgar art of exhibition; but what they have most to tell us is that, all unconsciously and with the best faith in the world, all by mere force of the terms of their superior passion combined with their superior diplomacy, they are laying a trap for the great innocence to come. If I like, as I have confessed, the "portentous" look, I was perhaps never to set so high a value on it as for all this prompt provision of forces unwittingly waiting to close round my eager heroine (to the eventual deep chill of her eagerness) as the result of her mere lifting of a latch. Infinitely interesting to have built up the relation of the others to the point at which its aching restlessness, its need to affirm itself otherwise than by an exasperated patience, meets as with instinctive relief and recognition the possibilities shining out of Milly Theale. Infinitely interesting to have prepared and organised, correspondingly, that young woman's precipitations and liabilities, to have constructed, for Drama essentially to take possession, the whole bright house of her exposure.

These references, however, reflect too little of the detail of the treatment imposed; such a detail as I for instance get hold of in the fact of Densher's interview with Mrs. Lowder before he goes to America. It forms, in this preliminary picture, the one patch not strictly seen over Kate Croy's shoulder; though it 's notable that immediately after, at the first possible moment, we surrender again to our major convenience, as it happens to be at the time, that of our drawing breath through the young woman's lungs. Once more, in other words, before we know it, Densher's direct vision of the scene at Lancaster Gate is replaced by her apprehension, her contributive assimilation, of his experience: it melts back into that accumulation, which we have been, as it were, saving up. Does my apparent deviation here count accordingly as a muddle?—one of the muddles ever blooming so thick in any soil that fails to grow reasons and determinants. No, distinctly not; for I had definitely opened the door, as attention of perusal of the first two Books will show, to the subjective community of my young pair. (Attention of perusal, I thus confess by the way, is what I at every point, as well as here, absolutely invoke and take for granted; a truth I avail myself of this occasion to note once for all—in the interest of that variety of ideal reigning, I gather, in the connexion. The enjoyment of a work of art, the acceptance of an irresistible illusion, constituting, to my sense, our highest experience of "luxury," the luxury is not greatest, by my consequent measure, when the work asks for as little attention as possible. It is greatest, it is delightfully, divinely great, when we feel the surface, like the thick ice of the skater's pond, bear without cracking

the strongest pressure we throw on it. The sound of the crack
one may recognise, but never surely to call it a luxury.) That
I had scarce availed myself of the privilege of seeing with
Densher's eyes is another matter; the point is that I had intelligently marked my possible, my occasional need of it. So, at all
events, the constructional "block" of the first two Books com-
pactly forms itself. A new block, all of the squarest and not a
little of the smoothest, begins with the Third—by which I mean
of course a new mass of interest governed from a new centre.
Here again I make prudent *provision*—to be sure to keep my
centre strong. It dwells mainly, we at once see, in the depths
of Milly Theale's "case," where, close beside it, however, we
meet a supplementary reflector, that of the lucid even though
so quivering spirit of her dedicated friend.

The more or less associated consciousness of the two women
deals thus, unequally, with the next presented face of the
subject—deals with it to the exclusion of the dealing of others;
and if, for a highly particular moment, I allot to Mrs. Stringham the responsibility of the direct appeal to us, it is again,
charming to relate, on behalf of that play of the portentous
which I cherish so as a "value" and am accordingly for ever
setting in motion. There is an hour of evening, on the alpine
height, at which it becomes of the last importance that our
young woman should testify eminently in this direction. But
as I was to find it long since of a blest wisdom that no expense
should be incurred or met, in any corner of picture of mine,
without some concrete image of the account kept of it, that is
of its being organically re-economised, so under that dispen-
sation Mrs. Stringham has to register the transaction. Book
Fifth is a new block mainly in its provision of a new set of
occasions, which readopt, for their order, the previous centre,
Milly's now almost full-blown consciousness. At my game,
with renewed zest, of driving portents home, I have by this
time all the choice of those that are to brush that surface with a
dark wing. They are used, to our profit, on an elastic but a

definite system; by which I mean that having to sound here and there a little deep, as a test, for my basis of method, I find it everywhere obstinately present. It draws the "occasion" into tune and keeps it so, to repeat my tiresome term; my nearest approach to muddlement is to have sometimes—but not too often—to break my occasions small. Some of them succeed in remaining ample and in really aspiring then to the higher, the sustained lucidity. The whole actual centre of the work, resting on a misplaced pivot and lodged in Book Fifth, pretends to a long reach, or at any rate to the larger foreshortening—though bringing home to me, on re-perusal, what I find striking, charming and curious, the author's instinct everywhere for the *indirect* presentation of his main image. I note how, again and again, I go but a little way with the direct—that is with the straight exhibition of Milly; it resorts for relief, this process, whenever it can, to some kinder, some merciful indirection: all as if to approach her circuitously, deal with her at second hand, as an unspotted princess is ever dealt with; the pressure all round her kept easy for her, the sounds, the movements regulated, the forms and ambiguities made charming. All of which proceeds, obviously, from her painter's tenderness of imagination about her, which reduces him to watching her, as it were, through the successive windows of other people's interest in her. So, if we talk of princesses, do the balconies opposite the palace gates, do the coigns of vantage and respect enjoyed for a fee, rake from afar the mystic figure in the gilded coach as it comes forth into the great *place*. But my use of windows and balconies is doubtless at best an extravagance by itself, and as to what there may be to note, of this and other supersubtleties, other arch-refinements, of tact and taste, of design and instinct, in "The Wings of the Dove," I become conscious of overstepping my space without having brought the full quantity to light. The failure leaves me with a burden of residuary comment of which I yet boldly hope elsewhere to discharge myself.

XVII

PREFACE TO "THE AMBASSADORS"

NOTHING is more easy than to state the subject of "The Ambassadors," which first appeared in twelve numbers of "The North American Review" (1903) and was published as a whole the same year. The situation involved is gathered up betimes, that is in the second chapter of Book Fifth, for the reader's benefit, into as few words as possible—planted or "sunk," stiffly and saliently, in the centre of the current, almost perhaps to the obstruction of traffic. Never can a composition of this sort have sprung straighter from a dropped grain of suggestion, and never can that grain, developed, overgrown and smothered, have yet lurked more in the mass as an independent particle. The whole case, in fine, is in Lambert Strether's irrepressible outbreak to little Bilham on the Sunday afternoon in Gloriani's garden, the candour with which he yields, for his young friend's enlightenment, to the charming admonition of that crisis. The idea of the tale resides indeed in the very fact that an hour of such unprecedented ease should have been felt by him *as* a crisis, and he is at pains to express it for us as neatly as we could desire. The remarks to which he thus gives utterance contain the essence of "The Ambassadors," his fingers close, before he has done, round the stem of the full-blown flower; which, after that fashion, he continues officiously to present to us. "Live all you can; it's a mistake not to. It does n't so much matter what you do in particular so long as you have your life. If you have n't had that what *have* you had? I'm too old—too old at any rate for what I see. What one loses one

loses; make no mistake about that. Still, we have the illusion of freedom; therefore don't, like me to-day, be without
the memory of that illusion. I was either, at the right time,
too stupid or too intelligent to have it, and now I'm a case
of reaction against the mistake. Do what you like so long
as you don't make it. For it *was* a mistake. Live, live!"
Such is the gist of Strether's appeal to the impressed youth,
whom he likes and whom he desires to befriend; the word
"mistake" occurs several times, it will be seen, in the course
of his remarks—which gives the measure of the signal warning he feels attached to his case. He has accordingly missed
too much, though perhaps after all constitutionally qualified
for a better part, and he wakes up to it in conditions that
press the spring of a terrible question. *Would* there yet perhaps be time for reparation?—reparation, that is, for the injury
done his character; for the affront, he is quite ready to say, so
stupidly put upon it and in which he has even himself had so
clumsy a hand? The answer to which is that he now at all
events *sees;* so that the business of my tale and the march of my
action, not to say the precious moral of everything, is just my
demonstration of this process of vision.

Nothing can exceed the closeness with which the whole
fits again into its germ. That had been given me bodily, as
usual, by the spoken word, for I was to take the image over
exactly as I happened to have met it. A friend had repeated
to me, with great appreciation, a thing or two said to him
by a man of distinction, much his senior, and to which a
sense akin to that of Strether's melancholy eloquence might
be imputed—said as chance would have, and so easily might,
in Paris, and in a charming old garden attached to a house
of art, and on a Sunday afternoon of summer, many persons
of great interest being present. The observation there listened
to and gathered up had contained part of the "note" that I was
to recognise on the spot as to my purpose—had contained in
fact the greater part; the rest was in the place and the time and

the scene they sketched: these constituents clustered and combined to give me further support, to give me what I may call the note absolute. There it stands, accordingly, full in the tideway; driven in, with hard taps, like some strong stake for the noose of a cable, the swirl of the current roundabout it. What amplified the hint to more than the bulk of hints in general was the gift with it of the old Paris garden, for in that token were sealed up values infinitely precious. There was of course the seal to break and each item of the packet to count over and handle and estimate; but somehow, in the light of the hint, all the elements of a situation of the sort most to my taste were there. I could even remember no occasion on which, so confronted, I had found it of a livelier interest to take stock, in this fashion, of suggested wealth. For I think, verily, that there are degrees of merit in subjects—in spite of the fact that to treat even one of the most ambiguous with due decency we must for the time, for the feverish and prejudiced hour, at least figure its merit and its dignity as *possibly* absolute. What it comes to, doubtless, is that even among the supremely good—since with such alone is it one's theory of one's honour to be concerned—there is an ideal *beauty* of goodness the invoked action of which is to raise the artistic faith to its maximum. Then truly, I hold, one's theme may be said to shine, and that of "The Ambassadors," I confess, wore this glow for me from beginning to end. Fortunately thus I am able to estimate this as, frankly, quite the best, "all round," of my productions; any failure of that justification would have made such an extreme of complacency publicly fatuous.

I recall then in this connexion no moment of subjective intermittence, never one of those alarms as for a suspected hollow beneath one's feet, a felt ingratitude in the scheme adopted, under which confidence fails and opportunity seems but to mock. If the motive of "The Wings of the Dove," as I have noted, was to worry me at moments by a sealing-

up of its face—though without prejudice to its again, of
a sudden, fairly grimacing with expression—so in this other
business I had absolute conviction and constant clearness to
deal with; it had been a frank proposition, the whole bunch
of data, installed on my premises like a monotony of fine
weather. (The order of composition, in these things, I may
mention, was reversed by the order of publication; the earlier
written of the two books having appeared as the later.) Even
under the weight of my hero's years I could feel my postulate
firm; even under the strain of the difference between those of
Madame de Vionnet and those of Chad Newsome, a difference liable to be denounced as shocking, I could still feel it
serene. Nothing resisted, nothing betrayed, I seem to make
out, in this full and sound sense of the matter; it shed from any
side I could turn it to the same golden glow. I rejoiced in the
promise of a hero so mature, who would give me thereby the
more to bite into—since it's only into thickened motive and
accumulated character, I think, that the painter of life bites
more than a little. My poor friend should have accumulated
character, certainly; or rather would be quite naturally and
handsomely possessed of it, in the sense that he would have,
and would always have felt he had, imagination galore, and
that this yet would n't have wrecked him. It was immeasurable,
the opportunity to "do" a man of imagination, for if *there*
might n't be a chance to "bite," where in the world might it be?
This personage of course, so enriched, would n't give me, for
his type, imagination in *predominance* or as his prime faculty, nor should I, in view of other matters, have found that
convenient. So particular a luxury—some occasion, that is,
for study of the high gift in *supreme* command of a case or of
a career—would still doubtless come on the day I should be
ready to pay for it; and till then might, as from far back, remain hung up well in view and just out of reach. The comparative case meanwhile would serve—it was only on the
minor scale that I had treated myself even to comparative cases.

I was to hasten to add however that, happy stopgaps as the minor scale had thus yielded, the instance in hand should enjoy the advantage of the full range of the major; since most immediately to the point was the question of that *supplement* of situation logically involved in our gentleman's impulse to deliver himself in the Paris garden on the Sunday afternoon —or if not involved by strict logic then all ideally and enchantingly implied in it. (I say "ideally," because I need scarce mention that for development, for expression of its maximum, my glimmering story was, at the earliest stage, to have nipped the thread of connexion with the possibilities of the actual reported speaker. *He* remains but the happiest of accidents; his actualities, all too definite, precluded any range of possibilities; it had only been his charming office to project upon that wide field of the artist's vision—which hangs there ever in place like the white sheet suspended for the figures of a child's magic-lantern—a more fantastic and more moveable shadow.) No privilege of the teller of tales and the handler of puppets is more delightful, or has more of the suspense and the thrill of a game of difficulty breathlessly played, than just this business of looking for the unseen and the occult, in a scheme half-grasped, by the light or, so to speak, by the clinging scent, of the gage already in hand. No dreadful old pursuit of the hidden slave with bloodhounds and the rag of association can ever, for "excitement," I judge, have bettered it at its best. For the dramatist always, by the very law of his genius, believes not only in a possible right issue from the rightly-conceived tight place; he does much more than this—he believes, irresistibly, in the necessary, the precious "tightness" of the place (whatever the issue) on the strength of any respectable hint. It being thus the respectable hint that I had with such avidity picked up, what would be the story to which it would most inevitably form the centre? It is part of the charm attendant on such questions that the "story," with the omens true, as I say, puts on from this stage the authenticity of concrete existence. It then *is*, essentially—it begins to be, though it may more or less obscurely lurk; so that the point is not in the least what to make of it, but only, very delightfully and very damnably, where to put one's hand on it.

In which truth resides surely much of the interest of that admirable mixture for salutary application which we know as art. Art deals with what we see, it must first contribute full-handed. that ingredient; it plucks its material, otherwise expressed, in the garden of life—which material elsewhere grown is stale and uneatable. But it has no sooner done this than it has to take account of a *process*—from which only when it 's the basest of the servants of man, incurring ignominious dismissal with no "character," does it, and whether under some muddled pretext of morality or on any other, pusillanimously edge away. The process, that of the expression, the literal squeezing-out, of value is another affair—with which the happy luck of mere finding has little to do. The joys of finding, at this stage, are pretty well over; that quest of the subject as a whole by "matching," as the ladies say at the shops, the big piece with the snippet, having ended, we assume, with a capture. The subject is found, and if the problem is then transferred to the ground of what to do with it the field opens out for any amount of doing. This is precisely the infusion that, as I submit, completes the strong mixture. It is on the other hand the part of the business that can least be likened to the chase with horn and hound. It 's all a sedentary part—involves as much ciphering, of sorts, as would merit the highest salary paid to a chief accountant. Not, however, that the chief accountant has n't *his* gleams of bliss; for the felicity, or at least the equilibrium, of the artist's state dwells less, surely, in the further delightful complications he can smuggle in than in those he succeeds in keeping out. He sows his seed at the risk of too thick a crop; wherefore yet again, like the gentlemen who audit ledgers, he must keep his head at any price. In consequence of all which, for the interest of the matter, I might seem here to have my choice of narrating my "hunt" for Lambert Strether, of describing the capture of the shadow projected by my friend's anecdote, or of reporting on the occurrences subsequent to that triumph. But I had probably best attempt a little to glance in each direction; since it comes to me again and again, over this licentious record, that one's bag of adventures, conceived or conceivable, has been only half-emptied by the mere telling of one's story. It depends so on what one means by that equivocal quantity. There is the story of one's hero, and then, thanks to the intimate connexion of things, the story of one's story itself. I blush to confess it, but if one's a dramatist one's a dramatist, and the latter imbroglio is liable on occasion to strike me as really the more objective of the two.

The philosophy imputed to him in that beautiful outbreak, the hour there, amid such happy provision, striking for him, would have been then, on behalf of my man of imagination, to be logically and, as the artless craft of comedy has it, "led up" to; the probable course to such a goal, the goal of so conscious a predicament, would have in short to be finely calculated. Where has he come from and why has he come, what is he doing (as we Anglo-Saxons, and we only, say, in our foredoomed clutch of exotic aids to expression) in that *galère?* To answer these questions plausibly, to answer them as under cross-examination in the witness-box by counsel for the prosecution, in other words satisfactorily to account for Strether and for his "peculiar tone," was to possess myself of the entire fabric. At the same time the clue to its whereabouts would lie in a certain *principle* of probability: he wouldn't have indulged in his peculiar tone without a reason; it would take a felt predicament or a false position to give him so ironic an accent. One hadn't been noting "tones" all one's life without recognising when one heard it the voice of the false position. The dear man in the Paris garden was then admirably and unmistakeably *in* one—which was no small point gained; what next accordingly concerned us was the determination of *this* identity. One could only go by probabilities, but there was the advantage that the most general of the probabilities were virtual certainties. Possessed of our friend's nationality, to start with, there was a general probability in his narrower localism; which, for that matter, one had really but to keep under the lens for an hour to see it give up its secrets. He would have issued, our rueful worthy, from the very heart of New England—at the heels of which matter of course a perfect train of secrets tumbled for me into the light. They had to be sifted and sorted, and I shall not reproduce the detail of that process; but unmistakeably they were all there, and it was but a question, auspiciously, of picking among them. What the "position" would infallibly be, and why, on his hands, it had turned "false"—these inductive steps could only be as rapid as they were distinct. I accounted for everything—and "everything" had by this time become the most promising quantity—by the view that he had come to Paris in some state of mind which was literally undergoing, as a result of new and unexpected assaults and infusions, a change almost from hour to hour. He had come with a view that might have been figured by a clear green liquid, say, in a neat glass phial; and the liquid, once poured into the open cup of *application,* once exposed to the action of another air, had begun to turn from green to red, or whatever, and might, for all he knew, be on its way to purple, to black, to yellow. At the still wilder extremes represented perhaps, for all he could say to the contrary, by a variability so violent, he would at first, naturally, but have gazed in surprise and alarm; whereby the *situation* clearly would spring from the play of wildness and the development of extremes. I saw in a moment that, should this development proceed both with force and logic, my "story" would leave nothing to be desired. There is always, of course, for the story-teller, the irresistible determinant and the incalculable advantage of his interest in the story *as such;* it is ever, obviously, overwhelmingly, the prime and precious thing (as

other than this I have never been able to see it); as to which
what makes for it, with whatever headlong energy, may be said
to pale before the energy with which it simply makes for itself.
It rejoices, none the less, at its best, to seem to offer itself in a
light, to seem to know, and with the very last knowledge, what
it's about—liable as it yet is at moments to be caught by us with
its tongue in its cheek and absolutely no warrant but its splendid impudence. Let us grant then that the impudence is always
there—there, so to speak, for grace and effect and *allure;* there,
above all, because the Story is just the spoiled child of art, and
because, as we are always disappointed when the pampered
don't "play up," we like it, to that extent, to look all its character. It probably does so, in truth, even when we most flatter
ourselves that we negotiate with it by treaty.

All of which, again, is but to say that the *steps,* for my fable,
placed themselves with a prompt and, as it were, functional assurance—an air quite as of readiness to have dispensed with
logic had I been in fact too stupid for my clue. Never, positively, none the less, as the links multiplied, had I felt less
stupid than for the determination of poor Strether's errand and
for the apprehension of his issue. These things continued to
fall together, as by the neat action of their own weight and
form, even while their commentator scratched his head about
them; he easily sees now that they were always well in advance of him. As the case completed itself he had in fact, from
a good way behind, to catch up with them, breathless and a
little flurried, as he best could. *The* false position, for our belated man of the world—belated because he had endeavoured
so long to escape being one, and now at last had really to face
his doom—the false position for him, I say, was obviously to
have presented himself at the gate of that boundless menagerie
primed with a moral scheme of the most approved pattern
which was yet framed to break down on any approach to vivid
facts; that is to any at all liberal appreciation of them. There
would have been of course the case of the Strether prepared,

wherever presenting himself, only to judge and to feel meanly: but *he* would have moved for me, I confess, enveloped in no legend whatever. The actual man's note, from the first of our seeing it struck, is the note of discrimination, just as his drama is to become, under stress, the drama of discrimination. It would have been his blest imagination, we have seen, that had already helped him to discriminate; the element that was for so much of the pleasure of my cutting thick, as I have intimated, into his intellectual, into his moral substance. Yet here it was, at the same time, just here, that a shade for a moment fell across the scene.

There was the dreadful little old tradition, one of the platitudes of the human comedy, that people's moral scheme *does* break down in Paris; that nothing is more frequently observed; that hundreds of thousands of more or less hypocritical or more or less cynical persons annually visit the place for the sake of the probable catastrophe, and that I came late in the day to work myself up about it. There was in fine the *trivial* association, one of the vulgarest in the world; but which gave me pause no longer, I think, simply because its vulgarity is so advertised. The revolution performed by Strether under the influence of the most interesting of great cities was to have nothing to do with any *bêtise* of the imputably "tempted" state; he was to be thrown forward, rather, thrown quite with violence, upon his lifelong trick of intense reflexion: which friendly test indeed was to bring him out, through winding passages, through alternations of darkness and light, very much *in* Paris, but with the surrounding scene itself a minor matter, a mere symbol for more things than had been dreamt of in the philosophy of Woollett. Another surrounding scene would have done as well for our show could it have represented a place in which Strether's errand was likely to lie and his crisis to await him. The *likely* place had the great merit of sparing me preparations; there would have been too many involved—not at all impossibilities, only rather worrying and delaying difficulties—

in positing elsewhere Chad Newsome's interesting relation, his so interesting complexity of relations. Strether's appointed stage, in fine, could be but Chad's most luckily selected one. The young man had gone in, as they say, for circumjacent charm; and where he would have found it, by the turn of his mind, most "authentic," was where his earnest friend's analysis would most find *him;* as well as where, for that matter, the former's whole analytic faculty would be led such a wonderful dance.

"The Ambassadors" had been, all conveniently, "arranged for"; its first appearance was from month to month, in "The North American Review" during 1903, and I had been open from far back to any pleasant provocation for ingenuity that might reside in one's actively adopting—so as to make it, in its way, a small compositional law—recurrent breaks and resumptions. I had made up my mind here regularly to exploit and enjoy these often rather rude jolts—having found, as I believed, an admirable way to it; yet every question of form and pressure, I easily remember, paled in the light of the major propriety, recognised as soon as really weighed; that of employing but one centre and keeping it all within my hero's compass. The thing was to be so much this worthy's intimate adventure that even the projection of his consciousness upon it from beginning to end without intermission or deviation would probably still leave a part of its value for him, and *a fortiori* for ourselves, unexpressed. I might, however, express every grain of it that there would be room for—on condition of contriving a splendid particular economy. Other persons in no small number were to people the scene, and each with his or her axe to grind, his or her situation to treat, his or her coherency not to fail of, his or her relation to my leading motive, in a word, to establish and carry on. But Strether's sense of these things, and Strether's only, should avail me for showing them; I should know them but through his more or less groping knowledge of them, since his very gropings would figure among his most interesting motions, and a full observance of the rich rigour I speak of would give me more of the effect I should be most "after" than all other possible observances together. It would give me a large unity, and that in turn would crown me with the grace to which the enlightened story-teller will at any time, for his interest, sacrifice if need be all other graces whatever. I refer of course to the grace of intensity, which there are ways of signally achieving and ways of signally missing—as we see it, all round us, helplessly and woefully missed. Not that it isn't, on the other hand, a virtue eminently subject to appreciation—there being no strict, no absolute measure of it; so that one may hear it acclaimed where it has quite escaped one's perception, and see it unnoticed where one has gratefully hailed it. After all of which I am not sure, either, that the immense amusement of the whole cluster of difficulties so arrayed may not operate, for the fond fabulist, when judicious not less than fond, as his best of determinants. That charming principle is always there, at all events, to keep interest fresh: it is a principle, we remember, essentially ravenous, without scruple and without mercy, appeased with no cheap nor easy nourishment. It enjoys the costly sacrifice and rejoices thereby in the very odour of difficulty—even as ogres, with their "Fee-faw-fum!" rejoice in the smell of the blood of Englishmen.

Thus it was, at all events, that the ultimate, though after all so speedy, definition of my gentleman's job—his coming out, all solemnly appointed and deputed, to "save" Chad, and his then finding the young man so disobligingly and, at first, so bewilderingly not lost that a new issue altogether, in the connexion, prodigiously faces them, which has to be dealt with in a new light—promised as many calls on ingenuity and on the higher branches of the compositional art as one could possibly desire. Again and yet again, as, from book to book, I proceed with my survey, I find no source of interest equal to this verification after the fact, as I may call it, and the more in detail the better, of the scheme of consistency "gone in" for. As always—since the charm never fails—the retracing of the process from point to point brings back the old illusion. The old intentions bloom again and flower—in spite of all the blossoms they were to have dropped by the way. This is the charm, as I say, of adventure *transposed*—the thrilling ups and downs, the intricate ins and outs of the compositional problem, made after such a fashion admirably objective, becoming the question at issue and keeping the author's heart in his mouth. Such an element, for instance, as his intention that Mrs. Newsome, away off with her finger on the pulse of Massachusetts, should yet be no less intensely than circuitously present through the whole thing, should be no less felt as to be reckoned with than the most direct exhibition, the finest portrayal at first hand could make her, such a sign of artistic good faith, I say, once it's unmistakeably there, takes on again an actuality not too much impaired by the comparative dimness of the particular success. Cherished intention too inevitably acts and operates, in the book, about fifty times as little as I had fondly dreamt it might; but that scarce spoils for me the pleasure of recognising the fifty ways in which I had sought to provide for it. The mere charm of seeing such an idea constituent, in its degree; the fineness of the measures taken—a real extension, if successful, of the very terms and possibilities of representation and figuration—such things alone were, after this fashion, inspiring, such things alone were a gage of the probable success of that dissimulated calculation with which the whole effort was to square. But oh the cares begotten, none the less, of that same "judicious" sacrifice to a particular form of interest! One's work should have composition, because composition alone is positive beauty; but all the while—apart from one's inevitable consciousness too of the dire paucity of readers ever recognising or ever missing positive beauty—how, as to the cheap and easy, at every turn, how, as to immediacy and facility, and even as to the commoner vivacity, positive beauty might have to be

sweated for and paid for! Once achieved and installed it
may always be trusted to make the poor seeker feel he would
have blushed to the roots of his hair for failing of it; yet,
how, as its virtue can be essentially but the virtue of the
whole, the wayside traps set in the interest of muddlement
and pleading but the cause of the moment, of the particular bit in itself, have to be kicked out of the path! All the
sophistications in life, for example, might have appeared to
muster on behalf of the menace—the menace to a bright variety
—involved in Strether's having all the subjective "say," as it
were, to himself.

Had I meanwhile, made him at once hero and historian,
endowed him with the romantic privilege of the "first person"—the darkest abyss of romance this, inveterately, when
enjoyed on the grand scale—variety, and many other queer
matters as well, might have been smuggled in by a back door.
Suffice it, to be brief, that the first person, in the long piece, is a
form foredoomed to looseness, and that looseness, never much
my affair, had never been so little so as on this particular occasion. All of which reflexions flocked to the standard from the
moment—a very early one—the question of how to keep my
form amusing while sticking so close to my central figure and
constantly taking its pattern from him had to be faced. He
arrives (arrives at Chester) as for the dreadful purpose of giving his creator "no end" to tell about him—before which rigor-
ous mission the serenest of creators might well have quailed.
I was far from the serenest; I was more than agitated enough
to reflect that, grimly deprived of one alternative or one substitute for "telling," I must address myself tooth and nail
to another. I couldn't, save by implication, make other persons tell *each other* about him—blest resource, blest necessity, of the drama, which reaches its effects of unity, all remarkably, by paths absolutely opposite to the paths of the
novel: with other persons, save as they were primarily *his* persons (not he primarily but one of theirs), I had simply nothing

to do. I had relations for him none the less, by the mercy of Providence, quite as much as if my exhibition *was* to be a muddle; if I could only by implication and a show of consequence make other persons tell each other about him, I could at least make him tell *them* whatever in the world he must; and could so, by the same token—which was a further luxury thrown in—see straight into the deep differences between what that could do for me, or at all events for *him*, and the large ease of "autobiography." It may be asked why, if one so keeps to one's hero, one shouldn't make a single mouthful of "method," shouldn't throw the reins on his neck and, letting them flap there as free as in "Gil Blas" or in "David Copperfield," equip him with the double privilege of subject and object—a course that has at least the merit of brushing away questions at a sweep. The answer to which is, I think, that one makes that surrender only if one is prepared *not* to make certain precious discriminations.

The "first person" then, so employed, is addressed by the author directly to ourselves, his possible readers, whom he has to reckon with, at the best, by our English tradition, so loosely and vaguely after all, so little respectfully, on so scant a presumption of exposure to criticism. Strether, on the other hand, encaged and provided for as "The Ambassadors" encages and provides, has to keep in view proprieties much stiffer and more salutary than any our straight and credulous gape are likely to bring home to him, has exhibitional conditions to meet, in a word, that forbid the terrible *fluidity* of self-revelation. I may seem not to better the case for my discrimination if I say that, for my first care, I had thus inevitably to set him up a confidant or two, to wave away with energy the custom of the seated mass of explanation after the fact, the inserted block of merely referential narrative, which flourishes so, to the shame of the modern impatience, on the serried page of Balzac, but which seems simply to appal our actual, our general weaker, digestion. "Harking back to make up" took at any rate more doing, as the phrase is, not only than the reader of to-day demands, but than he will tolerate at any price any call upon him either to understand or remotely to measure; and for the beauty of the thing when done the current editorial mind in particular appears wholly without sense. It is not, however, primarily for either of these reasons, whatever their weight, that Strether's friend Waymarsh is so keenly clutched at, on the threshold of the book, or that no less a pounce is made on Maria Gostrey —without even the pretext, either, of *her* being, in essence, Strether's friend. She is the reader's friend much rather— in consequence of dispositions that make him so eminently require one; and she acts in that capacity, and *really* in that capacity alone, with exemplary devotion, from beginning to end of the book. She is an enrolled, a direct, aid to lucidity; she is in fine, to tear off her mask, the most unmitigated and abandoned of *ficelles*. Half the dramatist's art, as we well know—since if we don't it's not the fault of the proofs that lie scattered about us—is in the use of *ficelles;* by which I mean in a deep dissimulation of his dependence on them. Waymarsh only to a slighter degree belongs, in the whole business, less to my subject than to my treatment of it; the interesting proof, in these connexions, being that one has but to take one's subject for the stuff of drama to interweave with enthusiasm as many Gostreys as need be.

The material of "The Ambassadors," conforming in this respect exactly to that of "The Wings of the Dove," published just before it, is taken absolutely for the stuff of drama; so that, availing myself of the opportunity given me by this edition for some prefatory remarks on the latter work, I had mainly to make on its behalf the point of its scenic consistency. It disguises that virtue, in the oddest way in the world, by just *looking,* as we turn its pages, as little scenic as possible; but it sharply divides itself, just as the composition before us does, into the parts that prepare, that tend in fact to over-prepare, for scenes, and the parts, or otherwise into the scenes, that justify and crown the preparation. It may definitely be said, I think, that everything in it that is not scene (not, I of course mean, complete and functional scene, treating *all* the submitted matter, as by logical start, logical turn, and logical finish) is discriminated preparation, is the fusion and synthesis of picture. These alternations propose themselves all recogniseably, I think, from an early stage, as the very form and figure of "The Ambassadors"; so that, to repeat, such an agent as Miss Gostrey, pre-engaged at a high salary, but waits in the draughty wing with her shawl and her smelling-salts. Her function speaks at once for itself, and by the time she has dined with Strether in London and gone to a play with him her intervention as a *ficelle* is, I hold, expertly justified. Thanks to it we have treated scenically, and scenically alone, the whole lumpish question of Strether's "past," which has seen us more happily on the way than anything else could have done; we have strained to a high lucidity and vivacity (or at least we hope we have) certain indispensable facts; we have seen our two or three immediate friends all conveniently and profitably in "action"; to say nothing of our beginning to descry others, of a remoter intensity, getting into motion, even if a bit vaguely as yet, for our further enrichment. Let my first point be here that the scene in question, that in which the whole situation at Woollett and the complex forces that have propelled my hero to where this lively extractor of his value and distiller of his essence awaits him, is normal and entire, is really an excellent *standard* scene; copious, comprehensive, and accordingly never short, but with its office as definite as that of the hammer on the gong of the clock, the office of expressing *all that is in* the hour.

The "*ficelle*" character of the subordinate party is as artfully dissimulated, throughout, as may be, and to that extent that, with the seams or joints of Maria Gostrey's ostensible connectedness taken particular care of, duly smoothed over,

that is, and anxiously kept from showing as "pieced on," this
figure doubtless achieves, after a fashion, something of the
dignity of a prime idea: which circumstance but shows us
afresh how many quite incalculable but none the less clear
sources of enjoyment for the infatuated artist, how many copious springs of our never-to-be-slighted "fun" for the reader
and critic susceptible of contagion, may sound their incidental
plash as soon as an artistic process begins to enjoy free development. Exquisite—in illustration of this—the mere interest and
amusement of such at once "creative" and critical questions as
how and where and why to make Miss Gostrey's false connexion carry itself, under a due high polish, as a real one.
Nowhere is it more of an artful expedient for mere consistency
of form, to mention a case, than in the last "scene" of the book,
where its function is to give or to add nothing whatever, but
only to express as vividly as possible certain things quite other
than itself and that are of the already fixed and appointed
measure. Since, however, all art is *expression,* and is thereby
vividness, one was to find the door open here to any amount
of delightful dissimulation. These verily are the refinements
and ecstasies of method—amid which, or certainly under
the influence of any exhilarated demonstration of which, one
must keep one's head and not lose one's way. To cultivate
an adequate intelligence for them and to make that sense
operative is positively to find a charm in any produced ambiguity of appearance that is not by the same stroke, and
all helplessly, an ambiguity of sense. To project imaginatively,
for my hero, a relation that has nothing to do with the matter (the matter of my subject) but has everything to do with
the manner (the manner of my presentation of the same) and
yet to treat it, at close quarters and for fully economic expression's possible sake, as if it were important and essential—
to do that sort of thing and yet muddle nothing may easily
become, as one goes, a signally attaching proposition; even
though it all remains but part and parcel, I hasten to recognise,

of the merely general and related question of expressional curiosity and expressional decency.

I am moved to add after so much insistence on the scenic side of my labour that I have found the steps of re-perusal almost as much waylaid here by quite another style of effort in the same signal interest—or have in other words not failed to note how, even so associated and so discriminated, the finest proprieties and charms of the non-scenic may, under the right hand for them, still keep their intelligibility and assert their office. Infinitely suggestive such an observation as this last on the whole delightful head, where representation is concerned, of possible variety, of effective expressional change and contrast. One would like, at such an hour as this, for critical license, to go into the matter of the noted inevitable deviation (from too fond an original vision) that the exquisite treachery even of the straightest execution may ever be trusted to inflict even on the most mature plan—the case being that, though one's last reconsidered production always seems to bristle with that particular evidence, "The Ambassadors," would place a flood of such light at my service. I must attach to my final remark here a different import; noting in the other connexion I just glanced at that such passages as that of my hero's first encounter with Chad Newsome, absolute attestations of the non-scenic form though they be, yet lay the firmest hand too—so far at least as intention goes—on representational effect. To report at all closely and completely of what "passes" on a given occasion is inevitably to become more or less scenic; and yet in the instance I allude to, *with* the conveyance, expressional curiosity and expressional decency are sought and arrived at under quite another law. The true inwardness of this may be at bottom but that one of the suffered treacheries has consisted precisely, for Chad's whole figure and presence, of a direct presentability diminished and compromised—despoiled, that is, of its *proportional* advantage; so that, in a word, the whole economy of his author's relation to him has at important points to be redetermined. The book, however, critically viewed, is touchingly full of these disguised and repaired losses, these insidious recoveries, these intensely redemptive consistencies. The pages in which Mamie Pocock gives her appointed and, I can't but think, duly felt lift to the whole action by the so inscrutably-applied side-stroke or short-cut of our just watching, and as quite at an angle of vision as yet untried, her single hour of suspense in the hotel salon, in our partaking of her concentrated study of the sense of matters bearing on her own case, all the bright warm Paris afternoon, from the balcony that overlooks the Tuileries garden—these are as marked an example of the representational virtue that insists here and there on being, for the charm of opposition and renewal, other than the scenic. It would n't take much to make me further argue that from an equal play of such oppositions the book gathers an intensity that fairly adds to the dramatic—though the latter is supposed to be the sum of all intensities; or that has at any rate nothing to fear from juxtaposition with it. I consciously fail to shrink in fact from that extravagance—I risk it, rather, for the sake of the moral involved; which is not that the particular production before us exhausts the interesting questions it raises, but that the Novel remains still, under the right persuasion, the most independent, most elastic, most prodigious of literary forms.

XVIII

PREFACE TO "THE GOLDEN BOWL"

(VOLUME XXIII IN THE NEW YORK EDITION)

AMONG many matters thrown into relief by a refreshed acquaintance with "The Golden Bowl" what perhaps most stands out for me is the still marked inveteracy of a certain indirect and oblique view of my presented action; unless indeed I make up my mind to call this mode of treatment, on the contrary, any superficial appearance notwithstanding, the very straightest and closest possible. I have already betrayed, as an accepted habit, and even to extravagance commented on, my preference for dealing with my subject-matter, for "seeing my story," through the opportunity and the sensibility of some more or less detached, some not strictly involved, though thoroughly interested and intelligent, witness or reporter, some person who contributes to the case mainly a certain amount of criticism and interpretation of it. Again and again, on review, the shorter things in especial that I have gathered into this Series have ranged themselves not as my own impersonal account of the affair in hand, but as my account of somebody's impression of it—the terms of this person's access to it and estimate of it contributing thus by some fine little law to intensification of interest. The somebody is often, among my shorter tales I recognise, but an unnamed, unintroduced and (save by right of intrinsic wit) unwarranted participant, the impersonal author's concrete deputy or delegate, a convenient substitute or apologist for the creative power otherwise so veiled and disembodied. My instinct appears repeatedly to have been that to arrive at the facts retailed and the figures introduced by the given help of some other conscious and confessed agent is essentially to find the whole business—that is, as I say, its effective interest—enriched *by the way.* I have in other words constantly inclined to the idea of the particular attaching case *plus* some near individual view of it; that nearness quite having thus to become an imagined observer's, a projected, charmed painter's or poet's—however avowed the "minor" quality in the latter—close and sensitive contact with it. Anything, in short, I now reflect, must always have seemed to me better—better for the process and the effect of representation, my irrepressible ideal—than the mere muffled majesty of irresponsible "authorship." Beset constantly with the sense that the painter of the picture or the chanter of the ballad (whatever we may call him) can never be responsible *enough,* and for every inch of his surface and note of his song, I track my uncontrollable footsteps, right and left, after the fact, while they take their quick turn, even on stealthiest tiptoe, toward the point of view that, within the compass, will give me most instead of least to answer for.

I am aware of having glanced a good deal already in the direction of this embarrassed truth—which I give for what it is worth; but I feel it come home to me afresh on recognising that the manner in which it betrays itself may be one of the liveliest sources of amusement in "The Golden Bowl." It's not that the muffled majesty of authorship does n't here *ostensibly* reign; but I catch myself again shaking it off and disavowing the pretence of it while I get down into the arena and do my best to live and breathe and rub shoulders and converse with the persons engaged in the struggle that provides for the others in the circling tiers the entertainment of the great game. There is no other participant, of course, than each of the real, the deeply involved and immersed and more or less bleeding participants; but I nevertheless affect myself as having held my system fast and fondly, with one hand at least, by the manner in which the whole thing remains subject to the register, ever so closely kept, of the consciousness of but two of the characters. The Prince, in the first half of the book, virtually sees and knows and makes out, virtually represents to himself everything that concerns us—very nearly (though he does n't speak in the first person) after the fashion of other reporters and critics of other situations. Having a consciousness highly susceptible of registration, he thus makes us see the things that may most interest us reflected in it as in the clean glass held up to so many of the "short stories" of our long list; and yet after all never a whit to the prejudice of his being just as consistently a foredoomed, entangled, embarrassed agent in the general imbroglio, actor in the offered play. The function of the Princess, in the remainder, matches exactly with his; the register of *her* consciousness is as closely kept—as closely, say, not only as his own, but as that (to cite examples) either of the intelligent but quite unindividualised witness of the destruction of "The Aspern Papers," or of the all-noting heroine of "The Spoils of Poynton," highly individualised *though* highly intelligent; the Princess, in fine, in addition to feeling everything she has to, and to playing her part just in that proportion, duplicates, as it were, her value and becomes a compositional resource, and of the finest order, as well as a value intrinsic. So it is that the admirably-endowed pair, between them, as I retrace their fortune and my own method, point again for me the moral of the endless interest, endless worth for "delight," of the compositional contribution. Their chronicle strikes me as quite of the stuff to keep us from forgetting that absolutely *no* refinement of ingenuity or of precaution need be dreamed of as wasted in that most exquisite of all good causes the appeal to variety, the appeal to incalculability, the appeal to a high refinement and a handsome wholeness of effect.

There are other things I might remark here, despite its perhaps seeming a general connexion that I have elsewhere sufficiently shown as suggestive; but I have other matter is hand and I take a moment only to meet a possible objection—should any reader be so far solicitous or even attentive —to what I have just said. It may be noted, that is, that the Prince, in the volume over which he nominally presides, is represented as in comprehensive cognition only of those aspects as to which Mrs. Assingham does n't functionally—perhaps all too officiously, as the reader may sometimes feel it—supersede him. This disparity in my plan is, however, but superficial; the thing abides rigidly by its law of showing Maggie Verver at first through her suitor's and her husband's exhibitory vision of her, and of then showing the Prince, with at least an equal intensity, through his wife's; the advantage thus being that these attributions of experience display the sentient subjects themselves at the same time and by the same stroke with the nearest possible approach to a desirable vividness. It is the Prince who opens the door to half our light upon Maggie, just as it is she who opens it to half our light upon himself; the rest of our impression, in either case, coming straight from the very motion with which that act is performed. We see Charlotte also at first, and we see Adam Verver, let alone our seeing Mrs. Assingham, and every one and every thing else, but as they are visible in the Prince's interest, so to speak—by which I mean of course in the interest of his being himself handed over to us. With a like consistency we see the same persons and things again but as Maggie's interest, *her* exhibitional charm, determines the view. In making which remark, with its apparently so limited enumeration of my elements, I naturally am brought up against the fact of the fundamental fewness of these latter—of the fact that my large demand is made for a group of agents who may be counted on the fingers of one hand. We see very few persons in "The Golden Bowl," but the scheme of the book, to make up for that, is that we shall really see about as much of them as a coherent literary form permits. That was my problem, so to speak, and my *gageure*—to play the small hand ful of values really for all they were worth—and to work my system, my particular propriety of appeal, particular degree of pressure on the spring of interest, for all that this specific ingenuity itself might be. To have a scheme and a view of its dignity is of course congruously to work it out, and the "amusement" of the chronicle in question—by which, once more, I always mean the gathered cluster of all the *kinds* of interest—was exactly to see what a consummate application of such sincerities would give.

So much for some only of the suggestions of re-perusal here —since, all the while, I feel myself awaited by a pair of appeals really more pressing than either of those just met; a minor and a major appeal, as I may call them: the former of which I take first. I have so thoroughly "gone into" things, in an expository way, on the ground covered by this collection of my writings, that I should still judge it superficial to have spoken no word for so salient a feature of our Edition as the couple of dozen decorative "illustrations." This series of frontispieces contribute less to ornament, I recognise, than if Mr. Alvin Langdon Coburn's beautiful photographs, which they reproduce, had had to suffer less reduction; but of those that have suffered least the beauty, to my sense, remains great, and I indulge at any rate in this glance at our general intention for the sake of the small page of history thereby added to my already voluminous, yet on the whole so unabashed, memoranda. I should in fact be tempted here, but for lack of space, by the very question itself at large—that question of the general acceptability of illustration coming up sooner or later, in these days, for the author of any text putting forward illustrative claims (that is producing an effect of illustration) by its own intrinsic virtue and so finding itself elbowed, on that ground, by another and a competitive process. The essence of any representational work is of course to bristle with immediate images; and I, for one, should have looked much askance at the proposal, on the part of my associates in the whole business, to graft or "grow," at whatever point, a picture by another hand on my own picture—this being always, to my sense, a lawless incident. Which remark reflects heavily, of course, on the "picture-book" quality that contemporary English and American prose appears more and more destined, by the conditions of publication, to consent, however grudgingly, to see imputed to it. But a moment's thought points the moral of the danger.

Anything that relieves responsible prose of the duty of being, while placed before us, good enough, interesting enough and, if the question be of picture, pictorial enough, above all *in itself,* does it the worst of services, and may well inspire in the lover of literature certain lively questions as to the future of that institution. That one should, as an author, reduce one's reader, "artistically" inclined, to such a state of hallucination by the images one has evoked as does n't permit him to rest till he has noted or recorded them, set up some semblance of them in his own other medium, by his own other art—nothing could better consort than *that,* I naturally allow, with the desire or the pretension to cast a literary spell. Charming, that is, for the projector and creator of figures and scenes that are as nought from the moment they fail to become more or less visible appearances, charming for this manipulator of aspects to see such power as he may possess approved and registered by the springing of such fruit from his seed. His own garden, however, remains one thing, and the garden he has prompted the cultivation of at other hands becomes quite another; which means that the frame of one's own work no more provides place for such a plot than we expect flesh and fish to be served on the same platter. One welcomes illustration, in other words, with pride and joy; but also with the emphatic view that, might one's "literary jealousy" be duly deferred to, it would quite stand off and on its own feet and thus, as a separate and independent subject of publication, carrying its text in its spirit, just as that text correspondingly carries the plastic possibility, become a still more glorious tribute. So far my invidious distinction between the writer's "frame" and the draughtsman's; and if in spite of it I could still make place for the idea of a contribution of value by Mr. A. L. Coburn to each of these volumes—and a contribution in as different a "medium" as possible—this was just because the proposed photographic studies were to seek the way, which they have happily found, I think, not to keep, or to pretend to keep, anything like dramatic step with their suggestive matter. This would quite have disqualified them, to my rigour; but they were "all right," in the so analytic modern critical phrase, through their discreetly disavowing emulation. Nothing in fact could more have amused the author than the opportunity of a hunt for a series of reproducible subjects—such moreover as might best consort with photography—the reference of which to Novel or Tale should exactly be *not* competitive and obvious, should on the contrary plead its case with some shyness, that of images always confessing themselves mere optical symbols or echoes, expressions of no particular thing in the text, but only of the type or idea of this or that thing. They were to remain at the most small pictures of our "set" stage with the actors left out; and what was above all interesting was that they were first to be constituted.

This involved an amusing search which I would fain more fully commemorate; since it took, to a great degree, and rather unexpectedly and incalculably, the vastly, though but incidentally, instructive form of an enquiry into the street-scenery of London; a field yielding a ripe harvest of treasure from the moment I held up to it, in my fellow artist's company, the light of our fond idea—the idea, that is, of the aspect of things or the combination of objects that might, by a latent virtue in it, speak for its connexion with something in the book, and yet at the same time speak enough for its odd or interesting self. It will be noticed that our series of frontispieces, while doing all justice to our need, largely consists in a "rendering" of certain inanimate characteristics of London streets; the ability of which to suffice to this furnishing forth of my Volumes ministered alike to surprise and convenience. Even at the cost of inconsistency of attitude in the matter of the "grafted" image, I should have been tempted, I confess, by the mere pleasure of exploration, abounding as the business at once began to do in those prizes of curiosity for which the London-lover is at any time ready to "back" the prodigious city. It wasn't always that I straightway found, with my fellow searcher, what we were looking for, but that the looking itself so often flooded with light the question of what a "subject," what "character," what a saving sense in things, is and isn't; and that when our quest was rewarded, it was, I make bold to say, rewarded in perfection. On the question, for instance, of the proper preliminary compliment to the first volume of "The Golden Bowl" we easily felt that nothing would so serve as a view of the small shop in which the Bowl is first encountered.

The problem thus was thrilling, for though the small shop was but a shop of the mind, of the author's projected world, in which objects are primarily related to each other, and therefore not "taken from" a particular establishment anywhere, only an image distilled and intensified, as it were, from a drop of the essence of such establishments in general, our need (since the picture was, as I have said, also completely to speak for itself) prescribed a concrete, independent, vivid instance, the instance that should oblige us by the marvel of an accidental rightness. It might so easily be wrong—by the act of being at all. It would have to be in the first place what London and chance and an extreme improbability should have made it, and then it would have to let us truthfully read into it the Prince's and Charlotte's and the Princess's visits. It of course on these terms long evaded us, but all the while really without prejudice to our fond confidence that, as London ends by giving one absolutely everything one asks, so it awaited us somewhere. It awaited us in fact—but I check myself; nothing, I find now, would induce me to say where. Just so, to conclude, it was equally obvious that for the second volume of the same fiction nothing would so nobly serve as some generalised vision of Portland Place. Both our limit and the very extent of our occasion, however, lay in the fact that, unlike wanton designers, we had, not to "create" but simply to recognise—recognise, that is, with the last fineness. The thing was to induce the vision of Portland Place *to* generalise itself. This is precisely, however, the fashion after which the prodigious city, as I have called it, does on occasion meet halfway those forms of intelligence of it that *it* recognises. All of which meant that at a given moment the great featureless Philistine vista would itself perform a miracle, would become interesting, for a splendid atmospheric hour, as only London knows how; and that our business would be then to understand. But my record of that lesson takes me too far.

So much for some only of the suggestions of re-perusal, and some of those of re-representation here, since, all the while, I feel myself awaited by an occasion more urgent than any of these. To re-read in their order my final things, all of comparatively recent date, has been to become aware of my putting the process through, for the latter end of my series (as well as, throughout, for most of its later constituents) quite in the same terms as the apparent and actual, the contemporary terms; to become aware in other words that the march of my present attention coincides sufficiently with the march of my original expression; that my apprehension fits, more concretely stated, without an effort or a struggle, certainly without bewilderment or anguish, into the innumerable places prepared for it. As the historian of the matter sees and speaks, so my intelligence of it, as a reader, meets him halfway, passive, receptive, appreciative, often even grateful; unconscious, quite blissfully, of any bar to intercourse, any disparity of sense between us. Into his very footprints the responsive, the imaginative steps of the docile reader that I consentingly become for him all comfortably sink; his vision, superimposed on my own as an image in cut paper is applied to a sharp shadow on a wall, matches, at every point, without excess or deficiency. This truth throws into relief for me the very different dance that the taking in hand of my earlier productions was to lead me; the quite other kind of consciousness proceeding from *that* return. Nothing in my whole renewal of attention to these things, to almost any instance of my work previous to some dozen years ago, was more evident than that no such active, appreciative process could take place on the mere palpable lines of expression—thanks to the so frequent lapse of harmony between my present mode of motion and that to which the existing footprints were due. It was, all sensibly, as if the clear matter being still there, even as a shining expanse of snow spread over a plain, my exploring tread, for application to it, had quite unlearned the old pace and found itself naturally falling into another, which might sometimes indeed more or less agree with the original tracks, but might most often, or very nearly, break the surface in other places. What was thus predominantly interesting to note, at all events, was the high spontaneity of these deviations and differences, which became thus things not of choice, but of immediate and perfect necessity: necessity to the end of dealing with the quantities in question at all.

No march, accordingly, I was soon enough aware, could possibly be more confident and free than this infinitely interesting and amusing *act* of re-appropriation; shaking off all shackles of theory, unattended, as was speedily to appear, with humiliating uncertainties, and almost as enlivening, or at least as momentous, as, to a philosophic mind, a sudden large apprehension of the Absolute. What indeed could be more delightful than to enjoy a sense of the absolute in such easy conditions? The deviations and differences might of course not have broken out at all, but from the moment they began so naturally to multiply they became, as I say, my very terms of cognition. The question of the "revision" of existing work had loomed large for me, had seemed even at moments to bristle with difficulties; but that phase of anxiety, I was rejoicingly to learn, belonged all but to the state of postponed experience or to that of a prolonged and fatalistic indifference. Since to get and to keep finished and dismissed work well behind one, and to have as little to say to it and about it as possible, had been for years one's only law, so, during that flat interregnum, involving, as who should say, the very cultivation of unacquaintedness, creeping superstitions as to what it might really have been had time to grow up and flourish. Not least among these rioted doubtless the fond fear that any tidying-up of the uncanny brood, any removal of accumulated dust, any washing of wizened faces, or straightening of grizzled locks, or twitching, to a better effect, of superannuated garments, might let one in, as the phrase is, for expensive renovations. I make use here of the figure of age and infirmity, but in point of fact I had rather viewed the reappearance of the first-born of my progeny—a reappearance unimaginable save to some inheritance of brighter and more congruous material form, of stored-up braveries of type and margin and ample page, of general dignity and attitude, than had mostly waited on their respective casual cradles—as a descent of awkward infants from the nursery to the drawing-room under the kind appeal of enquiring, of possibly interested, visitors. I had accordingly taken for granted the common decencies of such a case—the responsible glance of some power above from one nursling to another, the rapid flash of an anxious needle, the not imperceptible effect of a certain audible splash of soap-and-water; all in consideration of the searching radiance of drawing-room lamps as compared with nursery candles. But it had been all the while present to me that from the moment a stitch should be taken or a hair-brush applied the *principle* of my making my brood more presentable under the nobler illumination would be accepted and established, and it was there complications might await me. I am afraid I had at stray moments wasted time in wondering what discrimination against the freedom of the needle and the sponge would be able to describe itself as not arbitrary. For it to confess to that taint would be of course to write itself detestable.

"Hands off altogether on the nurse's part!" was, as a merely barbarous injunction, strictly conceivable; but only in the light of the truth that it had never taken effect in any fair and stately, in any not vulgarly irresponsible re-issue of anything. Therefore it was easy to see that any such apologetic suppression as that of the "altogether," any such admission as that of a single dab of the soap, left the door very much ajar. Any request that an indulgent objector to drawing-room discipline, to the purification, in other words, of innocent childhood, should kindly measure out then the appropriate amount of ablutional fluid for the whole case, would, on twenty grounds, indubitably leave that invoked judge gaping. I had none the less, I repeat, at muddled moments, seemed to see myself confusedly invoke him; thanks to my but too naturally not being able to forecast the perfect grace with which an answer to all my questions was meanwhile awaiting me. To expose the case frankly to a test—in other words to begin to re-read—was at once to get nearer all its elements and so, as by the next felicity, feel it purged of every doubt. It was the nervous postponement of that respectful approach that I spoke of just now as, in the connexion, my waste of time. This felt awkwardness sprang, as I was at a given moment to perceive, from my too abject acceptance of the grand air with which the term Revision had somehow, to my imagination, carried itself— and from my frivolous failure to analyse the content of the word. To revise is to see, or to look over, again—which means in the case of a written thing neither more nor less than to re-

read it. I had attached to it, in a brooding spirit, the idea of re-writing—with which it was to have in the event, for my *conscious* play of mind, almost nothing in common. I had thought of re-writing as so difficult, and even so absurd, as to be impossible—having also indeed, for that matter, thought of re-reading in the same light. But the felicity under the test was that where I had thus ruefully prefigured two efforts there proved to be but one—and this an effort but at the first blush. What re-writing might be was to remain—it has remained for me to this hour—a mystery. On the other hand the act of revision, the act of seeing it again, caused whatever I looked at on any page to flower before me as into the only terms that honourably expressed it; and the "revised" element in the present Edition is accordingly these terms, these rigid conditions of re-persual, registered; so many close notes, as who should say, on the particular vision of the matter itself that experience had at last made the only possible one.

What it would be really interesting, and I dare say admirably difficult, to go into would be the very history of this effect of experience; the history, in other words, of the growth of the immense array of terms, perceptional and expressional, that, after the fashion I have indicated, in sentence, passage and page, simply looked over the heads of the standing terms—or perhaps rather, like alert winged creatures, perched on those diminished summits and aspired to a clearer air. What it comes back to, for the maturer mind—granting of course, to begin with, a mind accessible to questions of such an order—is this attaching speculative interest of the matter, or in vulgar parlance the inordinate intellectual "sport" of it: the how and the whence and the why these intenser lights of experience come into being and insist on shining. The interest of the question is attaching, as I say, because really half the artist's life seems involved in it—or doubtless, to speak more justly, the whole of his life intellectual. The "old" matter is there, re-accepted, re-tasted, exquisitely re-assimilated and re-enjoyed—

believed in, to be brief, with the same "old" grateful faith (since wherever the faith, in a particular case, has become aware of a twinge of doubt I have simply concluded against the matter itself and left it out); yet for due testimony, for re-assertion of value, perforating as by some strange and fine, some latent and gathered force, a myriad more adequate channels. It is over the fact of such a phenomenon and its so possibly rich little history that I am moved just fondly to linger— and for the reason I glanced at above, that to do so is in a manner to retrace the whole growth of one's "taste," as our fathers used to say: a blessed comprehensive name for many of the things deepest in us. The "taste" of the poet is, at bottom and so far as the poet in him prevails over everything else, his active sense of life: in accordance with which truth to keep one's hand on it is to hold the silver clue to the whole labyrinth of his consciousness. He feels this himself, good man —he recognises an attached importance—whenever he feels that consciousness bristle with the notes, as I have called them, of consenting re-perusal; as has again and again publicly befallen him, to our no small edification, on occasions within recent view. It has befallen him most frequently, I recognise, when the supersessive terms of his expression have happened to be verse; but that does n't in the least isolate his case, since it is clear to the most limited intelligence that the title we give him is the only title of *general* application and convenience for those who passionately cultivate the image of life and the art, on the whole so beneficial, of projecting it. The seer and speaker under the descent of the god is the "poet," whatever his form, and he ceases to be one only when his form, whatever else it may nominally or superficially or vulgarly be, is unworthy of the god: in which event, we promptly submit, he is n't worth talking of at all. He becomes so worth it, and the god so adopts him, and so confirms his charming office and name, in the degree in which his impulse and passion are general and comprehensive—a definitional provision for them that makes but a mouthful of so minor a distinction, in the fields of light, as that between verse and prose.

The circumstance that the poets then, and the more charming ones, *have* in a number of instances, with existing matter in hand, "registered" their renewals of vision, attests quite enough the attraction deeply working whenever the mind is, as I have said, accessible—accessible, that is, to the finer appeal of accumulated "good stuff" and to the interest of taking it in hand at all. For myself, I am prompted to note, the "taking" has been to my consciousness, through the whole procession of this re-issue, the least part of the affair: under the first touch of the spring my hands were to feel themselves full; so much more did it become a question, on the part of the accumulated good stuff, of seeming insistently to give and give. I have alluded indeed to certain lapses of that munificence— or at least to certain connexions in which I found myself declining to receive again on *any* terms; but for the rest the sense of receiving has borne me company without a break; a luxury making for its sole condition that I should intelligently attend. The blest good stuff, sitting up, in its myriad forms, so touchingly responsive to new care of any sort whatever, seemed to pass with me a delightful bargain, and in the fewest possible words. "Actively believe in us and then you'll see!"—it wasn't more complicated than that, and yet was to become as thrilling as if conditioned on depth within depth. I saw therefore what I saw, and what these numerous pages record, I trust, with clearness; though one element of fascination tended all the while to rule the business—a fascination, at each stage of my journey, on the noted score of that so shifting and uneven character of the tracks of my original passage. This by itself introduced the charm of suspense: what would the operative terms, in the given case, prove, under criticism, to have been—a series of waiting satisfactions or an array of waiting misfits? The misfits had but to be positive and concordant, in the special intenser light, to represent together (as the two sides of a coin show different legends) just so many effective felicities and substitutes. But I could n't at all, in general, forecast these chances and changes and proportions; they could but show for what they were as I went; criticism after the fact was to find in them arrests and surprises, emotions alike of disappointment and of elation: all of which means, obviously, that the whole thing was a *living* affair.

The rate at which new readings, new conductors of sense interposed, to make any total sense at all right, became, to this wonderful tune, the very record and mirror of the general adventure of one's intelligence; so that one at all times quite marvelled at the fair reach, the very length of arm, of such a developed difference of measure as to what might and what might n't constitute, all round, a due decency of "rendering." What I have been most aware of asking myself, however, is how writers, on such occasions of "revision," arrive at that successful resistance to the confident assault of the new reading which appears in the great majority of examples to have marked their course. The term that superlatively, that finally "renders," is a flower that blooms by a beautiful law of its own (the fiftieth part of a second often so sufficing it) in the very heart of the gathered sheaf; it is *there* already, at any moment, almost before one can either miss or suspect it— so that in short we shall never guess, I think, the working secret of the revisionist for whom its colour and scent stir the air but as immediately to be assimilated. Failing our divination, too, we shall apparently not otherwise learn, for the simple reason that no revisionist I can recall has ever been communicative. "People don't do such things," we remember to have heard it, in this connexion, declared; in other words they don't really re-read—no, not *really;* at least they do so to the effect either of seeing the buried, the latent life of a past composition vibrate, at renewal of touch, into no activity and break through its settled and "sunk" surface at no point whatever— on which conclusion, I hasten to add, the situation remains simple and their responsibility may lie down beside their work even as the lion beside the lamb; or else they have in advance and on system stopped their ears, their eyes and even their very noses. This latter heroic policy I find myself glancing at, however, to wonder in what particular cases—failing, as I say, all the really confessed—it can have been applied. The actual non-revisionists (on any terms) are of course numerous enough, and with plenty to say for themselves; their faith, clearly, is great, their lot serene and their peace, above all, equally protected and undisturbed. But the tantalising image of the revisionist who is n't one, the partial, the piecemeal revisionist, inconsequent and insincere, this obscure and decidedly *louche* personage hovers before me mainly, I think, but to challenge my belief. Where have we met him, when it comes to that, in the walks of interesting prose literature, and why assume that we *have* to believe in him before we are absolutely forced?

If I turn for relief and contrast to some image of his opposite I at once encounter it, and with a completeness that leaves nothing to be desired, on any "old" ground, in presence of any "old" life, in the vast example of Balzac. He (and these things, as we know, grew behind him at an extraordinary rate) re-assaulted by supersessive terms, re-penetrated by finer channels, never had on the one hand seen or said all or had on the other ceased to press forward. His case has equal mass and authority—and beneath its protecting shade, at any rate, I move for the brief remainder of these remarks. We owe to the never-extinct operation of his sensibility, we have but meanwhile to recall, our greatest exhibition of felt finalities, our richest and hugest inheritance of imaginative prose. That by itself might intensify for me the interest of this general question of the reviving and reacting vision—did n't my very own lucky experience, all so publicly incurred, give me, as my reader may easily make out, quite enough to think of. I almost lose myself, it may perhaps seem to him, in that obscure quantity; obscure doubt-

343

less because of its consisting of the manifold delicate things, the shy and illusive, the inscrutable, the indefinable, that minister to deep and quite confident processes of change. It is enough, in any event, to be both beguiled and mystified by evolutions so near home, without sounding strange and probably even more abysmal waters. Since, however, an agreeable flurry and an imperfect presence of mind might, on the former ground, still be such a source of refreshment, so the constant refrain humming through the agitation, "If only one *could* re-write, if only one *could* do better justice to the patches of crude surface, the poor morsels of consciously-decent matter that catch one's eye with their rueful reproach for old stupidities of touch!"—so that yearning reflexion, I say, was to have its superlative as well as its positive moments. It was to reach its maximum, no doubt, over many of the sorry businesses of "The American," for instance, where, given the elements and the essence, the long-stored grievance of the subject bristling with a sense of over-prolonged exposure in a garment misfitted, a garment cheaply embroidered and unworthy of it, thereby most proportionately sounded their plaint. This sharpness of appeal, the claim for exemplary damages, or at least for poetic justice, was reduced to nothing, on the other hand, in presence of the altogether better literary manners of "The Ambassadors" and "The Golden Bowl"—a list I might much extend by the mention of several shorter pieces.

Inevitably, in such a case as that of "The American," and scarce less indeed in those of "The Portrait of a Lady" and "The Princess Casamassima," each of these efforts so redolent of good intentions baffled by a treacherous vehicle, an expertness too retarded, I could but dream the whole thing over as I went—as I read; and, bathing it, so to speak, in that medium, hope that, some still newer and shrewder critic's intelligence subtly operating, I should n't have breathed upon the old catastrophes and accidents, the old wounds and mutilations and disfigurements, wholly in vain. The same is true of the possible effect of this process of re-dreaming on many of these gathered compositions, shorter and longer; I have prayed that the finer air of the better form may sufficiently seem to hang about them and gild them over—at least for readers, however few, at all *curious* of questions of air and form. Nothing even at this point, and in these quite final remarks, I confess, could strike me as more pertinent than—with a great wealth of margin— to attempt to scatter here a few gleams of the light in which some of my visions have all sturdily and complacently repeated and others have, according to their kind and law, all joyously and blushingly renewed themselves. These have doubtless both been ways of remaining unshamed; though, for myself, on the whole, as I seem to make out, the interest of the watched re- newal has been livelier than that of the accepted repetition. What has the affair been at the worst, I am most moved to ask, but an earnest invitation to the reader to dream again in my company and in the interest of his own larger absorption of my sense? The prime consequence on one's own part of re- perusal is a sense for ever so many more of the shining silver fish afloat in the deep sea of one's endeavour than the net of widest casting could pretend to gather in; an author's common courtesy dictating thus the best general course for making that sense contagious—so beautifully tangled a web, when not so glorious a crown, does he weave by having at heart, and by cherishing there, the confidence he has invited or imagined. There is then absolutely no release to his pledged honour on the question of repaying that confidence.

The ideally handsome way is for him to multiply in any given connexion all the possible sources of entertainment—or, more grossly expressing it again, to intensify his whole chance of pleasure. (It all comes back to that, to my and your "fun"— if we but allow the term its full extension; to the production of which no humblest question involved, even to that of the shade of a cadence or the position of a comma, is not richly pertinent.)

We have but to think a moment of such a matter as the play of *representational* values, those that make it a part, and an important part, of our taking offered things in that we should take them as aspects and visibilities—take them to the utmost as appearances, images, figures, objects, so many important, so many contributive items of the furniture of the world—in order to feel immediately the effect of such a condition at every turn of our adventure and every point of the representative surface. One has but to open the door to any forces of exhibition at all worthy of the name in order to see the imaging and qualifying agency called at once into play and put on its mettle. We may traverse acres of pretended exhibitory prose from which the touch that directly evokes and finely presents, the touch that operates for closeness and for charm, for conviction and illusion, for communication, in a word, is unsurpassably absent. All of which but means of course that the reader is, in the common phrase, "sold"—even when, poor passive spirit, systematically bewildered and bamboozled on the article of his dues, he may be but dimly aware of it. He has by the same token and for the most part, I fear, a scarce quicker sensibility on other heads, least of all perhaps on such a matter as his really quite swindled state when the pledge given for his true beguilement fails to ensure him that fullest experience of his pleasure which waits but on a direct reading *out* of the addressed appeal. It is scarce necessary to note that the highest test of any literary form conceived in the light of "poetry"—to apply that term in its largest literary sense—hangs back unpardonably from its office when it fails to lend itself to *vivâ-voce* treatment. We talk here, naturally, not of non-poetic forms, but of those whose highest bid is addressed to the imagination, to the spiritual and the æsthetic vision, the mind led captive by a charm and a spell, an incalculable art. The essential property of such a form as that is to give out its finest and most numerous secrets, and to give them out most gratefully, under the closest pressure—which is of course the pressure of the attention articulately *sounded.* Let it reward as much as it will and can the soundless, the "quiet" reading, it still deplorably "muffs" its chance and its success, still trifles with the roused appetite to which it can never honestly be indifferent, by not having so arranged itself as to owe the flower of its effect to the act and process of apprehension that so beautifully asks most from it. It then infallibly, and not less beautifully, most responds; for I have nowhere found vindicated the queer thesis that the right values of interesting prose depend all on withheld tests—that is on its being, for very pity and shame, but skimmed and scanted, shuffled and mumbled. Gustave Flaubert has somewhere in this connexion an excellent word—to the effect that any imaged prose that fails to be richly rewarding in return for a competent utterance ranks itself as wrong through not being "in the conditions of life." The more we remain in *them,* all round, the more pleasure we dispense; the moral of which is —and there would be fifty other pertinent things to say about this—that I have found revision intensify at every step my impulse intimately to answer, by my light, to those conditions.

All of which amounts doubtless but to saying that as the whole conduct of life consists of things done, which do other things in their turn, just so our behaviour and its fruits are essentially one and continuous and persistent and unquenchable, so the act has its way of abiding and showing and testifying, and so, among our innumerable acts, are no arbitrary, no senseless separations. The more we are capable of acting the less gropingly we plead such differences; whereby, with any capability, we recognise betimes that to "put" things is very exactly and responsibly and interminably to do them. Our expression of them, and the terms on which we understand that, belong as nearly to our conduct and our life as every other feature of our freedom; these things yield in fact some of its most exquisite material to the religion of doing. More than that, our literary deeds enjoy this marked advantage over many of our acts, that, though they go forth into the world and stray even in the desert, they don't to the same extent lose themselves: their attachment and reference to us, however strained, need n't necessarily lapse—while of the tie that binds us to *them* we may make almost anything we like. We are condemned, in other words, whether we will or no, to abandon and outlive, to forget and disown and hand over to desolation, many vital or social performances—if only because the traces, records, connexions, the very memorials we would fain preserve, are practically impossible to rescue for that purpose from the general mixture. We give them up even when we would n't—it is not a question of choice. Not so on the other hand our really "done" things of this superior and more appreciable order—which leave us indeed all licence of disconnexion and disavowal, but positively impose on us no such necessity. Our relation to them is essentially traceable, and in that fact abides, we feel, the incomparable luxury of the artist. It rests altogether with himself not to break with his values, not to "give away" his importances. Not to *be* disconnected, for the tradition of behaviour, he has but to feel that he is not; by his lightest touch the whole chain of relation and responsibility is reconstituted. Thus if he is always doing he can scarce, by his own measure, ever have done. All of which means for him conduct with a vengeance, since it is conduct minutely and publicly attested. Our noted behaviour at large may show for ragged, because it perpetually escapes our control; we have again and again to consent to its appearing in undress—that is in no state to brook criticism. But on all the ground to which the pretension of performance by a series of exquisite laws may apply there reigns one sovereign truth—which decrees that, as art is nothing if not exemplary, care nothing if not active, finish nothing if not consistent, the proved error is the base apologetic deed, the helpless regret is the barren commentary, and "connexions" are employable for finer purposes than mere gaping contrition.